Dynamics of Skill Acquisition

An Ecological Dynamics Approach

Second Edition

Chris Button, PhD

Ludovic Seifert, PhD

Jia Yi Chow, PhD

Duarte Araújo, PhD

Keith Davids, PhD

HUMAN KINETICS

Library of Congress Cataloging-in-Publication Data

Names: Button, Chris, 1973- author.
Title: Dynamics of skill acquisition: an ecological dynamics approach / Christopher Button, Ludovic Seifert, Jia Yi Chow, Duarte Araújo, Keith Davids.
Description: Second edition. | Champaign, IL : Human Kinetics, Inc., 2021.
  | Revised edition of: Dynamics of skill acquisition : a constraints-led approach / Keith Davids, Chris Button, Simon Bennett. 2008. | Includes bibliographical references and index.
Identifiers: LCCN 2019032443 (print) | LCCN 2019032444 (ebook) | ISBN 9781492563228 (paperback) | ISBN 9781492594741 (epub) | ISBN 9781492563235 (pdf)
Subjects: LCSH: Physical education and training. | Physical education and training--Psychological aspects. | Movement, Psychology of. | Human mechanics. | Physical fitness.
Classification: LCC GV342 .D28 2020 (print) | LCC GV342 (ebook) | DDC 613.7--dc23
LC record available at https://lccn.loc.gov/2019032443
LC ebook record available at https://lccn.loc.gov/2019032444

ISBN: 978-1-4925-6322-8 (print)

The web addresses cited in this text were current as of July 2019, unless otherwise noted.

Acquisitions Editor: Diana Vincer; **Senior Developmental Editor:** Amanda S. Ewing; **Managing Editor:** Julia R. Smith; **Copyeditor:** Annette Pierce; **Proofreader:** Leigh Keylock; **Indexer:** Nancy Ball; **Permissions Manager:** Dalene Reeder; **Graphic Designer:** Denise Lowry; **Cover Designer:** Keri Evans; **Cover Design Specialist:** Susan Rothermel Allen; **Photographs (cover):** © Ludovic Seifert; **Photo Asset Manager:** Laura Fitch; **Photo Production Manager:** Jason Allen; **Senior Art Manager:** Kelly Hendren; **Printer:** Versa Press

Printed in the United States of America   10 9 8 7 6 5 4 3 2 1

The paper in this book is certified under a sustainable forestry program.

Human Kinetics
1607 N. Market St.
Champaign, IL 61820
Website: www.HumanKinetics.com

In the United States, email info@hkusa.com or call 800-747-4457.
In Canada, email info@hkcanada.com.
In the United Kingdom/Europe, email hk@hkeurope.com.

For information about Human Kinetics' coverage in other areas of the world, please visit our website: **www.HumanKinetics.com**

Tell us what you think!
Human Kinetics would love to hear what we can do to improve the customer experience. Use this QR code to take our brief survey.

E7282

CONTENTS

PREFACE

Skill acquisition is a recurring process that continually challenges each of us throughout the life span. It is fundamental to survival, because humans need to become skilled in a variety of different tasks such as feeding, communicating and socializing. Actions in daily activities such as sports and work differ in the nature of the demands they impose on performers. Some actions, such as racket sports or driving on an expressway, are performed at high speeds; others, such as dance, American football, martial arts, and physical therapy, may involve a significant amount of body contact. Many actions, such as playing golf or performing surgery, require a high degree of precision and accuracy of movement. Others, such as synchronized marching and ice-skating, emphasize the challenge of performing graceful, stylized sequences of aesthetic movement. We are pitted against the wild elements of nature when doing activities such as hiking, climbing, kayaking, or surfing. Despite the huge variety of constraints imposed by various sports and daily activities, one thing they all share is a requirement for performers to coordinate and control movements effectively.

Movement practitioners in various physical activities understand that skilled learners are able to

- produce functional, efficient, and effective movement patterns that appear smooth and effortless;
- typically demonstrate precise timing between their movements and ongoing environmental events;
- consistently reproduce patterns of coordinated movement, even under severe time constraints or competitive pressures;
- perform movements that are not automated in the sense of being identical from one performance to the next, but are subtly varied and precisely adapted to immediate changes in the environment; and
- integrate different limb movements into an aesthetically pleasing pattern when necessary.

Purpose of the Book

Humans operate in information-rich, dynamic environments and require complex coordination patterns to interact with surfaces, objects, and events. An important challenge for movement scientists is to understand how coordination patterns are assembled, controlled, and acquired. In the early 21st century there has been an increasing interest in the societal constraints that shape and influence the acquisition of movement skills. Do the resources of the digital age affect how we learn skills? Will our changing environment invite us to move in different ways?

The study of human movement now bridges many related disciplines, including motor development, motor control, psychology, biology, and physical therapy. Although we attempt to apply our discussion of movement as broadly as possible throughout this book, we will often use movement models from sports and exercise as examples to describe key ideas. As sports and recreation enthusiasts ourselves, we recognize that such movement models can provide particularly rich task constraints in which to study and understand important aspects of movement behavior (Davids, Button, Araújo, Renshaw, and Hristovski, 2006). One of the main objectives of physical educators, sport scientists, movement scientists, psychologists, and physiotherapists is to develop valid conceptual models of human movement behavior that are based on research (Post, Pijpers, Bosch, and Boschker, 1998). The development of a comprehensive model of motor control is necessary before one can consider issues related to learning, but this in itself is not a simple task, because "the story of even a simple movement will have intentional, mechanical, informational, neural and muscular chapters" (Michaels, 1998, p. 65). It is now clear that a rigorous model of human movement requires a multidisciplinary framework to capture the interlocking scales of analysis (e.g., neural, behavioral, psychological) and the many subsystems (e.g., perceptual and movement) involved in producing behavior.

From a practical perspective, understanding how coordination and control are achieved promotes an informed organization of learning and rehabilitation environments and more effective use of practice and therapy time (Vaz, Silva, Mancini, Carello, and Kinsella-Shaw, 2017). Studying these processes in human movement systems is vital for considering issues involved in

- becoming familiar with children's movement capabilities at various stages of development;
- interpreting movement disabilities and disorders and their effects on perceptual-motor function;
- designing ergonomic equipment;
- designing coaching, teaching, and training tasks;
- planning and managing exercise prescription, therapeutic, and rehabilitation programs;
- understanding the nature of individual differences at various levels of performance;
- preventing injury and taking health and safety precautions;
- understanding how to transmit information to learners and patients in rehabilitation; and

- enhancing and maintaining quality of life for elderly people as their movement capabilities change.

A conceptual model of coordination and control is important for designing learning environments, but it is also important for ensuring that learners have positive experiences when acquiring motor skills. Given the concern about the lack of physical activity and the poor movement competency shown in affluent societies (e.g., the United Kingdom's *Our Healthy Nation* report, the World Health Organization's *World Health Report*, and New Zealand's *Healthy Eating–Healthy Action* report), this type of knowledge is vital for the design of physical activity programs to provide the basic skills necessary for subelite sport and exercise participation (Clark, 1995). The goal of this book is to outline a reliable and comprehensive model of human movement to provide a valid framework (i.e., concepts, methodological tools, and language) through which students and practitioners can understand and address these issues.

Organization

The first edition was divided into two sections, the first part dealing with theory and second part applying the theory to practice. This second edition integrates the two into each chapter throughout the book, providing a holistic text that captures the interrelationship of theory, data, and practice. This new and innovative structure will give readers an understanding of motor learning from an ecological dynamics perspective.

As in the first edition, we include special features that show how practice tasks can be designed to enhance skill acquisition and expertise in sport; these features include research highlights, self-test questions, and case studies. The case studies use the experiences of elite coaches, physical therapists, athletes, and sport scientists to demonstrate how theory informs the design of practice, training, and rehabilitation environments. Laboratory activities that increase student understanding and illustrate key ideas are also included.

New Content

In this second edition of *Dynamics of Skill Acquisition*, we have added new chapters and updated the book with important new empirical research findings and theoretical insights that have emerged since the first edition was written. These new insights include knowledge and data on

- variation in the timing of learning;
- adaptive flexibility in sport and its role in expertise development in athletes;
- realistic practice tasks in sports practice, training, and rehabilitation through representative design;

- attention and decision making in learning;
- social and cultural constraints on sport performance and motor learning; and
- talent development that aims to avoid burnout, stress injuries, and an overemphasis on competition in developing athletes.

These new insights have underpinned the introduction of nonlinear pedagogy (Chow, 2013; Chow, Davids, Button, and Renshaw, 2016), a framework to guide movement practitioners in designing practice environments in different sport and physical activity contexts. Nonlinear pedagogy is useful for helping coaches and teachers to design affordances into practice landscapes, helping practitioners to understand how to use constraints to channel learning, and providing information on designing tests of performance evaluation.

The second edition also includes many new practical examples that are based on empirical evidence that was not yet published when the first edition was being written. For example, there has been research on the role of ball projection machines, the use of indoor climbing walls to simulate outdoor climbing task constraints, the practice approaches of elite springboard divers, the use of small-sided games to simulate performance environments for team games, and the coordination of swimming strokes.

A new chapter (chapter 11) focuses on the experiential knowledge of elite coaches, athletes, and practitioners in sport in the United States, Europe, and Australasia to understand how constraints can be used during practice to enhance skill acquisition and expertise in specific sports. Other new content includes the following topics:

- Complex adaptive systems in sport
- The role of the coach or teacher as designer
- Representative task design in the construction of practice
- Performance evaluation tests and talent development programs
- Emotion-laden training
- The use of a constraints-based approach to enhance dynamics of skill acquisition

Audience

This book is written for people with an interest in movement coordination and control and skill acquisition. This includes movement scientists, sport scientists, psychologists, biomechanists, physiologists, coaches, teachers, physical educators, and physical therapists. Advanced undergraduates with a firm grounding in the traditional theories of motor behavior, beginning postgraduates, and academic faculty will all benefit from an understanding of ecological constraints on movement behavior.

ACKNOWLEDGMENTS

The second edition of *Dynamics of Skill Acquisition* is the culmination of a large amount of work carried out by many people, and we would like to acknowledge that effort here. First, we would like to pay tribute to and thank the seven movement practitioners who kindly provided invaluable contributions in chapter 11: Garrett Lucash, Jean François Gregoire, Mark O'Sullivan, Philippe Hellard, Tom Willmott, Richard Shuttleworth, and Anna Fitzpatrick. Your insightful real-world applications of the theoretical concepts described in this book have extended our efforts and helped us to illustrate some of the benefits and challenges of adopting the ecological dynamics approach for learners. Each of the authors has benefited from the help of numerous colleagues, both inside and outside of the academic world. The list is far too long to mention here, but we thank you for your valued, ongoing support. A special mention to Professor Simon Bennett, who was a coauthor on the first edition of the book but could not be involved in this version; thanks for your important groundwork and continued collaboration. We also wish to thank the publishing team at Human Kinetics who helped to coordinate the project and gave us helpful, constructive advice throughout. Thanks in particular to Diana Vincer, Ray Vallese, Bridget Melton, Dalene Reeder, and Julia Smith for keeping the team on track. Finally, we would like to recognize our families, who graciously accept and indulge our enduring fascination with motor learning. We are truly grateful for your love and support, and none of this would be possible without you.

CHAPTER 1

Athletes and Sports Teams Considered as Complex Adaptive Systems

---

CHAPTER OBJECTIVES

After completing this chapter, you will be able to do the following:

- List some of the characteristics of complex adaptive systems
- Understand what this characterization implies for designing practice tasks for the development of athletes and sports teams
- Describe adaptation in sports performance contexts
- Explain how coadaptation can be exploited as a coaching methodology
- Describe what affordances are and why they are important for skill acquisition
- Conceptualize the skill practitioner as a *designer* of affordance landscapes
- Discuss the relationship between information, specificity, and transfer of skill learning

---

Individual athletes and sports teams are impressive examples of complex adaptive systems. They have the capacity to reproduce high levels of performance consistently, yet respond to unexpected changes that commonly arise in performance. How adaptive systems develop this capacity and how practitioners can help to support this process is the focus of this first chapter. To understand the implications of conceptualizing athletes and sports teams as complex adaptive systems, you will need to become acquainted with the technical definition of *complexity* and what that implies for system adaptations.

A fundamental challenge for coaches, physical educators, strength and conditioning trainers, skill acquisition specialists, and performance analysts is to base their work on clear theoretical principles of performance and learning. A guiding theoretical framework can capture the nature of the learning process and key properties of the learner. Without such a foundation, sport practitioners are left to subjective opinions, traditional ways of doing things, and coaching manuals that need updating regularly, as we elucidated in the first edition of this book. The theoretical framework proposed within this chapter and used throughout the book is the **ecological dynamics** approach.

The updated second edition of this book conceptualizes athletes and sports teams as **complex adaptive systems**, providing a powerful theoretical conceptualization for skill acquisition, expertise, and talent development. Complex systems are technically defined as systems with many interacting components (Davids et al., 2013). It's the potential for interaction between components of complex systems that can lead to rich adaptive behaviors emerging from them. Neurobiological systems (i.e., systems with nervous systems that actively interact with their environment rather than merely react) exploit their inherent complexity, using surrounding informational constraints to continually reorganize their actions to achieve their intended task goals. Underpinned by information from the environment, rich patterns of behavior emerge from continuous interactions of many system components. For example, a coach does not need to instruct a competent games player on when to use the left, right, or both hands to intercept a ball in practice. Ball-flight trajectory is information the games player can use to reorganize a catching action if a ball is thrown to the left or right of or straight into the abdominal area of the athlete.

Complex adaptive systems are everywhere on earth and their goal-directed behaviors emerge as their system degrees of freedom (components) continually reorganize (adapting and adjusting to each other). Traditionally, a reductionist philosophy has been used in isolating neurobiological system components for scientific analysis, such as studying separate areas of the brain or investigating functions of components (e.g., visual system) independently. While useful to an extent, reductionism provides limited insights on how complex systems adapt their behaviors to achieve task goals during performance in dynamic environments (Teques, Araújo, Seifert, Del Campo, and Davids, 2017). Complexity science demands that we examine system behavior holistically because the behavior of the whole is richer than the sum of the contribution of individual parts.

THE PERCEPTION-ACTION COUPLE OF NEUROBIOLOGICAL SYSTEMS ALLOWS FOR THE EXPLOITATION OF COMPLEXITY INHERENT TO THE SYSTEM IN SERVICE OF GOAL-DIRECTED BEHAVIOR.

The Ecological Dynamics Theoretical Framework

Since the first edition of this book was published in 2008, the ecological dynamics theoretical framework has developed and gained prominence among researchers and many practitioners (see chapter 11). A major contributor to the ecological dynamics framework is **dynamical systems** theory, which originated in the field of mathematics to model how systems continually change over different timescales. Dynamical systems theory can describe the dynamical patterns that continually form as components of a complex system interact under constraints (Kelso, 2012). Constraints on a complex system are most important to study because they act as information that shapes and modifies these interactions. Dynamical systems theory explains how complex adaptive systems reorganize system components over time by exploiting inherent **self-organization** tendencies. Key ideas capture how athletes and sports teams undergo processes of adaptation at the timescale of performance (milliseconds, seconds, and minutes), learning (hours, days, and weeks) and expertise acquisition (months and years). Although self-organizing tendencies in athletes are spontaneous, their specific expression is always shaped by personal, task, and environmental constraints (Newell, 1986), which are boundaries that influence behaviors emerging from performers and learners in sport.

What Is Adaptation in Sport Performance Contexts?

Adaptation in sport performance refers to the continuous reorganization of system degrees of freedom to satisfy the ecological constraints of competition, for example, when an athlete or sports team can explore different coordination patterns to achieve a task goal. This process might involve an athlete reorganizing muscles, limb segments, or coordinative structures or involve teammates adjusting their relative positioning to exploit or cover space when attacking or defending. In this way, relations between these system components in athletes and sports teams are continually reorganized to achieve specific intentions and goals during performance. This constant adaptation requires the capacity to switch or transition between functional movement patterns, a process best refined and exploited during practice (Davids, Araújo, Seifert, and Orth, 2015).

Employing theory, models, and data, the behaviors of continuously changing, evolving, developing, and adapting systems can be explained at multiple scales of analysis with the same underlying abstract principles, regardless of system structure and composition (Kelso, 2012). To exemplify, consider how molecules of water in a stream change their organization from a fluid state to ice and steam as weather changes. Dynamical systems theory suggests that transitions between these system states can emerge as a result of changes in a key system variable. In dynamical systems, this type of variable is known

If you want to know a system, study its constraints.

How might unlocking affordances for a single athlete alter the behavior of the system at larger scales (team, organization, city, etc.)?

as an order parameter (e.g., H₂O compositional structure: liquid, ice, steam), which is influenced by critical changes in another variable, known as a control parameter (e.g., ambient temperature). Relations between an <u>order parameter</u> and a <u>control parameter</u> are instrumental in understanding how interactions are regulated in complex adaptive systems such as a flock of birds, a school of fish, and a swarm of insects (figure 1.1). Within an individual athlete (motor system degrees of freedom) or team sports performance, intra- and interindividual interactions have been formally modeled, theoretically conceptualized, and empirically studied in the same way (Davids et al., 2013). The same abstract principles (based on relations between order parameters and control parameters) can help us to understand how an athlete transits between one state of organization (e.g., walking) to another (e.g., running). They can also explain decision making in team sports, such as how a subgroup of players coordinates its movements to transit from defense to attack and vice versa.

Another relevant theoretical mechanism for explaining how coordination tendencies can emerge in athletes and sports teams exists in the concept of **coadaptation** in evolutionary systems (see Kauffman, 1993). In evolution, Kauffman (1993) noted how transitions in system organization most often occurred when

Courtesy of Ian Renshaw.

FIGURE 1.1   Self-organizing order in biological systems is exemplified by nesting gannets in Muriwai National Park, west of Auckland, New Zealand. Although the nesting order appears regimented, this functional behavior emerges because it protects against possible predators during nesting season. Outside of the nesting season, these birds have a tendency to be argumentative and do not maintain such close proximity.

Handwritten margin note: "ORDER" AND "CONTROL" PARAMETERS DEFINE THE POINTS OF CAUSALITY WITHIN A DYNAMICAL SYSTEM.

coevolving systems reorganized components in order to adapt to changes in their environments (over decades and centuries). An interesting question concerns when these systems are most open or ready to change. Kauffman (1993) argued that natural systems were most ready to evolve when they were in a metastable (dynamically stable) region. A metastable region exists between the edge of chaos (when it is open to random changes) and order (when it is highly structured). When a system finds itself in a metastable region, it is most open to coadaptation (changing in relation to the environment), which can be the most functional for enhancing system performance (Kelso, 2012). This idea from evolutionary biology is a valuable idea for scientists and practitioners working to enhance skill and expertise in sports over the timescale of learning (days, weeks, and months) (Passos, Araújo, and Davids, 2016). In sport, intrapersonal (within an athlete) and interpersonal (between athletes) coordination tendencies emerge as system components temporarily coadapt (reorganize) into synergies to achieve specific task goals. Within-individual interactions (i.e., movement coordination) display the same hallmark properties of synergy formation under constraint and sensitivity to surrounding information as in between-individual relations (Riley, Shockley, and Van Orden, 2012). What this means is that parts of a complex adaptive system are *open* to interactions with the environment because they can use surrounding information to constrain their tendency for self-organization (see chapter 3). For example and as seen in figure 1.2, in rock climbing, an individual athlete can use visual information from a crack or gap in a surface or a rock overhang to determine whether to form a grip with two or three fingers or the whole hand.

A growing body of research is also attempting to identify the information that constrains pattern formation in athletes and sports teams during performance and learning (Araújo and Davids, 2016). The capacity for continuous reorganization of system components (degrees of freedom in a complex adaptive system) delivers the functional variability to athletes and teams that is needed to coadapt to changing performance environments. This capacity for system reorganization also provides stability (i.e., robustness of actions) when athletes are confronted with internal and external fluctuations or disturbances (Seifert, Komar, Araújo, and Davids, 2016). Successful performance in sport is based on a subtle blend of persistence and change to achieve performance outcomes, which is founded on synergy formation. This balance between stability and adaptive variability in athletes and sports teams can be achieved because of inherent system **degeneracy** (i.e., where many coordinative structures can be recruited to achieve the same or different functional performance outcomes). Research has demonstrated that degeneracy in complex adaptive systems provides the neurobiological basis for diverse actions required in information-rich and dynamic environments for attaining task goals (Seifert, Komar, Araújo, and Davids, 2016). For example, in swimming, task constraints were manipulated for individuals swimming 200-meter freestyle by constraining

Handwritten margin notes:

Right margin: COMPLEXITY = THE SCIENCE OF METASTABILITY? CONSIDER AN OFFENSIVE PLAY AS ONE OF THESE GOAL-DIRECTED SYNERGIES, SUPPORTED BY ALL COMPONENT SCALES (e.g. INDIVIDUAL BIOMECHANICS, BIOENERGETICS, etc.)

Left margin: LINKS TO GENERAL PRINCIPLES OF ALLOSTASIS IN BIOLOGICAL SYSTEMS

© Ludovic Seifert

FIGURE 1.2 Haptic (touch) information from the hands and feet on the rock surface can provide information on stability. Using these sources of information, climbers can organize their finger, hand, and foot movements into synergies (coordination patterns) relevant to their interactions with the surface.

the glide duration (e.g., implementing a freely chosen condition versus maximal and minimal glide condition in practice). Without instruction, swimmers increased their kicking patterns (i.e., using 10-beat kicking, whereas 2-, 4-, and 6-beats are the normal kicking patterns) to functionally coadapt to the glide phase of the stroke. Seifert, Komar, Araújo, and Davids (2016) showed how swimmers can use inherent system degeneracy to satisfy a task constraint by coadapting existing movement patterns.

Coadaptation as a Coaching Strategy to Exploit the Learner's Degeneracy

Coadaptation is needed when athletes have to cope with change, such as new equipment technology, rule changes in a sport, and opposition innovations in performance. Coaches familiarize performers with the need to coadapt in training programs, rarely letting athletes settle into a comfort zone where it is in effect "business as usual" in terms of their performance (Rothwell, Stone, Davids, and Wright, 2017). They can exploit the coadaptation process by promoting a functional blend of safety and uncertainty for athletes during practice.

IS IMPROVING COADAPTATION A KEY TARGET WITH DELIBERATE PRACTICE STRATEGIES?

Safety is needed for athletes to feel secure in making mistakes and exploring tasks during practice, and uncertainty can be designed into practice tasks to help athletes explore different possibilities for action. Coadaptive moves are innovative and creative coaching methods that manipulate task constraints to challenge athletes to continuously seek innovative and more-functional performance solutions. When coaches emphasize problem-solving and adaptive behaviors in practice, athletes can experience autonomy and responsibility for their own performance and the resilience needed to perform under pressure.

For example, coadaptation in athletes was illustrated in a 2006 study by Hristovski, Davids, Araújo, and Button, who manipulated the distance between novice boxers and a punching bag (figure 1.3). During practice, participants received no specific instructions on how to hit the heavy bag and were asked to strike the target with any actions that felt natural. Varying the scaled distances from the target to the boxers resulted in emergence of different boxing patterns (e.g., hooks, jabs, uppercuts). At a critical scaled-body distance value (0.6), boxers entered a coadaptive state that allowed them to flexibly switch between any of the boxing action modes they had previously learned. The scaled-body distance value of 0.6 pushed the boxer-target system to a dynamically stable region (technically known as **metastability** in complex systems) (Kelso, 2012). In metastable regions of a performance landscape, many coordination tendencies can spontaneously emerge to satisfy specific task and environmental constraints (Hristovski et al., 2006). At other scaled-distance-to-target values, this level of flexibility in emergent actions was not

[margin handwritten note: SEEKING METASTABILITY ALLOWS A COMPLEX SYSTEM TO MAXIMIZE ITS FUNCTIONAL VARIANCE/DEGENERACY/EMERGENCE POTENTIAL. So WHAT KEY VARIABLES (e.g. DISTANCE FROM TARGET) "UNLOCK" METASTABILITY?]

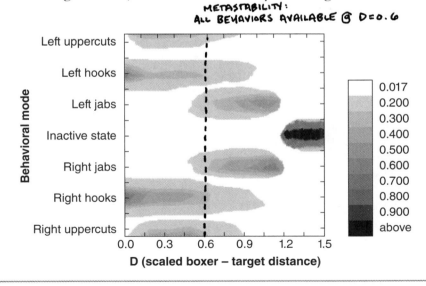

[handwritten above figure: METASTABILITY: ALL BEHAVIORS AVAILABLE @ D=0.6]

FIGURE 1.3 The likelihood of a certain type of punch emerging depends on the distance between the boxer and the punching bag. N.B.: The probability index on the right of the figure denotes that the darker shadings indicate more likely behaviors.

Reprinted by permission from R. Hristovski, K. Davids, D. Araújo, and C. Button, "How Boxers Decide to Punch a Target: Emergent Behavior in Nonlinear Dynamical Movement Systems," *Journal of Sports Science and Medicine* 5 (2006): 60-73.

observed because only isolated action patterns were displayed. The implication of this work is that interpersonal distance between boxers and a target (and in different forms of combat sports) is a vital source of information that constrains coordination and invites a range of functional behaviors in athletes. Coaches need to be aware of the values of key information variables, such as distance from a target, that can provide opportunities for certain actions in sport performance and practice.

Incorporating Coadaptation Into Sports Teams Practice

Team sports are dynamic performance environments, rich in information and changing from moment to moment (Passos et al., 2016). Team sports require continuous perception, decision making, and actions from players because of their continuous, coadaptive interactions. These are constrained in space and

Spotlight on Research

Player Interactions in Rugby Union

Pedro Passos and colleagues (2008) sought to investigate how attackers and defenders used information to regulate their actions in 1v1 dyads in rugby union. Near the try line, an attacker seeks to destabilize a dyadic system formed with an immediate defender. A defender, on the other hand, seeks to maintain system stability (remaining between the attacker with the ball and the try line at all times). Passos and colleagues found that near the try line, where an attacker can score a try if he moves past the defender with the ball without being tackled, relative velocity between the attacker and defender was a key variable. This variable was defined as the differential between the velocity at which an attacker and defender move in a 1v1 dyad. Passos and colleagues observed that, when the relative velocity value reached 2 meters per second or higher, the dyadic system could become destabilized as long as this value emerged within a critical region of 4 meters of interpersonal distance between the attacker and defender. Note that the information variables of relative velocity and interpersonal distance are closely related in the way that they influence the stability of a dyadic system. Reaching 2 meters per second or higher in relative velocity at a value of interpersonal distance of more than 4 meters did not have the same effect on destabilizing the dyadic system.

Application

The critical region of 4 meters of interpersonal distance in rugby union was a zone in which attackers needed to explore and exploit opportunities for actions for destabilizing a dyad with an immediate defender. These information variables are useful for rugby union coaches when designing learning environments for attackers and defenders in 1v1 situations near the try line.

time, including changes in direction, location, and positioning of competing and cooperating players. Sophisticated attacking and defending patterns of play emerge from these continuous attacker–defender interactions (for examples, see Passos, Araújo, and Davids, 2016). <u>Attackers and defenders are components of a complex adaptive system linked by visual</u>, <u>acoustic</u>, <u>and</u> <u>proprioceptive informational fields.</u> Processes of coadaptation in performance have been observed in several team sports, including rugby union, futsal, basketball, and soccer (Ribeiro, Silva, Duarte, Davids, and Garganta, 2017). Research in team sports has shown that information variables such as (1) relative angles between competing individuals, (2) values of interpersonal distances between attackers and defenders, (3) relative velocity of two moving competitors, and (4) variations in distances as gaps between opponents emerge from the continuous interpersonal interactions between players (see Passos, Araújo, and Davids, 2016). An important practical question concerns how we can use these information variables to design practice environments for athletes in team sports to make decisions and coordinate their actions when attacking and defending.

Learning Design in Ecological Dynamics

Ecological dynamics focuses on a relevant scale of analysis for understanding learning and performance: the *person–environment relationship*. Using the term *organismic asymmetry*, Dunwoody (2007) argued that the role of the environment was being neglected by a biased tendency toward seeking to explain human behaviors through internalized referents, schema, programs, and plans. This bias in thinking has influenced models of learning for decades, skewing practice task design in sport as Davids and Araújo (2010) highlighted. This weakness was more recently acknowledged in motor behavior research (Zelaznik, 2014).

In ecological dynamics, <u>the acquisition of skill in individual and team-based sports is based on the continuous information-based interactions between each athlete and a specific performance environment</u> (Davids et al., 2013). Athlete–environment interactions result in the coupling of goal-directed movements to available information sources during performance. This is a fundamental principle of learning design in individual and team sports. Coupling information and movement in practice emerges when athletes continuously interact with key objects (objects to avoid or intercept in ball games), surfaces (properties of a rock surface to climb or scramble over or an icy surface to ski or skate across), events (the sudden acceleration of a lead athlete in a marathon or the emergence of a three-person block in a volleyball attack), terrain dimensions (driving to greens on different golf courses or coping with different field width and length dimensions in soccer) and features (markings

Ecological Dynamics eschews the neurocentric view of motor behavior in favor of athlete-environment analysis.

Key Concept

The Performer–Environment Scale of Analysis

In 2014, Howard Zelaznik argued, in an address as a fellow of the U.S. National Academy of Kinesiology, that previous research had been too focused on understanding how nervous systems control movements. He proposed the following (p. 41):

- "Motor control and learning in kinesiology should move away from believing the brain holds the key to action and move out to examine the movement of people within their environment . . .future [kinesiologists] need to become a set of scholars using either the Newell framework or a Gibsonian approach."
- "We want to understand skills from the perspective of a person moving within an environment that provides affordances and challenges. We need to stress that the proper level of analysis is a whole person interacting with tasks and the environmental affordances."
- "Understanding the relations between these three factors and how individuals structure movement within this framework will lead to important understandings about the learning, performance, teaching, and rehabilitation of motor skills."

on an orienteering course and dealing with a crosswind on an archery course), and significant others (changes in positioning and movements of teammates and coping with alterations to tactical patterns of opponents). To prepare for these interactions, coaches could design *adaptive zones* in practice contexts for athletes to explore.

What Is an Adaptive Zone and How Can It Be Designed in Practice Programs?

An adaptive zone is the practice time between the planned repetition of action in rehearsal and the unstructured exploration and discovery of performance solutions. In the adaptive zone, performers cannot become completely *dependent* on the information available in a performance environment to regulate their actions. This control strategy would result in them merely reacting to information from events. Nor can athletes perform completely *independently* of their surrounding environment (through a shared plan or performance model or by strictly adhering to previous coaching instructions) (Davids et al., 2015). With skilled performance analysis, opponents can understand and disrupt the best-prepared plans during competition. In the adaptive zone, actions of an individual athlete or sports team need to combine intentions, perception,

FOR AN ATHLETE, THE ADAPTIVE ZONE OF TRAINING SHOULD AIM TO DEFINE AND BROADEN THE AFFORDANCE LANDSCAPE.

and action in an *emergent* manner to take advantage of the information that emerges in performance and learning environments. In the adaptive zone, athletes can be encouraged to anticipate events and outcomes and attune to information that is most relevant for their task goals.

This type of adaptive capacity needs to be practiced in training and cannot simply be turned on and off at will. Practice designs need to place athletes into an adaptive zone during preparation for competition. For example, small-sided and conditioned games provide adaptive zones for learners to explore the relationships between key sources of information, and actions can be exploited by developing athletes. Data from existing research studies in ecological dynamics suggest that information variables emerging during ongoing interpersonal interactions of athletes (e.g., gap widths, angular relations, relative velocities, and interpersonal distances in team games) provide *affordances* (they invite certain opportunities for action) that can be used by players and explored during practice. Adaptive zones should provide rich and varied fields of affordances from the available landscape (Davids, Renshaw, Pinder, Greenwood, and Barris, 2016).

What Are Affordances and Why Are They Important for Skill Acquisition in Sport?

James Gibson (1979) proposed how different perceptual variables support an individual's exploration and discovery of **affordances**, which he considered to be action-relevant properties of the environment. Gibson (1979) proposed that affordances were opportunities or possibilities for action offered by the environment. Affordances are everywhere on our planet. In human societies, affordances may even be signposted as in figure 1.4.

Photodisc

FIGURE 1.4 Affordances for pedestrians and cyclists on a walkway. A flat, firm surface invites different types of locomotion. The signs invite pedestrians and cyclists to use separate paths to prevent painful collisions. They even invite cyclists to move at specific speeds to maintain control of their bikes and avoid wayward pedestrians. After all, invitations can be rejected!

In sport, affordances capture relations between an athlete and a performance environment that may be directly perceived, inviting adaptive actions from individuals under different performance conditions (Davids, Güllich, Shuttleworth, and Araújo, 2017). Information designed into practice tasks can support the discovery of opportunities to act, emerging from continuous interactions of an athlete with key features of a performance environment. Perceiving an affordance is to perceive how one can act when faced with specific conditions in a performance environment. Recall the research examples discussed earlier of boxers hitting a target with a range of striking actions and the 1v1 dyadic system interactions in rugby union. It was clear that specific values of key information variables (D = 0.6 in scaled distance to a target in boxing and 2 meters per second relative velocity of an attacker running with a ball at a defender within 4 meters) invited specific actions from athletes. These ideas could help coaches design affordance fields in practice. These information variables, identified by research, provide the context for designing opportunities for athletes to explore important actions and variants of them during practice.

In an excellent theoretical position paper, Withagen, Araújo, and de Poel (2017) went even further than Gibson and proposed that affordances are action possibilities that *invite* behaviors from individuals. These invitations for action are specific to the individual and time based and depend on past experience, learning, and development for their use in performance. Affordances, therefore, have an objective (they are perceivable in a performance environment) and subjective (they need an actor to perceive them) dimension (Gibson, 1979). The specific skills, experiences, motivations, and intentions of each individual athlete guide performance as they reorganize movements to seek and use affordances in a performance environment.

This important advance in conceptualization since Gibson's initial insights highlights the subtle, nuanced interactions between athletes and affordances that emerge during performance: While affordances engage, attract, solicit, invite, and draw in athletes, individuals can accept or reject these invitations by modulating the strength of the couplings formed with affordances during practice and performance. Hence, performance and practice should be highly interactive, shaping the design work of coaches in athlete-development programs.

At particular instances during sport performance, athletes may have many available affordances that differ in their invitational strength over time. These ideas can be depicted by an *affordance landscape* (Rietveld and Kiverstein, 2014). In this landscape, affordances can differ in their strength to invite actions, which can change over time. For Gibson (1979) actions are not caused by a performance environment. Because a feature or event or another individual in a performance landscape may *invite* different interaction possibilities from an athlete, selecting from the plethora of inviting affordances is an important and demanding aspect of competitive performance that needs to be experienced in practice. Practice design should aim to allow an athlete to express her intentionality in performance, capturing how she can strive to achieve specific task goals through selecting specific affordances in the landscape. Intentionality and motivations of individual athletes can be drawn into practice task designs, requiring a significant level of problem solving, decision making, and selection that can simulate demands of competitive environments.

An affordance has the *potential* to invite an action (Withagen, de Poel, Araújo, and Pepping, 2012). Indeed, an object, event, surface, or another person affords many behaviors to individuals, and not all are perceived as invitations to act. Furthermore, people may decide not to accept the invitation. An important aspect of selection from an affordance landscape, considered from the perspective of the performer–environment relationship, refers to the action capabilities of a performer. Here constraints play a significant role, such as efficiency and effectiveness, which can be understood as an important part of the selectivity process. Many levels of constraints affect affordance use, including evolutionary influences, and these imply an emergent feature of selection (affordances that preserve an individual's safety may become more immediate if a sudden change in the environment occurs). They may also imply more persistent cultural constraints, which may lead to a particular dominant responsiveness in interacting with environmental objects and features in specific ways. In this way, affordances can be viewed as resources available in a performance environment that can constrain or make behaviors possible. They do not cause behaviors. The soliciting effect of affordances draws performers toward certain behaviors. This effect can be seen in individuals who may be immediately drawn toward certain actions, indeed being in a state of **action readiness**, in certain fields within the affordance landscape (Rietveld and Kiverstein, 2014). Fields stand out from all affordances that may be available in a landscape that is entirely dynamic. Some become more prominent in strength as events change and others become less solicitous depending on performance contexts. The strength of affordance solicitation can vary depending on contextual circumstances (figure 1.5).

Where does cognitive activity fit in, you may ask, as athletes detect and decide which affordances to select and use during performance? The dynamics of the coupling strength that governs our use of affordances in performance depends on many interacting constraints, such as intentions to perform certain actions, cultural factors, personal history, evolutionary influences (fight or flight), and many more (see chapter 4).

The level to which an affordance invites a response from an individual athlete can vary from instant to instant and could be different within and between performers from occasion to occasion. In parkour, an athlete may jump over a ledge on one occasion or land with the right foot and push off with the left foot on another. Use of affordances, therefore, depends on

An Individual's Action Capabilities + Embodied Perception Defines their Affordance Landscape, which is Shifting Moment by Moment via Interacting Constraints.

imacoconut/Getty Images/Getty Images

FIGURE 1.5 Engaging in activities like parkour can help an athlete develop athleticism while learning to select between different affordances in a landscape during interactions with objects, surfaces, ledges, inclines, and obstacles (e.g., jumping over, gripping, landing on, pushing off of, balancing on, avoiding). Parkour demands innovation in interacting with these properties of the environment, which involves accepting or rejecting invitations to interact in different ways with them.

interacting constraints pertaining to the individual, task, and environment. Withagen and colleagues (2017) provide a compelling theoretical argument and mathematical model that suggests how affordances can be conceived of as attractors in a personalized landscape that can be discovered, explored, and exploited.

Affordance Landscapes and Learning Design in Sport

These ideas emphasize the role of affordances in design of practice environments, supporting the notion that pedagogues should be conceived as learning designers (Davids, Araújo, Hristovski, Passos, and Chow, 2012). A key task for pedagogues is to understand how to design multiple affordances into practice task simulations of a competitive performance environment. Through practice, athletes can become entrained to specific affordances that attract them within the landscape. Not all affordances have the same degree of attraction for all

(handwritten margin note, left side, rotated:) COACH = DESIGNER — A METAPHORICAL LINK TO THE "DESIGN OF EVERDAY THINGS"?

athletes, and coupling strength can be varied in practice task designs. Clearly, practices that emphasize scripted play, rehearsal, and repetition in drills will restrict and reinforce coupling to very narrow fields within the affordance landscape. But many competitive sport contexts are highly dynamic and variable. They are not easy to choreograph into predictable performance sequences. During practice, other task designs are needed that can allow athletes to couple their actions to multiple affordances in a flexible manner. This type of task-constraint manipulation in practice is captured by Bernstein's view of practice as "repetition without repetition" (Bernstein, 1996, pg. 204). That is, it involves a search of the practice environment (affordance landscape) to explore functional movement solutions through continuous interactions with key objects, features, surfaces, and other people. Modulating the coupling strength with a range of affordances during practice can alter the dynamics of interactions so that athletes learn actions that go beyond merely reacting to environmental constraints. Rather, designing dynamical interactions with many different, but relevant, possibilities for action can help athletes select and use affordances to support their actions in sport.

The size and nature of a field of affordances in a practice task will depend on the needs of the learner. Almost by default it appears, coaches seem drawn to designing very narrow affordance fields that can restrict exploratory search activities. Evidence for a different pedagogical approach was demonstrated by Pinder, Renshaw, Davids, and Kerhervé (2011), who analyzed performance on a cricket batting task. Skilled young cricketers were asked to bat using different methods of ball projection (i.e., in different fields of an affordance landscape) and provided with no specific performance instructions. Against a ball-projection machine, advanced visual information from a bowler's actions was removed, causing significant adaptations in initiating movements earlier. These task constraints also resulted in reduced peak bat swing velocities and poorer quality of bat–ball contact than when participants batted against an actual bowler. Pinder, Renshaw, and colleagues (2011) also found that when batting against a two-dimensional video image of a bowler, batters were able to use information from the bowler's actions, enabling initial behavioral responses that were consistent with the task of batting against a live bowler. However, against the video image, without the requirements of actually intercepting a ball and without ball-flight information, significant variations in downswing initiation timing and peak bat velocities were observed. Another study (of one-handed catching) by Panchuk, Davids, Sakadjian, MacMahon, and Parrington (2013) observed similar variations in emergent coordination tendencies when different affordance fields were designed for performance. Data showed how kinematics of hand movements and gaze behaviors of participants were adapted as they attempted to use different affordances for catching balls projected from a ball machine with and without synchronization to video images of a thrower throwing a ball and its trajectory. Collectively,

TYPICAL PRACTICE DESIGN ACTUALLY RESTRICTS THE AFFORDANCE LANDSCAPE BY EMPHASIZING REHEARSAL AND REPETITION.

these studies demonstrate how learning designs can influence the manner in which athletes move and learn to couple perception with action (potentially resulting in poor transfer to competitive environments).

Representative Design in Practice

Transfer of training can be enhanced by ensuring that the informational constraints designed into a practice task simulate the affordance landscape in a performance environment, shaping emergent movement patterns and interpersonal interactions between athletes. Research shows how the athlete–environment interactions need to be carefully considered in designing *representative* practice tasks. **Representative design** is a concept proposed by Egon Brunswik (1956) that refers to the composition of experimental task constraints so that they *represent* a behavioral setting to which the results are intended to be generalized (for detailed discussions see Araújo, Davids, and Passos, 2007). In ecological dynamics, this concept has shaped understanding of how to design practice task constraints in learning environments that can be generalized to competitive performance constraints (Davids, 2012). *Representative learning design* captures how motor learning theorists and sport practitioners might use Brunswik's (1956) insights to design practice and training task constraints that are representative of a performance context that they are intended to simulate: competitive environments in individual or team sports (Pinder, Davids, Renshaw, and Araújo, 2011). Ecological dynamics proposes that in designing representative practice tasks in individual and team sports, practice simulations need to be based on a detailed sampling of the *informational variables* available in specific performance environments for athletes to use for regulating their behaviors. Representative practice tasks allow athletes to use their processes of cognition, perception, and action in a functionally integrated way during performance (Pinder, Davids, Renshaw, and Araújo, 2011). Representative learning design in practice is predicated on the key principle that movements typically need to be coupled to specifying perceptual variables in practice tasks that simulate competitive performance environments. Successful transfer between a learning and performance environment can be ensured by incorporating a *representative learning design* in the former to induce functional behaviors of learners (i.e., cognitions, perceptions, and actions). Ensuring availability of representative affordances and behavioral correspondence in practice simulations is the key to successful transfer of functional performance behaviors from one environment to another. For example, rather than practice dribbling a ball around static objects that bear little resemblance to the size and shape of defenders in a competitive soccer match (see figure 1.6), coaches can design more-representative learning tasks that include passive and then more-active defenders.

Similarly, it is worth reviewing the research of Pinder, Renshaw, and colleagues (2011), discussed earlier in this section. When batting against cricket

"REPRESENTATIVENESS" COULD BE CONCEPTUALIZED AS THE DEGREE OF AFFORDANCE LANDSCAPE MATCHING BETWEEN TRAINING AND COMPETITION.

bowlers (or pitchers in softball and baseball), some practice designs involve learners batting against ball-projection machines. The value of this practice task design is limited because the only information available for batters to coordinate their actions comes from ball-flight information. More representative learning designs involve batters facing real bowlers who provide advanced information on ball trajectory from the kinematics of their preparatory actions when running up to bowl. As we note next, the key point is that more representative (faithful) simulations of competitive performance environments in practice contain specifying information variables that support more effective transfer for learning.

FIGURE 1.6 The information provided by the static cones is less representative than the information provided by a moving defender. During the early stages of learning, the defender's movement might be restricted until a dribbler gains confidence in ball manipulation.

Practice task designs with **nonspecifying information** variables lead to slower rates of learning because of the less effective transfer between practice and competitive performance.

Transfer Conceptualized in Ecological Dynamics

An important question that ecological dynamics considers is this: What transfers from learning to performance? The answer lies in the *information–movement relationship* that transfers between the task constraints of a faithfully simulated practice task and a competitive performance environment (Seifert, Wattebled, L'Hermette, Bideault, Herault, and Davids, 2013). Key information sources of a performance environment need to be *represented* when designing a practice environment in both individual and team sports. Transfer of skill and learning occur when training in one context shapes performance and learning in a different context. Ensuring a high degree of skill transfer between a training environment (e.g., a climbing wall) and a particular performance context (e.g., a rocky outcrop) is a key challenge in sport. Ecological dynamics proposes that transfer is underpinned by how an individual's experiences in a practice simulation influence the process of exploring and adapting to constraints within a performance niche. Performance behaviors that support positive transfer emerge when the existing intrinsic dynamics (behavioral tendencies) of an individual cooperate with the dynamics of a new task to be learned. On the other hand, when intrinsic and task dynamics compete (for example when a skilled tennis player learns to play badminton), transfer must be accompanied by some form of relearning, requiring a period of transitional and exploratory behaviors. Some stable, well-learned behaviors may need to be suppressed or changed, whereas new movement patterns need to become more stable with learning.

Specificity and Generality of Transfer

Clearly, enhancing skill and expertise in sport requires *specificity* in transfer between practice and performance contexts that are similar in terms of information present and actions required of a learner. These practice task designs are high in representativeness and action fidelity (Pinder, Davids, Renshaw, and Araújo, 2011). However, specificity of transfer cannot be functional all the time because of problems caused by too much specialization of experiences, especially early in athletic development. Physical and psychological problems may be caused by too much intensity and not enough variation in practice regimens. After all, one cannot simply become an elite sprinter by sprinting in competitions alone. Research has shown that expert athletes typically participate in more sports during their developmental years and experience a greater number of hours of practice in different sports than nonexperts do (Davids, Gullich, Shuttleworth, and Araújo, 2017). This research shows that early specialization in sports practice and training in young children is typically less beneficial than early diversification of experience in different physical activities. Research has revealed the physical, psychological, emotional, and social problems (including dropout) that may result from early specialization (chapter 12). An ecological dynamics perspective suggests that a more balanced development experience focused on early diversification can enrich athletes' adaptive capacities in different sport domains. Transfer between practice and performance contexts that are not high in task representativeness can also be useful. Individual athletes may benefit from practice and experience in an activity that appears to have little resemblance to a performance context. *General* transfer to performance in a new context is facilitated through enhancing use of underlying performance processes such as perceptual search behaviors for information; development of fundamental abilities like balance, postural control, and agility; and cognitive processes such as intentionality, anticipation, and attention. For example, the capacity for visual exploration can support transfer between small-sided and conditioned games and performance in competitive field invasion sports (Davids, Araújo, Correia, and Vilar, 2013). In this way, athletes can gain benefits from swimming in a pool when

i.e. GPP (↑ GENERALITY vs. ↑ SPECIFICITY)

preparing for open-water swimming, and the use of an indoor climbing wall can benefit rock-climbing performance to a certain extent.

Ecological dynamics proposes that early in practice, developing athletes can be exposed to a mix of unstructured and structured play experiences. It advocates less attention to early specialization to prevent potential detrimental effects on athletes. Instead, more attention can be paid to enhancing athleticism and general perceptual, cognitive, and motor capacities through nonspecialized, but relevant, experiences and activities. Hence, coaches need to understand when and how practice task design can be modified to switch between specific and general activities to encourage athleticism as a foundation for later specialization in a sport. This type of practical intervention in coaching and learning designs requires a theoretically supported, nuanced notion of the concept of transfer and how it may work in practice. These theoretical ideas are aligned with practitioner models of athlete development such as the athletic skills model (ASM), which proposes that a dynamic transitioning can emerge between diverse sport experiences and specialization in a target sport (Wormhoudt et al., 2018). The ASM advocates the need to respect the development stages that individuals are exposed to in a variety of learning contexts that will help them explore functional movement solutions while expanding their psychological, physical, and physiological capabilities. The process of holistic development that emerges when interacting with different performance contexts contributes to improving the functional coadaptation of individuals to performance environment constraints (Araújo et al., 2010). The fun associated with the constant challenge of discovering new individual actions and possibilities for play in different performance contexts increases learners' engagement with long-term motives for practice (Wormhoudt et al., 2018). Key ideas in ecological dynamics and the ASM suggest that the overemphasis on specificity of transfer in practice in early specialization models of athlete development may result in physical, psychological, and emotional problems (Davids et al., 2017).

While clearly important in practice, there is a fundamental misconception that *only* specificity of transfer has utility in continuous athlete learning and development. The theory of ecological dynamics and the ASM propose the need for a more nuanced understanding of the concept of transfer. Generality of transfer is useful at different times in athlete development and performance, but especially early in learning to provide a foundation for more specialized experiences later. Therefore, it is useful to consider transfer to exist on a continuum between high specificity and high generality (see chapter 12). An appropriate question of theoretical and practical relevance is this: How does one use specificity and generality of transfer in sports practice and when?

Specifying Variables and Transfer

In life, people maintain contact with the environment by perceiving information to regulate their actions and by moving to create information that they

DESPITE POSSIBILITY OF REVERSE CAUSALITY (BETTER ATHLETES CAN PLAY MORE SPORTS), THERE IS PROBABLY A TRAINING EFFECT INTRODUCED BY VARIABLE TASK-ENVIRONMENT CONSTRAINTS OF DIFFERENT SPORTS THAT DRIVE TRANSFERABLE PHYSICAL-PERCEPTUAL ADAPTATIONS.

can use (Gibson, 1979). An important principle of ecological psychology is that specifying information is more functional for regulating actions in human behavior. It indicates that *specificity of transfer is enhanced by the inclusion of* **specifying information** *in practice tasks that can be used by athletes to regulate their actions* (see figure 1.7). *Specifying* variables are synonymous with the gold standard for information needed to regulate specific actions in sport. For example, in ice climbing, the design of *specific* task constraints is needed to enable climbers to pick up specifying information to become skilled in the use of ice hooks and crampons when climbing an icefall (Seifert, Orth, Boulanger, Dovgalecs, Hérault, and Davids, 2014). Seifert, Orth, and colleagues (2014) showed how experts explore subtle combinations of kinesthetic, haptic (touch), acoustic, and visual information to regulate their actions while climbing, whereas beginners fixed on one source of information. The inclusion of specifying information is needed to enhance the specificity of transfer, but athletes need to become adept at the task of coupling their actions to a variety of perceptual variables from different modalities (Chow, Davids, Shuttleworth, and Araújo, in press). It is neither possible nor desirable to practice under competitive performance conditions all the time, especially with young children and developing athletes or in certain sports like ice climbing. Many reasons exist for the use of practice task constraints that engender more *general* transfer. Perhaps most important is the need to develop athleticism in young athletes without forcing them to specialize too early in their development.

How can coaches use nonspecifying variables to exploit general transfer in athletic development? Whenever practice task design contains no specifying information in practice, it is likely that transfer will be more *general*,

© Ludovic Seifert

FIGURE 1.7 Skilled ice climbers use tools such as hooks and crampons that provide a variety of sources of information to regulate actions.

leading to slower rates of learning. This idea can be captured by using cones to mark boundaries in a team sport practice drill (nonspecifying information), rather than using court or field markings as (specifying) information to constrain actions in team game contexts. Sometimes it is not possible to design the microstructure of practice in a highly specific way, depending on availability of facilities, equipment, space, time, and number of learners involved in practice. Low- to medium-skilled athletes (developing athletes and beginners) can find it useful to train with general (nonspecific) information sources. Highly skilled athletes (elite, professional, and international-standard athletes) typically need more exposure to specific information sources during practice. Coaches and sport scientists can design specifying perceptual variables into practice task constraints with more-advanced learners and skilled athletes when they need to focus on specific performance outcomes (e.g., countering a specific tactical strategy or formation adopted by specific opponents in team games or sailing a boat under specific weather conditions). This will ensure a specificity of transfer during practice, which is imperative for advanced learners in team and individual sports. However, beginners can improve performance to a limited extent when they pick up nonspecifying perceptual variables in practice. The process of general transfer can help learners develop their athleticism and relevant performance behaviors.

Another important feature of *transfer* in ecological dynamics is the need to enhance use of intertwined processes of cognitions, perceptions, and actions used by athletes during practice for performance regulation. For example, this can occur when behaviors used in indoor climbing environments or in small-sided games generalize to a competitive performance context (e.g., when climbing a cliffside or playing full-sided team games). A key challenge for sport practitioners is to ensure a behavioral correspondence between practice and performance contexts (Araújo et al., 2007). This important idea was investigated in a study of traditional training practices in elite springboard diving. Barris, Farrow, and Davids (2014) studied preparation for takeoff in Olympic-level springboard divers when diving into a pool and under the different task constraints of training in a dryland facility comprising a foam pit. Elite divers routinely practiced in separate training environments (dryland and pool), exhibiting differences in action fidelity, especially landing (feet first and hands first, respectively). Divers practiced the same preparation phase, takeoff, and initial aerial rotation in both practice environments, although it was unclear whether the dryland training environment offered the same affordances as those available in the pool environment. It was expected that the different affordance fields in the two distinct practice environments would lead to differences in preparation phases. Barris and colleagues (2014) observed similar *global topological* characteristics in all participants who used the same joint coordination patterns during dive takeoffs completed in the dryland and aquatic environments. However, as a group, participants showed statistically significant differences in performance at key events (second approach step, hurdle step, hurdle jump height, and board angles during the hurdle and at landing) during the preparation phase of dive takeoffs completed in dryland and aquatic training environments. Specifically, there was significantly less board angle depression at landing (after the hurdle jump) during takeoffs completed in the dryland area ($M = 14.27$, $SE = 0.24$) than those completed in the pool ($M = 15.99$, $SE = 0.26$), perhaps caused by landing feet or head first. Such research demonstrates how the informational constraints of practice tasks can promote movement attributes different from those desired for competition.

Summary

Informational constraints, or *affordances,* are designed into practice task simulations by coaches and physical education teachers to facilitate exploratory interactions of athletes with their performance environments. An important task is to ascertain how affordances need to be *represented* in simulated practice environments. Practice task design should result in an affordance landscape, allowing learners to perceive information that specifies a property of interest (e.g., the movement interactions between an attacker and defender invites affordances such as dribbling into a gap or moving to close a gap). Learning design should facilitate continuous, coadaptive interactions of athletes with objects, features, events, and others in performance. This aspect of learning design should allow learners to make reliable judgements and actions about environmental properties such as values of interpersonal distance between an attacker and a defender in 1v1 team game subphases. Tasks should also be designed to continuously evolve over time, requiring interrelated decisions and actions so that athletes learn to perceive and use affordances for regulating behaviors. Task design should also enable learners to act in context in order to perceive affordances to achieve performance goals. The inherent degeneracy of complex adaptive systems can be recognized and exploited in learning design by allowing performers to solve performance problems through perceiving different affordances and using variations in action to achieve the same task goals. Finally, relevant fields in the affordance landscape of practice can be modified through constraints manipulation to increase exploratory adaptive behaviors in individuals. Placing individuals in a well-designed field of affordances operationalized by principled constraints manipulation will increase exploration and enhance the capacity for movement adaptation (Davids et al., 2015).

(margin notes) "REPETITION WITHOUT REPETITION"

Self-Test Questions

1. Explain some of the important characteristics of a complex adaptive system with reference to an example from sport or physical activity.

2. What implications does understanding behavior at the performer–environment scale have for movement practitioners such as coaches?

3. How does the affordance concept help us to understand how individual athletes make decisions in sport?

4. Describe two practice environments for a skill of your choice that promote either specific or general transfer depending on the nature of information (i.e., specifying or nonspecifying).

CHAPTER 2

Physical Constraints on Coordination: Dynamical Systems Theory

---

CHAPTER OBJECTIVES

After completing this chapter, you will be able to do the following:

- Identify complex systems in sport and movement contexts
- Understand why a dynamical systems approach is a useful lens through which to consider the complexity of human movement coordination
- Use dynamical systems terminology to discuss important characteristics of human movement (such as stability, transitions, and movement preferences)
- Explain how constraints act on a system to shape its self-organization
- List different types of constraints on the human movement system and how they interact
- Identify how coordination patterns differ as we acquire skill and relate these characteristics to the degrees of freedom problem

---

In this chapter we introduce concepts from dynamical systems theory as part of the ecological dynamics framework. Dynamical systems theory provides a relevant model of understanding movement coordination and control in neurobiological systems. This approach views <u>the learner as a complex biological</u>

THE SYSTEM'S BEHAVIOR IS IN FACT DETERMINISTIC, BUT EXTREMELY COMPLICATED

system composed of many independent but interacting subsystems governed by physical laws that could be modeled by mathematic equations. In many complex structures, the dynamical interaction between components can actually enhance the intrinsic system organization. These interactions can produce rich order within the system through a process known as *self-organization*. Self-organization processes exemplify the coordination tendencies that are inherent in many complex systems and are influenced by many constraints that act on the system. It means assemblage and implementation of the components result from the system itself without prescription from a higher-order system (Haken, 1996).

We begin this chapter by defining complex systems and explaining why the human performer can be considered a complex system. Then we describe how the process of skill acquisition takes place via the self-organizing properties of the human movement system. We explain how, during motor performance and learning, self-organizing properties are subjected to a range of constraints that shape the emergence of coordinated action. Self-organization under constraints is a fundamental process that can be exploited when practitioners design task constraints that encourage skill acquisition.

Complex Systems: A Definition

Dynamical systems theory emphasizes the need to understand natural phenomena as systems with many interacting component parts (e.g., Clarke and Crossland, 1985; Davids and Araújo, 2010). A systems perspective provides an excellent rationale for studying human behavior because

> structures and configurations of things should be considered as a whole, rather than examined piece by piece. In a highly complex system like the human mind or human body all the parts affect each other in an intricate way, and studying them individually often disrupts their usual interactions so much that an isolated unit may behave quite differently from the way that it would behave in its normal context (Clarke and Crossland, 1985, p. 16).

What do we mean by the term *complex system*? The word *complex* comes from the Latin word *complexus,* meaning "interwoven," and describes a network of related, interacting parts. So, complex systems are highly integrated systems that are made up of many interacting parts, each of which is capable of affecting other parts.

Complex Systems as Dynamical Systems

When we examine the microcomponents of a complex system, we observe constant interactions and fluctuations. The interactions among the individual parts of the system appear random, and there is the potential for much

Characteristics of Complex Systems

Complex systems are fairly common in daily life. For example, the weather, the traffic flow in a large city, an ant colony, your favorite sport team, and even your own body are all phenomena that exhibit complexity. These systems share several fundamental attributes, as shown in table 2.1.

Table 2.1 Attributes of Complex Systems and Examples

Complex system attribute	Examples
Many independent and variable degrees of freedom (dfs) exist. In the physical sciences, the term **degrees of freedom** typically refers to the independent components of a system that can fit together in many different ways (Bernstein, 1967).	• Performers in a dance troupe • Workers in a commercial organization • The muscles of your body
Complexity is characterized by the number of potential configurations available to the independent parts of such a system (see Newell and Vaillancourt, 2001).	The members of a dance troupe can take part in several performance routines, which requires different members to take on different roles. Larger dance troupes are capable of more diverse and complex routines, whereas the capacity for diversity and complexity in smaller troupes is less.
Many different levels are in the system.	• Lead dancers and supporting crew • The neural, hormonal, biomechanical, and psychological levels in the human body
There is potential for **nonlinearity** and **nonproportionality** between the modifications of the initial conditions and the emerging behavior because the component parts can interact in many different ways.	An example of an influential initial condition would be the dimensions of a performance stage, which can shape emerging behaviors (such as the types of dance moves possible and the resulting coordination of the troupe).
The capacity for **stable** and **unstable** patterned relationships among system parts occur through system self-organization.	The members of a dance troupe can arrange themselves in many collective configurations but can also exhibit their individual expression.
Subsystem components have the ability to limit or influence the behavior of other subsystems (see Gleick, 1987; Kaplan and Glass, 1995).	Subgroups within the dance troupe will influence the timing and expressive behaviors of other subgroups through their own actions.

disorder within the whole system. For example, think of molecules of water in a stream, neurons in the nervous system, or individual blood cells in the human body. These microcomponents could potentially interact in unpredictable ways and thus result in system disorder, such as when the flow of water molecules becomes unpredictable after turbulence or when neurons in the cortex are induced by strobe lighting to fire at random, causing a seizure in people with epilepsy. However, <u>analysis at the macroscopic</u> (<u>large-scale</u>) <u>level typically reveals surprisingly ordered patterns of behavior</u> (Kauffman, 1993, 1995). <u>At this level of analysis</u>, <u>complex systems exhibit coordination tendencies</u> because individual components are capable of linking together to move in and out of functional and coherent patterns or synergies (Haken, 1996; Kelso and Engström, 2006).

A key to understanding the behavior of complex systems concerns how coordination occurs among the vast numbers of component parts. Dynamical systems theory embraces this challenge by deriving nonlinear mathematical descriptions to characterize the order that emerges within complex systems. Van Gelder and Port (1995) offer a liberal definition of a dynamical system as "<u>any state-determined system with a numerical phase space and a rule of evolution</u> (including differential equations and discrete maps) specifying trajectories in this space" (p. 9). The numerical **phase space** refers to all the hypothetical states of organization into which a dynamical system can evolve. In neurobiological movement systems, these states correspond to patterns of coordination that correspond to the smallest unit of analysis to capture the individual–environment coupling. In the ecological dynamics framework, <u>one can define these states through a collective variable capturing the coupling between the individual and the environment</u>. For instance, in rock climbing, Seifert, Boulanger, Orth, and Davids (2015) considered the rolling motion of the trunk relative to the wall as a collective variable in order to understand whether the climber is positioned facing or side toward the wall rather than to compute the rolling motion around the head–feet axis (which is individual centered).

Because they are relatively open systems, dynamical systems can adopt different states of organization and harness surrounding energy sources to form stable patterns of organization. For example, in a physical system formed by billions of molecules of water in a stream, a stable region of system state space is where the resulting force vector (that is, the direction and magnitude of any interacting forces on system flow) converges to a minimum (e.g., as in a vortex). In nature, open systems are capable of receiving and outputting energy into the flows surrounding them, which means that they are sensitive to changes in their surroundings. The <u>stable and functional patterns of organization exhibited by open systems are called</u> **attractors.**

This situation results in a stable state of organization for any system, suggesting that <u>a large perturbing force will be required to destabilize the particular</u>

[margin handwritten note:] IN SKILL ACQUISITION TRAINING, A "PERTURBING FORCE" CAN BE INTRODUCED VIA CONSTRAINT TO PUSH THE LEARNER OUT OF THEIR CURRENT ATTRACTOR "VALLEY." IN FACT, TO MAKE A CHANGE, IT IS LIKELY REQUIRED.

order of the system at that time (e.g., an eddy or a strong current acting on a vortex) (Kugler, Shaw, Vincente, and Kinsella-Shaw, 1990). In neurobiological systems, attractors represent coordination tendencies among system components and are roughly synonymous with functional coordination patterns in the repertoire of a movement system. A good example of coordination tendencies relates to front crawl swimming where the two arms could be either in a catchup, opposition, or superposition mode of coordination (according to swimming speed, active drag, and skill) (Chollet, Chalies, and Chatard, 2000; Chollet and Seifert, 2011).

Constraints on Complex Systems

In complex systems, states of order emerge under constraints. This idea has been imported into human movement science from physics and biology, where scientists have been engaged in studying the emergence of movement behaviors under constraints (e.g., Kelso, 1995; Kugler and Turvey, 1987). Newell (1986) proposed the idea of constraints as boundaries or features that limit the motion of the minute parts of a system. In other words, constraints are the numerous variables that define the phase space of a complex system.

Constraints both limit *and* enable the number of behavioral trajectories that the system can adopt (Seifert, Button, and Davids, 2013). While the dictionary definition of constraint (to limit or to restrict) inevitably directs attention to the boundaries that they create, within those boundaries the same constraints cause behaviors to emerge. Indeed, it seems that complex systems are able to exploit the constraints that surround them in order to allow functional patterns of behavior to emerge in specific contexts (for example, how humans organize their movements in crowd evacuation situations in the case of fire or emergencies). Immediately, we can see how this process of emergent behavior is helpful if we want to adapt our movements to ever-changing performance contexts or to alterations in the skeletomuscular system as a result of aging or injury (Davids and Araújo, 2010).

Physical and Informational Constraints

Constraints can be either physical or informational. **Physical constraints** can be structural or functional in the human movement system. For example, the size and grip strength of a child's hands are structural physical constraints that influence how or whether that child can pick up and manipulate an object such as a toy train or a large ball during play. Functional physical constraints include processes such as reactions and perceptual abilities, which support movement performance. In young children, these characteristics are still maturing and can hamper their ability to coordinate actions effectively. Some physical constraints can persist throughout our life span, whereas others change over time, and in some situations need to be carefully monitored. For instance, in most countries, learning drivers must demonstrate an acceptable standard of visual acuity in order to pass their driving test.

Informational constraints (the focus of chapter 3), on the other hand, are the various forms of energy flowing through the system, such as the pheromones for insects, light reflected from a toy train, or sound waves that a child perceives when a ball bounces across the floor. Young children explore haptic (touch) informational constraints as they pick up and play with objects in their environment. Informational constraints help to shape requisite movement responses and support the coordination of actions with respect to dynamic environments. For instance, the shape of an object (e.g., a cylindrical versus concave shape of a bottle) might change the reaching-to-grasp movement pattern (Sartori, Straulino, and Castiello, 2011).

Self-Organization and Constraints

As noted earlier, complex open systems are capable of exchanging energy with the environment. A good example is a weather system whose behavior is generally difficult to predict more than a few days in advance. Weather systems can contain different amounts of energy because of air flows that vary in pressure and movement of water molecules from the oceans to clouds and back again. Achieving and maintaining stability is a challenge for open complex systems because of their potential for interacting with the environment. The problem for weather forecasters is that a tiny change in the energy flows into and within a weather system can cause large-scale fluctuations in system output on some occasions (i.e., extreme weather events like droughts or monsoons) and have minor effects at other times because the energy that exists within the system is never constant.

Given the longstanding laws of nonlinear thermodynamics, which predict a tendency toward entropy, or disorder, in nature, how can we explain the surprising amount of order that exists at a macroscopic level in many complex systems? To answer that question, we need to consider how open systems in nature can harness energy created by the interaction of their components at the local (microscopic) level to sustain order of the system at the macroscopic level. The capacity of an open complex system to exchange energy and matter with its environment provides it with natural tendencies to settle into attractors or stable patterns of organization; that is, it can take advantage of the physical process that we referred to earlier as **self-organization**.

To recap, biological systems such as flocks of birds, an insect colony, or schools of fish seem to have developed the capacity to use environmental energy to sustain functional periods of stability that benefit the whole system (for a good example in an ant colony, see Gordon, 2007). These systems are able to seek and settle into functional attractors because they have a propensity for pattern formation (e.g., Prigogine and Stengers, 1984). In birds and fish, this spontaneous coordination tendency is manifested as flocking or schooling behavior. For example, in the case of flying birds, a V-like flocking pattern is common because it benefits the navigation of the whole flock without one bird acting as the controlling agent to direct the flight path. Similarly, sea birds adopt highly patterned nesting arrangements (about the length of one bird between nests) during the mating season without the need for a principal bird to dictate spacing. Fish swim randomly as they go about important daily activities such as feeding or mating, but they coalesce into highly synchronized schools when a predator approaches.

These examples from nature show that the openness of a system to surrounding energy flows is useful because energy is a source of information that acts as a constraint on the system. This informational constraint benefits the system by supporting functional and stable behavior patterns for relatively short periods of time, known as a *metastable regime* or expressing *metastability* (Kelso and Engström, 2006) (see Spotlight on Research on Metastability).

Spotlight on Research

Metastability: A Regime for Emergence of New Functional Solutions

Metastability corresponds to a behavioral state in which no pattern of stable coordination actually exists, but some attraction to preferred patterns still persists (Kelso, 2008). In a metastable regime, "there is attractiveness but, strictly speaking, no attractor" (Kelso and Engström, 2006, p. 172). Thus, metastability can be defined as the simultaneous production of two *opposing tendencies*: the tendency of several components to couple (*integrative* tendency) and the tendency of these components to each express their individual behavior (*segregative* tendency) (Kello, Anderson, Holden, and Van Orden, 2008; Kelso and Engström, 2006; Kelso, 2012). Metastability corresponds to the balance between the phases of order and disorder in a complex system close to the critical state (Kello, Beltz, Holden, and Van Orden, 2007). This behavioral state is related to the phenomenon of *intermittency*, which defines a system equilibrium that is close to a critical state, from which it can shift spontaneously from a coordinated to a disordered state (Kelso, 1995).

Thus metastable regimes do not define a coordination state, but rather the "traces of coordination" (Kelso, 2008, p. 190). For instance, in a cricket batting task, Pinder, Davids, and Renshaw (2012) reported a bouncing zone on the pitch for which the batsmen did not show any preferred or stable behavior while hitting the ball. When the ball bounced roughly 7.5 meters away from the batsmen, they sometimes moved forward and sometimes backward in order to strike. The movement, the contact time, and the direction of the batting shot showed great variability when the ball was delivered into this zone. In contrast, these parameters

(continued)

Metastability: A Regime for Emergence
of New Functional Solutions *(continued)*

showed high stability when the ball bounced in zones closer to or more distant from the batsmen. Another example was provided with novice boxers. Hristovski, Davids, Araújo, and Button (2006) showed how the ratio of the distance between the boxing bag and the boxer's arm length could be used to define zones of stable behavior and zones of metastable behaviors. At greater distances from the boxing bag (e.g., 1 to 1.2 of each boxer's arm length scaled to the target distance) a jab movement pattern emerged, whereas at closer distances (e.g. 0.3) uppercut and hook patterns were observed (Hristovski et al., 2006). A critical value of 0.6 scaled distance to the target seemed to lie within the metastable regime where the novice boxers explored a rich, varied, and creative range of movement patterns involving uppercuts, hooks, and jabs (Hristovski et al., 2006).

Application

By placing individuals in metastable regions, via principled constraint manipulation, a practitioner can theoretically increase the learner's exploration of different states of movement organization and requisite information–movement couplings. Coaches and instructors could act as designers by manipulating constraints to encourage performers to explore as exemplified by Seifert and colleagues (2015) in a climbing task. These researchers designed three climbing routes by manipulating the hold orientation and the number of available edges for grasping. A horizontal-edge route was designed to allow horizontal holds in which the trunk faces the wall. A vertical-edge route was designed to allow vertical holds. Experienced climbers were able to grasp these with the side of their body toward the wall. Finally, a double-edge route was designed to create a metastable regime of performance inviting both horizontal and vertical holds. Because a route with only vertical-edge holds was challenging for novice climbers, the double-edge route allowed safe and functional exploration because climbers could both exploit their preexisting behavioral repertoire (i.e., horizontal-hold grasping pattern with their trunk toward the wall) and explore new behaviors (i.e., vertical-hold grasping with their side toward the wall). The results indicate that metastable practice can be useful because perceptual-motor exploration appears less risky and the learner is more inclined to experiment in these regions.

In the study of open systems, scientists have been interested in the phase transitions that can emerge spontaneously in complex systems. Phase transitions are movements of the microcomponents of a system into and out of different states of organization. In weather systems, for example, the dynamics among system components typically don't lead to large-scale changes in system behavior. Instead, a lot of underlying fluctuation mildly affects system stability. However, critical changes in the energy arrays surrounding the system, such as a rise in atmospheric pressure within a weather system, can alter system stability and lead to macroscopic changes and reorganization into a different state (e.g., thunderstorms in tropical regions). Phase transitions form the basis of self-organization in complex systems, and examples of such pattern formations have been observed in open biological, physical, and social systems, such as when large audiences synchronize their clapping at concerts.

Emergent Behavior in Human Movement

Self-organization is a powerful process that can help us adapt movement patterns to changing environmental circumstances, such as performing tennis strokes on different surfaces or driving in traffic. How do we harness this natural process? To begin, self-organization in complex systems is not a completely blind process in which any random pattern can result. Typically, a dynamical system takes on few states of organization, and research has shown that we are not very good at producing random patterns of movement behavior (Newell, Deutsch, Sosnoff, and Mayer-Kress, 2006). These findings support observations that natural dynamical systems tend to inhabit only certain parts of the total landscape of all possible states that a system can hypothetically adopt (i.e., the state space) (Kauffman, 1993, 1995). The type of order that emerges in the behavior of a system depends a great deal on existing environmental conditions and the constraints that shape the behavior (see Spotlight on Research on the HKB Model).

Spotlight on Research_____

From Humble Beginnings to the HKB Model

When Scott Kelso published his series of studies (1981b, 1984) examining changes in coordination between rhythmic finger movements, he may not have predicted how significant his ideas would become in the human movement sciences. In his original work, Kelso examined the spontaneous coordination dynamics emerging from the relative oscillations of the left and right index fingers during rhythmic movements. Surprisingly, when participants performed these movements, they exhibited a spontaneous switch of coordination patterns as the frequency of finger movements was constrained by the beat of a metronome (i.e., a gradual increase from 1.25 to 3.5 hertz).

It was consistently shown that the relative phasing between each finger demonstrated stability in coordination dynamics at only two isolated attractor regions: fingers oscillating either in-phase (fingers moving toward the midline of the body together) or antiphase (one finger moving toward the body's midline while the other finger moves away from the midline) (see figure 2.1). The relative phase of any

(continued)

From Humble Beginnings to the HKB Model *(continued)*

two oscillating systems (e.g., each leg used in walking) is the phase lag in one system's cycle of movement compared with the other. When the study participants began oscillating in the antiphase pattern, they eventually switched to an in-phase pattern as the metronome frequency increased. The sudden phase transitions from one state of coordination to the other were not brought about by an intentional change prescribed by the participant, but through the self-organizing properties of the motor system.

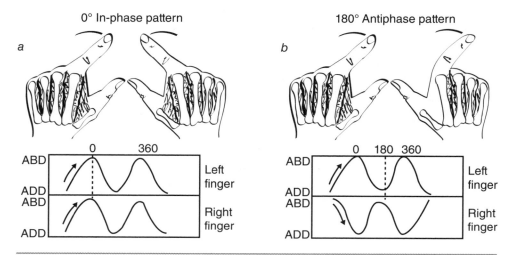

FIGURE 2.1 In the movements performed in Kelso's (1981b, 1984) original experiments, *(a)* we can observe the 0° in-phase pattern, and *(b)* we can observe the 180° antiphase pattern. These patterns are thought to be intrinsically stable in rhythmic, bimanual movements. (ABD = abduction movements; ADD = adduction.)

Reprinted by permission from S.A. Wallace, Dynamic pattern perspective of rhythmic movement: An introduction. In *Advances in Motor Learning and Control*, edited by H.N. Zelaznik (Champaign, IL: Human Kinetics, 1996), 170.

Haken, Kelso, and Bunz (1985) proposed a mathematical model—the HKB model—that formally demonstrated how the movement behavior observed in the finger-waggling paradigm could emerge as the potential function of the movement system changed. The model demonstrated that scaling of a control parameter (e.g., metronomic beat frequency) could lead to a reduction in stability of the order parameter (e.g., relative phase of finger movements). This behavior resulted from an alteration in the potential energy of the system, which Haken and colleagues (1985) modeled as two stable movement patterns. As a control parameter changes, the attractor landscape is deformed and system behavior switches from the least stable organization (antiphase) to the most stable (in-phase). In more dynamic environments where random forces are present, the degree of system stability is associated with the degree of fluctuations the movement system exhibits (Haken, 1996; Schöner, Haken, and Kelso, 1987).

The HKB model also acknowledged other important features of the dynamical movement system, such as the relationship between attractor stability and the relaxation time, which is the speed at which the system would return to an attractor (stable motor patterning) following an external **perturbation**. Relaxation time has been used to test the stability of attractors in a variety of situations (e.g., Court, Bennett, Williams, and Davids, 2002, 2005; Scholz and Kelso, 1989). Since the innovative work of Haken, Kelso, and Bunz, researchers have found similar coordination tendencies, such as transitions, multistability (i.e., coexistent stable states for the same condition of performance), and sensitivity to frequency and amplitude, with a whole host of rhythmic movements. Although it seems that different rhythmic tasks may have different potential functions and, hence, different attractor regimes, the same self-organizational principles hold. From relatively simple beginnings, a new paradigm for studying motor behavior was born.

Application

Re-create Kelso's classic studies. Oscillate your index fingers together in an antiphase fashion, slowly increase the speed, and explore the self-organization tendencies of your own movement system. Based on your miniexperiment, what are some of the control parameters that could affect when transitions might occur?

The exercise in the application of the Spotlight on Research on the HKB Model is not just a frivolous party trick; it is of considerable significance when studying movement coordination. Consider, for example, how a skier's body position might self-organize to produce a perfectly timed turn on the ski trail. Because of the demanding nature of the ski trail, the skier's actions are not completely determined in advance. Instead, both internal constraints, such as the skier's anatomical organization, and external constraints, such as visual information and the contact of the skis with the snow, influence the emergence of the skier's precise movement patterns on the trail (e.g., Bernstein, 1967; Warren, 1990). A change in environmental conditions, such as the gradient of the slope, the wind direction, or a patch of ice, could significantly affect the existing patterns of movement coordination. For instance, a steep slope would typically force a novice skier to adopt a pattern of traversing from side to side on the trail. By shifting the weight distribution over the inside ski and changing the alignment of the skis, the skier does not generate excessive downhill speed. This strategy provides a task-specific solution without a significant loss in postural stability.

Constraints and Movement Coordination

An important implication of the ideas we've discussed so far is that perceptions, memories, intentions, plans, and actions do not have to be considered as entities stored in the central nervous system. Rather, they may be better understood as self-organizing, macroscopic patterns formed by the interaction of the many system components and key constraints in the environment (Kelso, 1995; Kugler and Turvey, 1987). For example, the system components could be neurons in the brain firing together to form ideas, memories, or plans, or they might involve groups of muscles spanning several joints to form coordination patterns. Constraints are central to the self-organization process in human movement systems. A dynamical systems interpretation emphasizes environmental and physical constraints as well as individual constraints, such as one's cognitions, memories, and intentions (Williams, Davids, and Williams, 1999).

According to Newell (1986), constraints can be classified into three categories: organismic, environmental, and task. These categories provide a coherent framework for understanding how coordination patterns emerge during goal-directed behavior (see figure 2.2).

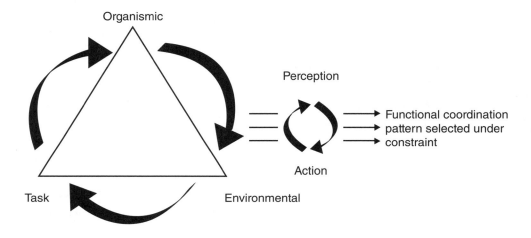

FIGURE 2.2 Three classes of constraints—organismic, environmental, and task— provide a coherent framework for understanding how coordination patterns emerge during goal-directed behavior.

Organismic Constraints

Organismic constraints refer to a person's characteristics, such as genotypes, height, weight, muscle-to-fat ratio, connective strength of synapses in the brain, cognitions, motivations, and emotions. Customary thought patterns, levels of practice, sensory defects (or even a disrupted night's sleep!) can act as organismic constraints to shape the way a person approaches a particular performance goal. These unique characteristics represent resources that are brought to bear on the task problem or limitations that can lead to individual-specific adaptations (see chapter 5 about biological constraints). For instance, males and females are known to have different muscle-to-fat ratios and adipose tissue distributions leading to differences in buoyancy, stroke length, and arm coordination in swimming (Seifert et al., 2011). A crucial distinction between many biological organisms and humans is that humans can use internal energy sources to intentionally constrain their actions to achieve goals or desired outcomes. That is, human behavior is not deterministic but can be intentionally driven (Kugler et al., 1990).

Environmental Constraints

Environmental constraints are global, physical variables in nature, such as ambient light, temperature, or altitude. On Earth, gravity is a key environmental constraint on movement coordination for all tasks, as our example of a skier traversing a steep mountain slope showed. Considering our skier once more, we can use the visual flow presented by a ski mogul to regulate the torques generated across the hip and knee joints. Larger mounds of snow require the skier to flex the hips and knees in order to absorb the reaction imparted to the legs, and ambient temperature can affect the skier's muscle properties.

When we move in water, our actions are shaped by a different set of environmental constraints. Because water is roughly 800 times denser than air, swimmers must take into account the fluid density to minimize drag by hydrodynamic body position and movement coordination (for an example in breaststroke, see Chollet and Seifert, 2011). Moreover, Archimedes buoyancy force is another key environmental constraint that swimmers attempt to exploit with a horizontal body position. Additionally, some environmental constraints are social rather than physical, including family support, peer groups, societal expectations, values, and cultural norms (Haywood and Getchell, 2005) (see chapter 6 about social and cultural constraints).

Task Constraints

Task constraints are usually more specific to performance contexts (than environmental constraints) and include task goals; specific rules associated with an activity; implements or tools; surfaces; ground areas and pitches; and boundary markings such as pavements, barriers, line markings, and posts. Even with apparently stable activities, such as playing a musical instrument or swinging a golf club, motor behavior can fluctuate because the task constraints may vary from performance to performance. For example, musicians have to adapt to playing in different settings (e.g., small concert rooms, large auditoriums, outdoor venues), each with distinctive acoustics, sound systems, and stage layouts. They may even have to adapt to performing with different instruments on occasion, which may affect the nuances of the performance.

Being able to vary motor performance according to the different contexts of action is an integral part of skill acquisition, and adaptive learning allows people to cope with novel task constraints as performance conditions change. For instance, Rein, Davids, and Button (2010) nicely demonstrate how basketball players adapt their shooting technique depending on factors such their distance to the basket and the presence of an opponent. To encourage flexibility and adaptability in patients, physical therapists often manipulate task constraints. For example, a therapist might encourage a patient using a wheelchair to negotiate a busy and cluttered enclosed area in an attempt to improve the patient's control and ability to maneuver the wheelchair. Such practices also encourage the patient to explore alternative coordination solutions and optimize techniques in daily motor skills.

The Fluid Nature of Constraints

During goal-directed activity, the fluid interaction of organismic, environmental, and task constraints on the neuromuscular system results in the emergence of different states of coordination that become optimized with practice and experience. For example, how a climbing instructor scales a rocky outcrop is a consequence of many constraints at any one time, including the climber's genes, physical endurance levels, and injury status; the nature of the climbing surface; and the climber's overall goals such as getting to the top as quickly as possible or demonstrating a safe path to students.

Because the three classes of constraints can interact, it is sometimes difficult to distinguish among them. An organismic constraint such as whether the learner has understood an instruction may depend on how effectively the instruction was delivered by the practitioner (task constraint). Furthermore, environmental constraints include surrounding energy flows (e.g., ambient light), whereas the specific nature of information sources is a key task constraint for learners (e.g., light reflected off the walls and floor of a swimming pool). In this example, the surrounding energy flows are the same, but the different task constraints lead to specific information sources being useful under varying performance contexts.

Thus, instead of isolating constraints that could lead the learner to focus on *structural* features of the task, it could be assumed that by guiding the learner toward *functional* features (i.e., to perceive the possibilities for action), he or she might perceive invariant reflecting interacting constraints. For instance, in climbing, Boschker, Bakker, and Michaels (2002) found that inexperienced climbers exclusively perceived structural features of holds (e.g., location, shape, and orientation) when looking at a climbing wall, whereas experienced climbers mainly focused on the functional features such as the grasping, reaching, and standing opportunities of individual holds as well as the chains of climbing moves possible from using multiple holds.

Another key idea from the study of nonlinear systems is that constraints on behavior (and thereby their interactions) are by no means permanent (Guerin and Kunkle, 2004). Research has taught us that constraints on motor performance are often temporary, and they can strengthen or decay on different timescales. For example, we can consider an infant's developing body as a slowly decaying constraint on its walking capability as the muscle-to-fat ratio of the lower limbs alters over time. However, if the mother calls out to her infant with a toy, this new constraint might have a temporary but irresistible emergent influence on the infant's coordination (Cordovil, Araújo, Pepping, and Barreiros, 2015). The consequence for the behavior of emerging or decaying constraints is an increase or decrease in the self-organizing entropy of the system. This is an important point to consider in skill acquisition, and it is of particular importance when designing practice and rehabilitation environments, a topic we will develop further in chapter 8. Practitioners should expect that the constraints on each individual are fluid and interacting as a result of influences such as development, learning, aging, and experience.

Coordinating Degrees of Freedom in the Human Movement System

Understanding how order emerges among the degrees of freedom (dfs) of complex, dynamical systems is the fundamental problem for researchers of skill acquisition. During the 1980s and 1990s, when theoreticians introduced dynamical systems theory to the study of human movement coordination, they immediately recognized the links between their theories and the insights of Russian physiologist Nikolai Bernstein. This timely interaction of ideas stimulated interest in the role of constraints on motor control and skill acquisition.

Bernstein and the Degrees of Freedom Problem

How do humans coordinate the activity of all the movement subsystems, such as postural control, transport, and object manipulation? Russian movement physiologist Nikolai Bernstein (1967) reminded us that studying the processes of movement coordination is necessary to help us understand this question. He was concerned with how the many microcomponents of the human movement system—muscles, joints, and limb segments—are coordinated during the performance of complex tasks. For example, gymnasts bringing together parts of their lower and upper body while somersaulting, drivers using their foot and both hands to steer a car by braking and moving the wheel, and dancers coordinating arms and legs during a pas de deux neatly illustrate this coordination problem.

Understanding how the learner employs and constrains the large number of relevant motor system dfs during actions like reaching and grasping has become known as Bernstein's (1967) degrees of freedom problem. Bernstein's definition of acquiring movement coordination neatly captures the fundamental issue in a dynamical systems interpretation of human movement. The acquisition of coordination is viewed as "the process of mastering redundant degrees of freedom of the moving organ, in other words its conversion to a controllable system" (p. 127).

Bernstein (1967) proposed that learners initially form specific functional muscle–joint linkages or synergies to manage the large number of dfs that are controlled in the human movement system. He suggested that such functional groupings compress the physical components of the movement system and specify how the relevant dfs for an action become mutually dependent. Synergies among motor system components help learners discover and assemble the relevant couplings between limbs (e.g., coordinating the braking action of a foot with the steering action of both hands when turning a car) to cope with the abundance of dfs (Mitra, Amazeen, and Turvey, 1998). In this way, fluctuations in the number of dfs used over repetitions of a task are managed by constraining variability in their implementation to a small subspace of the total number available (Scholz, Schöner, and Latash, 2000; Todorov and Jordan, 2002). For example, when learning to drive a car, learners could potentially use either foot to depress the brake pedal and use a variety of shoulder, elbow, or wrist movements to turn the steering wheel. These limb segments constitute a considerable number of different motor system dfs that might be used to achieve the movement goal. With practice, eventually this large number of dfs is reduced to a smaller subset that is easier to manage and regulate (i.e., the wrists and right foot).

According to Bernstein (1967), the initial coordination patterns for tasks such as casting a fishing rod or maintaining balance on a surfboard begin as fixed, rigid linkages between body parts. This early learning strategy helps people cope with the extreme abundance of dfs in the motor system. The assembly of a functional coordination solution is beyond the learner's capacity and so the problem of controlling the movement system is managed by "dysfunctionally, suboptimally or overly" constraining the available motor system dfs (Broderick and Newell, 1999, p. 166). A common, but by no means universal, observation is that learners reduce the active regulation of individual mechanical dfs at the motor system periphery to a minimum. With learning and experience, the fixed characteristic of coordination is progressively altered as movement system dfs are released and allowed to re-form into different configurations or synergies for specific purposes. Typically, as a result of extended practice, the initially strong couplings between muscles and joints are gradually unfixed and formed into task-specific coordinative structures so that internal and external forces can be better exploited to increase movement economy and efficiency (Bernstein, 1967; Newell, Broderick, Deutsch, and Slifkin, 2003; Vereijken, Van Emmerik, Whiting, and Newell, 1992). For example, the stiff upright stance adopted by the rigid coupling of hip, knee, and ankle joints in a novice surfer gradually becomes loosened with practice. Eventually there is a greater reliance on a coupling between only a few key dfs, such as the knee joints, for producing appropriate muscle torques to guide the board and harness the energetic impulses from currents and waves to create rapid transitions in the water.

Interestingly, it may be necessary for people recovering from injury or illness to temporarily reshape learned movement patterns with their reconfigured or altered dfs (e.g., walking on crutches with a broken leg, grasping an object after a finger amputation). The coordination patterns that arise early in relearning a skill have been given different names, such as *task-specific devices* (e.g., Bingham, 1988), *information–movement couplings* (Bootsma and van Wieringen, 1990; Davids, Kingsbury, Bennett, and Handford, 2001; Savelsbergh and van der Kamp, 2000), and *coordinative structures* (Schmidt and Fitzpatrick, 1996; Turvey, 1990).

Coordinative Structures in Action: Kicking a Soccer Ball

Coordinative structures harness the coordination tendencies that exist in neurobiological systems. They are designed for a specific purpose or activity, such as when groups of muscles are temporarily assembled into coherent units to achieve specific task goals, like throwing a Frisbee or hammering a nail. Quality perceptual information is necessary for assembling coordinative structures because the details of their organization are not completely predetermined and are tuned by the constraints of each activity. The assembly of coordinative structures is a dynamical process that depends on relevant sources of perceptual information related to a performer's key properties (e.g., proprioceptive information from muscles and joints) and the environment (e.g., vision of a target or surface). With practice, coordinative structures become more flexible and emerge from the rigidly fixed configurations that learners use early on to manage the multitude of motor system dfs. With each task goal, coordinative structures are assembled anew and may slightly vary each time the performer constructs an action in a dynamic environment.

For example, soccer players learn to adapt their coordinative structure for kicking a ball so that they can use it under changing conditions. These conditions may include side-foot passes, goal chips, or shots; fields that vary in dimensions; changing weather conditions; and motor system fatigue. This characteristic of skill-based differences can be observed in qualitative form in figure 2.3, which depicts the kicking skills of a novice soccer player and an experienced soccer player. These images qualitatively show that skill-based differences in coordination characteristics remain obvious throughout the kick, from the preparation phase to the follow-through phase, where the expert kicker shows greater hip extension and knee flexion than the novice kicker (Chow, Davids, Button, and Koh, 2007).

In a study by Chow, Button, Davids, and Koh (2007), participants across three skill levels (skilled, intermediate, and novice) demonstrated various coordination patterns in a soccer chipping task (i.e., task goal required participants

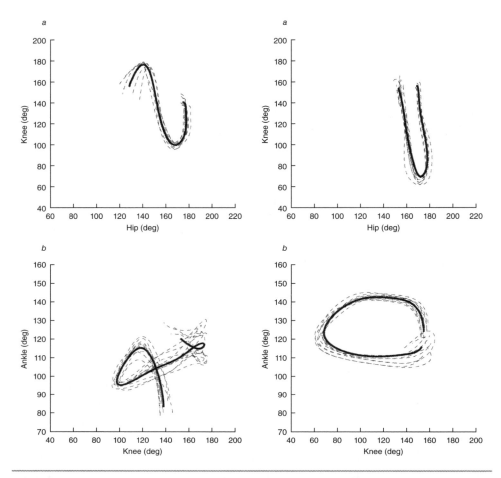

FIGURE 2.3 Skill-based differences in coordination characteristics remain obvious throughout the kick where the expert kicker *(right panels)* shows greater hip extension *(a)* and knee flexion *(b)* than the novice kicker *(left panels)*.

Reprinted by permission from J.Y. Chow, K. Davids, C. Button, and M. Koh, "Variation in Coordination of a Discrete Multiarticular Action as a Function of Skill Level," *Journal of Motor Behavior* 39, no. 6 (2007): 463-479.

to accurately and comfortably kick a ball over a height barrier to a live receiver). It was observed that novice participants exhibited large ranges of motion in the kicking limb in an attempt to drive the ball over the barrier because height clearance was an emerging constraint for them. In contrast, the skilled and intermediate participants tended to use a more restricted range of motion in their kicking actions to provide better control during ball contact to get the ball over the barrier and at the same time position the ball accurately and comfortably for the live receiver. Key interactions between the task, performer, and environment a play significant role in how coordination is shaped (see figure 2.4).

During the performance of motor tasks, the central nervous system typically can select from a large number of dfs for regulating movements (see Latash, 2000). Hasan and Thomas (1999) have referred to this abundance of dfs as

a

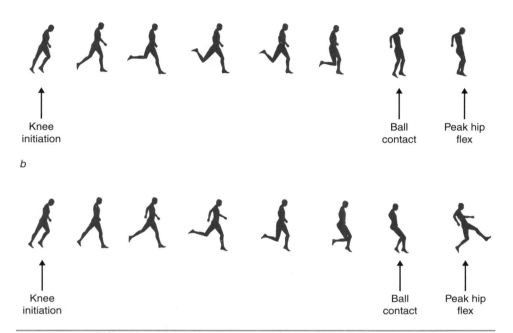

b

FIGURE 2.4 Representation of *(a)* skilled and intermediate participants performing a chipping action (more constrained motion of the kicking limb) and *(b)* novice participants performing a driving action with a larger range of motion of the kicking limb.

Reprinted by permission from J.Y. Chow, K. Davids, C. Button, and M. Koh, "Variation in Coordination of a Discrete Multiarticular Action as a Function of Skill Level," *Journal of Motor Behavior* 39, no. 6 (2007): 463-479.

"an embarrassment of riches" (p. 380) for the human central nervous system, and it has even been proposed that many dfs become redundant in some actions because they do not actively contribute to the regulation of an action.

It is important to understand the relationship between the controllability of the motor system and the flexibility of movement coordination. On the one hand, the abundance of motor system dfs can provide the opportunity for much-needed flexibility in adapting movement patterns to dynamic environments. On the other hand, the central nervous system has the problem of controlling the behavior of the motor system dfs in dynamic environments, which it achieves through the assembly of functional coordinative structures. By being connected to the environment (i.e., open to information from the environment), physical constraints on motor system dfs can be adapted to function within each unique performance situation. In other words, movement coordination is controlled with respect to environmental events, surfaces, and objects during performance of many activities. This quality of the movement system invokes a second definition of coordination: taking into account how performers are connected to environment and exploit affordances, which is what we turn to in the next chapter.

Summary

In this chapter, we discussed how researchers have applied dynamical systems theory to the study of coordination in human movement systems. We outlined the significance of key ideas borrowed from mathematics, physics, and biology, such as complexity, self-organization processes, and constraints. Understanding coordination in dynamical movement systems represents an important scientific challenge for human movement specialists. Bernstein (1967) was among the first to emphasize the need to understand coordination among motor system components. He argued that early in learning, people rigidly fix motor system dfs to cope with the redundant number available. Later in learning, synergies (i.e., coordinative structures) are imposed to functionally group motor system dfs to ensure that movements are adapted to changing circumstances of performance.

From a dynamical systems view, coordination is a property that emerges from each individual movement system in response to the constraints that need to be satisfied. Newell's (1986) model of interacting constraints highlights how dynamical movement systems can take advantage of inherent self-organization processes at different levels of the human body. Newell's model identifies the main categories of constraints—organismic, environmental, and task—that shape the coordination patterns emerging during performance and, as we shall discover, skill acquisition. Because each person is different and performance circumstances are constantly changing, individual motor output reflects how people adapt to the constraints of a dynamic environment and take advantage of the richness and diversity of the various performance contexts. This idea is at the heart of the ecological dynamics approach to skill acquisition.

Self-Test Questions

1. Think of an example of a complex system in a sport, exercise, or rehabilitation setting. What characteristics does this system share with other complex systems, such as the weather or the central nervous system?

2. What are some of the key constraints that influence the organization of systems such as crowds of people, an infant playing with a toy, and a stroke patient relearning how to move?

3. Describe how the control of a complex multijoint movement, for example the front crawl in swimming, may be explained from the dynamical systems approach.

4. How would you explain to athletes that metastability in the motor system can reflect functional exploration of the perceptual-motor workspace and is an important part of skill acquisition?

Laboratory Activity

Make Your Own Multistable Regimes

We have introduced several important concepts in this chapter that originate from the dynamical systems theory. Our hope is that it will help you to better understand these complex ideas if you were to conduct a practical activity that draws from them. Is it possible to use the prompts below to explore how learners regulate their degrees of freedom as a function of practice? Can you conceive how a metastable regime influences the likelihood of a performer adopting different movement patterns?

Experimental Problems

- Identify a movement task with which you have limited familiarity (e.g., kicking a ball over a barrier onto a target).
- As the learner, practice the activity until you reach an acceptable level of skill as defined by a relevant performance criterion (e.g., success on at least three out of four attempts).
- Identify a key control parameter for the task that you can systematically manipulate or change (e.g., height of barrier, distance to target).
- Attempt the task under the constraints of a scanning procedure to explore whether a metastable regime exists.

Equipment and Resources

- Selection of balls, discs, bats, rackets, and targets
- Open laboratory space or gymnasium
- Video camera
- Measuring tape

Hint: Many task choices are available, but it might be helpful to consider general activities that have multiple possible solutions, such as throwing, kicking, balance, or locomotion. Consider the best ways to record the movement patterns and outcomes associated with performance.

CHAPTER 3

Informational Constraints on Coordination: An Ecological Psychology Perspective

CHAPTER OBJECTIVES

After reading this chapter, you will be able to do the following:

- Explain why biological organisms are open systems and the benefits this bestows on them
- Describe how Gibson's ecological interpretation of information differs from traditional, indirect accounts of perception
- Explain how perceptual exploration can reveal sensory invariants that may then be used to regulate action
- Discuss the concept of affordances and how it might impinge on decision making and intentional behavior
- Provide examples of information–movement coupling in human coordination
- Apply the concepts of attunement and calibration to help explain the process of perceptual learning

The ecological dynamics approach to skill acquisition is built on two theoretical pillars. In the previous chapter, we discussed the first pillar: Bernstein's (1967) insights regarding physical constraints on organization of motor system degrees of freedom (dfs). The second theoretical pillar concerns how performers coordinate actions with respect to important informational constraints such as environmental events, objects, and surfaces, which is the basis for James Gibson's (1979) perspective in ecological psychology.

This chapter focuses on affordances and informational constraints on movement and skill acquisition, explaining how information and movement are so intimately related (van der Kamp and Renshaw, 2015). Healthy humans typically place significant emphasis on vision while learning to coordinate actions with their environment. Hence, our focus in this chapter will initially be on the role of optical information in regulating actions. In later sections we will discuss how other informational constraints, such as haptic (touch) and acoustic (sound) flows, can be harnessed during skill acquisition.

Conditions for a Satisfactory Theoretical Account of Coordination

Most actions require coordination between the relevant parts of the movement system, and between the environment (e.g., object or surface to be intercepted). For example, how does a child learn to stand from sitting or to pick up a toy? What information does a surgeon use when making a delicate incision during an operation? When coordinating their movements with respect to their environment, people use precise information to locate objects, obstacles, and surfaces in space (*where* information) at a specific instant in time (*when* information) (Araújo and Davids, 2009; Davids, Savelsbergh, Bennett, and van der Kamp, 2002; Fajen, Riley, and Turvey, 2009). Fajen and colleagues (2009) indicated that five conditions need to be met in order for a satisfactory theoretical account to explain coordination of movements with environmental events (see table 3.1). These conditions clearly highlight the importance for theoreticians to account for how perception and action become linked as we navigate our environment.

Open Systems and Energy Exchange

To understand how information constrains movement, we need to return to the concept of an open system, which we discussed briefly in chapter 2. Open systems are common in nature. Biological organisms are open systems because they are continually exchanging energy with the environment at any given moment. Whenever forces are applied within an open system, there are usually changes to system organization because internal energy within the system (e.g., as a result of the mechanics of limb movements) interacts with the available forces in the environment (e.g., reactive forces, gravity,

Table 3.1 Conditions for a Satisfactory Theoretical Account of Coordination

Condition	Theoretical requirements
1.	Place more importance on explaining the success and reliability of perception than on misperceptions and illusions (favored in many laboratory studies of perception, but are much less frequent in life).
2.	Emphasize the critical role of movement in perception, just as perception plays a critical role in regulating movement.
3.	Highlight how performers perceive the properties of the world that are most directly relevant to how they move to achieve goals.
4.	Account for the coupling between perception and action.
5.	Capture changes in perception–action coupling that accompany learning.

Based on Fajen and colleagues (2009).

friction, air resistance) (Warren, 2006). For example, it is this openness that skilled figure skaters are able to exploit as they use the momentum created by applying muscle forces of the lower legs, trunk, and arms in a jump and spin (internal source of energy), with additional force available from the low coefficient of friction offered by the ice surface (external source). On the one hand, this combination allows skilled skaters to become more energy efficient and to fluidly generate more vertical and rotational forces. On the other hand, novice skaters are unable to control the additional forces offered by the ice surface, and changes to their movement patterns can be more abrupt and unintended.

The point is that humans and other animals have onboard sources of energy (e.g., stored in muscle) that allow them to be self-sustaining and adaptive. With experience, they can also learn to exploit a range of surrounding patterned energy flows offered by environmental properties that they can harness to act more efficiently (Warren, 2006). This is good news for those of us who want to save energy, and particularly for athletes and professionals with physically demanding jobs. With task practice, they can become increasingly efficient in using their precious internal energy sources while also becoming skilled at exploiting freely available energy from forces such as gravity and friction, as evidenced by the skilled movements of acrobats and circus artists (e.g., see Sparrow, 2000). In accordance with Bernstein's (1967) ideas, coordination and control of movement do not occur in a vacuum and do not result from applying internal muscular forces alone.

A hallmark of increasing expertise in many physical activities is energy conservation, signaled by the capacity to exploit available forces in the surrounding environment as a source of energy to be harnessed during action. For example, skilled surfers have learned to time their approach into a wave so that the energy of the wave can lift and carry them while turning into and

Coordination in the Stream of Action

Open systems are able to exchange energy and matter with their environment. Their behaviors should be studied with reference to the specific environments in which they are located (Gordon, 2007). An important implication of this idea is that coordination in open movement systems is best analyzed in the midst of the stream of action (Reed, 1982). The study of perception and action should take place in representative environments provided by natural activities in work, sport, and other performance settings.

out of the gathering break. Skilled performers are also able to use surrounding patterned energy flows, such as optical energy in the form of light reflected off objects and surfaces, as information to constrain their actions (Gibson, 1979). We can begin to understand how energy can constrain actions by considering two important ecological concepts (Gibson, 1979): information and direct perception.

Information

To explain how humans and other animals establish perceptual contact with their environment, Gibson (1966, 1979) introduced a radical new theory of the stimulus information available to the receptors. He argued that the assumption of impoverished stimulus information, on which most inferential theories of perception are based, is fallacious. Traditional information-processing theories argue that, for perceivers to be informed about sources of stimulation, they must store a large set of alternatives in their memory and select among them according to those stimulating conditions. In other words, stimulation to the receptors does not directly inform about its sources. For example, one cannot know from the light ray itself whether its source is near or distant. Receptors in an eye stimulated by a ray of light can only be informed of the presence of the ray of light. For a stimulation to act informatively, a perceiver must have some means of interpreting or decoding the stimulation according to a limited set of memorized possibilities.

Contrary to this classical viewpoint, Gibson argued for a very different conceptualization of information that he considered to be the more appropriate way to understand perception and cognition among living organisms. From this ecological view, the structure of light, for example, could be intrinsically informative. Gibson's theory implies that sensitivity to information structure must exist in a perceiver, but an added interpretation process is not necessary (Richardson, Shockley, Fajen, and Turvey, 2008). Ecological psychologists assume that perceptual information resides in the ambient energy arrays and flows (Gibson, 1979) and that it can directly inform an individual about the environmental properties of our world.

Gibson also stressed the importance of an individual's movement in both the detection and discovery of specifying information. In his view, perceivers are rarely passive: To detect information, perceptual systems scan the ambient arrays to actively detect information. Furthermore, by *moving*, performers can create spatiotemporal energy patterns that are specific to environmental properties. The moving body of an observer contributes to the structure of an array at any observed place. Because performers exploit spatiotemporal energy patterns that are specific to the properties of the environment that are to be perceived or to be acted on, inferential processes are dispensable, and direct perceptual contact with a performance environment is possible.

Because Gibson wanted to understand perception of the environment, instead of working with primitives such as points, lines, planes, and projections, he began with the ambient **optic array**. The ambient optic array is structured light surrounding a point of observation. It consists of multiple reflected light rays filling a medium (in this case, the air). This means that there must be sources of light, reflecting surfaces, and a medium. The same set of reflecting surfaces that make the light-filled medium possible also accounts for differences of intensity in different directions from any point of observation. These differences exist by virtue of differences in arrangement (layout) relative to one another and to the illumination, differences in texture, and differences in pigment structure.

In the case of light, the optic array (i.e., information), just exists; it is not coming to the eye. Gibson (1979) used the fact that animals with compound eyes, as well as animals with chambered eyes, show visually guided behavior (such as avoidance in the presence of an expanding shadow specifying a looming object) as evidence that they are designed to use optical information in the array, even though they have no retinal images. Thus, retinal images are not necessary for vision, but information is (Mace, 1986). Gibson maintained that such optical changes (variants) and nonchanges (invariants) in the surrounding array are used by perceivers to control their movements relative to the environment.

Variants and Invariants in Structured Ambient Energy

As a structure surrounding a performer, patterned ambient energy (e.g., optic array, sound waves) can be explored or observed in the active sense of the word. When this occurs, the patterned energy flow changes in some ways, but not in all. For example, an important way that the optical array of an idealized frozen environment changes occurs when an observer moves. Everything in the array flows, and regular exchanges of array components are revealed and hidden. But within the flow, some relations between components stay invariant.

These **invariants** specify (i.e., inform an individual about) stable features of the environment. The changes, or variants, specify movement of the observer relative to the stable environment. Because invariants are defined only with respect to variants, it follows that change is necessary to reveal nonchange. It also follows that coordinated movements of an observer can be specified only relative to invariant structure of the surrounding energy arrays (Mace, 1986).

Variants and invariants of the ambient optic array allow for the separation of that which belongs to the environment from that which belongs to the performer. As the performer's point of view changes, one can perceive when it is the point of view changing and when it is the environment changing. When the point of view changes in a stable environment, the persistence of that environment is specified by invariants (Gibson, 1979). A consequence of the optics of occlusion is that as one uncovers new surfaces by exploration, one is extending the amount of connected, concurrently existing surface that one has detected.

To understand what these ideas imply for understanding skill performance and acquisition, it may be helpful to consider an example from golf. In figure 3.1, the golfer is exploring the invariant structure of a putting green as he moves around the ball and hole to study a required putt. The invariant structure of each putting green includes the information sources that are always available in each circumstance, regardless of whether one is playing on Pebble Beach (United States), Royal Lytham and St. Annes (United Kingdom), or a local golf course. Experienced golfers know that as they move between the ball and the hole, important characteristics, such as the cut of the grass and subtle contours of the putting surface, become more apparent (Button and Pepping, 2002). Movements of the performer reveal these invariant information sources for subsequent putting actions.

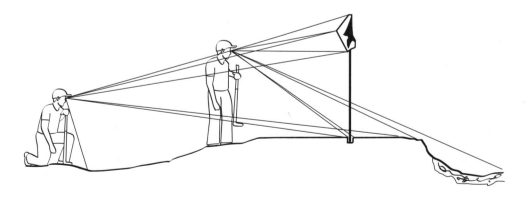

FIGURE 3.1 The golfer explores the invariant structure of a putting green as he moves around the ball and hole to study a required putt. Experienced golfers know that as they move between the ball and the hole, important characteristics of the putting green become more apparent.

Given the far-reaching implications of these theoretical ideas, it is not surprising that much research time and effort has been devoted to identifying those invariants that can specify actions. One of the most closely studied invariants in the informational array is an optic variable known as *tau*. Since its conceptualization and operationalization by the experimental psychologist David Lee in the 1970s and 1980s, it has generated a significant amount of research and debate in the literature.

When a nondeforming object, such as a ball, moves toward an observer, the contours of the ball form a solid visual angle (see figure 3.2). This optic flow is perceived over time as a nested hierarchy of solid angles that expands symmetrically as it approaches the observer. The optical information specified by the relative rate of expansion of the visual solid angle enclosed by these contours is **tau**. Tau provides the individual with direct information about the remaining time to contact (TC) between the point of observation and an approaching object (Lee, 1976).

Assuming that an approaching object has a constant velocity and is traveling toward the point of observation, there are considerable advantages of being able to perceive TC. For instance, the individual does not need to indirectly process ambiguous cues on distance, object size, and velocity and perform mental calculations to compute the object's time of arrival. Not needing to rely on indirect processing of cues is particularly beneficial in dynamic activities such as driving on an expressway, playing tennis, or skating rapidly on an ice rink. In these activities, performers may have little time to react and need not spend the time to calculate the time of arrival of an object or surface while interpreting events in the environment.

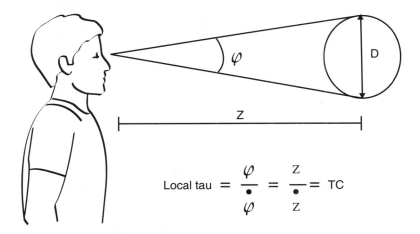

$$\text{Local tau} = \frac{\varphi}{\overset{\bullet}{\varphi}} = \frac{Z}{\overset{\bullet}{Z}} = TC$$

FIGURE 3.2 Tau provides information about the remaining TC between the point of observation and an approaching object. φ corresponds to the visual angle subtended by the approaching object on the observer. Z corresponds to the distance of the object from the point of observation.

Travassos, Araújo, Davids, Vilar, Esteves, and Correia (2012) developed an interesting application of the tau concept to the study of team sports performance. They studied how futsal defenders intercept the trajectory of a ball (passed between attackers) by comparing how they regulated their actions using critical information sources, such as time to intercept the ball, in successful and unsuccessful interceptions. Time to ball interception was measured by the difference between the time for each defender to reach an interception point in ball trajectory and the time of the ball's arrival at the same interception point. Results showed positive values of time to ball interception when passes were not intercepted, and negative to zero values when passes were intercepted. Analysis of defenders' adaptations to the environment revealed that continuous changes in their velocities toward the ball constrained their exploitation of these informational variables and the success of the interception.

Spotlight on Research

Grasping Tau

Savelsbergh, Whiting, and Bootsma (1991) attempted to determine whether the timing of an interceptive action was consistent with the use of first-order Tc information. Unlike previous research that inferred the use of tau, Savelsbergh and colleagues (1991) used a clever method to manipulate the relative rate of retinal expansion (tau) of the image of an approaching object. Under conditions of binocular viewing (experiment 1) and monocular viewing (experiment 2), participants were required to catch balls that approached on an inverted parabolic trajectory attached to a pendulum. They used three balls with different diameters: a large (7.5-centimeter) and small (5.5-centimeter) ball with a constant diameter, and a gradually deflating ball that changed in diameter from 7.5 to 5.5 centimeters during approach. To create the deflating ball without the participants' knowledge, the researchers encased a small ball with a balloon that was mechanically deflated with a vacuum pump. Although seemingly artificial, this is precisely the sort of controlled setting that scientists need to identify specific invariant sources of information through experimental manipulation.

The relative rate of expansion of the deflating ball did not correspond to the movement pattern generated by a nondeflating ball approaching with a constant velocity. In effect, the expansion of a deflating ball specified a longer Tc than a nondeflating ball. Logically, if tau regulated timing of the one-handed catch, then key aspects in the interceptive movement should occur later for the deflating ball compared with the large and small balls of constant diameter. In addition, the researchers observed no expected differences in the participants' response to the large and small balls of constant diameter because tau (the invariant) is independent of object size (the variant). No differences were expected for binocular and monocular viewing conditions because tau, which is specified in monocular geometry of the structure of light reflected from the ball's surface onto the retina, was available in both conditions.

The experiment showed that participants opened the hand to a wider aperture for the large and deflating balls compared with the small ball, but they took longer to grasp the deflating and small balls compared with the large ball. In effect, they treated the deflating ball as a large ball in the early part of the movement response and then as a small ball during the latter part of the response. Whereas peak velocity of the grasp was achieved simultaneously for the small and large balls, it was achieved significantly later for the deflating ball (see table 3.2). Savelsbergh and colleagues (1991) concluded that data on the timing of the events in the grasp were "consistent with the subjects' use of relative expansion information" (p. 321). An interesting aspect of the study was that participants were not aware of physical changes to the ball in its deflating condition.

Table 3.2 Kinematic Characteristics of One-Handed Catching From the "Grasping Tau" Study

Kinematic variable	Ball		
	Large	Small	Deflating
Initiation time[ns]	1,575 (68)	1,580 (65)	1,585 (67)
Movement time[*]	140 (51)	154 (48)	153 (51)
Time of catch[***]	1,716 (39)	1,738 (36)	1,739 (36)
Time of peak closing velocity[*]	41 (10)	42 (11)	36 (14)

Note: All values are in milliseconds; standard deviations are in parentheses; ns = not significant; *p = 0.06; ***p<0.001. The perceived contour of approaching balls that were deflating was altered, with a consequent effect on the grasping action. Data from Savelsbergh and colleagues (1991).

Data from G.J.P. Savelsbergh et al., "Auditory Perception and the Control of Spatially Coordinated Action in Deaf and Hearing Children," Journal of Child Psychology and Psychiatry 32, no. 4 (1991): 89-500.

The "Grasping Tau" paper has received a significant amount of scrutiny, perhaps because it was the first study that sought direct evidence for humans using the relative rate of expansion in guiding the timing of an interceptive action. The most important criticisms relate to (1) the need for quantitative predictions regarding the magnitude of the effect of the altered relative rate of expansion on the timing of the grasp, (2) the need for justifying the relevance of the dependent variables chosen for analysis, and (3) the difference in magnitude of effect between the monocular and binocular viewing conditions.

Application

Because of the demonstrable effects of other variables such as approach velocity, object size, and background structure, there is now consensus that tau is not used in isolation in temporal judgments (Michaels and Beek, 1995). Researchers have used the psychophysical paradigm to demonstrate whether humans are

(continued)

Grasping Tau *(continued)*

sensitive to tau and whether they use it to judge TC with approaching objects. This paradigm includes prediction motion tasks that require a person to make a simple response that coincides with the time at which a previously visible, moving target will arrive at a contact point, given that its motion before disappearance remains constant. Also popular within this paradigm have been relative judgment tasks, in which people are required to make perceptual judgments regarding which of two or more approaching objects will arrive first at a specified contact point. For excellent analyses of the weaknesses of classical psychophysical methods in the study of real-world vision, see Tresilian (1995) and also Harris and Jenkin (1998).

Affordances

The experiment by Savelsbergh and colleagues (1991, see Spotlight on Research) was a useful attempt in the challenging task of isolating optic invariants for study. Using a basic interceptive timing task, the experiment tried to show how different informational constraints could afford different coordination patterns. How the environment is perceived in behavioral terms (i.e., **affordances**) is another major idea from James Gibson (1979) that contributes to our understanding of perception and action in ecological psychology. Gibson (1979) proposed that humans perceive action possibilities or affordances offered by the environment. His ideas imply that performers perceive objects, surfaces, or events by what they offer, invite, or demand in terms of action opportunities. Affordances are properties of performer–environment systems that can be exploited in patterns of stimulus energy and that can, therefore, be directly perceived. For example, surfaces in the environment afford different actions for different people because of, among other constraints, their distinct physical properties, such as limb lengths (see Fajen et al., 2009), for key features of affordances discussed in the context of sport). For instance, does the surface afford stepping on with the feet or climbing on with the legs and arms (in the case of a young child), given key physical properties of the person?

Affordances can, therefore, be objective (a surface invites an action), subjective (the specific *invited* action depends on critical boundaries of each person's action capabilities), or neither of these adjectives, because the concept of affordances cuts across this objective–subjective divide (Heft, 2013). For Gibson (1979), affordance was a central concept of ecological psychology, which captured the complementary relationship of an animal with its environment. Gibson pointed out a fundamental criticism in indirect theories of perception, stating that "psychologists assume that objects are composed of their qualities . . . what we perceive when we look at objects are their affordances, not their qualities" (p. 134). Perceiving the environment in terms of affordances renders dispensable those cognitive processes that transform action-independent perceptions into action-oriented perceptions. That is, in the process of perception, there is no integration and combination of cues involved. The primary objects of an individual's perceptual experience are the action possibilities that the environment affords.

An important notion is that of a *landscape of affordances* (Rietveld and Kiverstein, 2014), which indicates that the daily environment offers a range of more or less inviting affordances (Withagen, de Poel, Araújo, and Pepping, 2012). However, these affordances are only accessible to individuals with the necessary skills to act on them. Rietveld and Kiverstein (2014) define the landscape of affordances as the possibilities for action available in a particular *form of life* (equivalent to distinct social, physical, and psychological contexts in a specific sport like golf, swimming, or soccer) because of the patterned and coordinated activities in which members of this form of life are *able* to partake in. For example, where one basketball player with excellent passing ability perceives a gap between defenders as an opportunity to play a long pass to a teammate, another player who is highly skilled at running with the ball may perceive it as an opportunity to dribble between the opposing defenders. Thus, athletes interact with a surrounding environment through skilled engagement with the affordances that a specific environment offers them because of their unique skills. From this viewpoint, the process of perceptual learning brings an attunement to affordances enhanced by skill acquisition.

Example of Affordance: An Approaching Ball

Let's consider more closely how the invariant optic flow specified by an approaching ball may invite an interceptive action such as hitting, catching, or avoidance. As noted previously, an affordance is constrained by rules or social conventions, as well as by personal characteristics, inviting a specific action that depends on perception from a person's environmental location and biomechanical characteristics (Fajen et al., 2009). For instance, the change in local flow created by an approaching squash ball may enable a player to intercept the ball by volleying it with the racket, but not to drive it. Given a different type of local flow, information may be provided that results in avoidance behavior such as moving out of the way to avoid being hit.

The differences between the optic structures stipulate a different affordance for the player. However, the same changes in local flow can afford different actions depending on the action capabilities of the individual. For example, toward the end of a hard, five-set game of squash, the affordances for one player may be to let the ball pass because it cannot be reached given the current level of fatigue in the muscular system. There is no physical standard prescribing affordances for each player. Each person's perception and action cycles will reveal the affordance in each situation. In this respect, affordances can provide a useful theoretical framework for understanding intra- and interindividual levels of decision making and movement variability, a concept we will revisit in chapter 4.

Information–Movement Coupling

Perceiving, as conceived by Gibson, is an activity of the whole body acting on and in the environment to obtain information (Gibson, 1966; Reed, 1996) and requires coordinated movement. That is, the legs function by bringing one in a perceptually controlled way to a place where nested adjustments of head turning, eye movements, lens accommodation, hand positioning, finger movement, and so forth can perform their functions in a coordinated act. Perceiving is guided by the practical requirements of a person's intentional goals, achievements, and circumstances. A person has to perceive enough of the environment to accomplish intentional goals, but that's all. There are no final right or wrong perceptions. Moreover, the ability to perceive can improve. If there is always more structure that can be clarified with more exploration, then the possibility for enhanced perceiving is always present. Perceiving involves modulating the complex adjustments of the body performing goal-directed activities in the environment (Mace, 1986). Perception, like action, is a coordinated activity, an *achievement* of the performer–environment system (Guignard et al., 2017).

Earlier we discussed how a golfer moves to create changes in optic flow that will provide information for action (see figure 3.1). This strategy exemplifies a central tenet of Gibson's (1979) ideas: that movement generates information that, in turn, supports further movements, leading to a cyclical relationship between information and movement. Gibson summarized this position, saying that "we must perceive in order to move, but we must also move in order to perceive" (p. 223). The interdependency between the perception of information and the generation of movement implies that perception and action should not be studied separately (Araújo, Davids, and Hristovski, 2006). Only in practice contexts where perception and action processes are expressed within representative environments will we observe the smartness of evolutionary-designed perceptual mechanisms (see Davids, Button, Araújo, Renshaw, and Hristovski, 2006; Runeson, 1977). In this context, *smartness* refers to the dedicated function for which a perceptual mechanism has evolved. Recognizing the tight couplings that emerge between perceptual and action systems reveals several interesting implications for movement practitioners, as we discover throughout this book.

Early research on balancing in children and adults supported the notion of the tight coupling between the optic array and movement (Lee and Lishman, 1975). In a purpose-built room with a fixed floor and moveable walls, researchers induced postural sway by moving the walls slowly forward or backward. The direction of the participants' sway depended on the direction in which the walls moved (see figure 3.3). Although participants were unaware that the walls were moving, they "unconsciously and unavoidably" (p. 162) corrected posture to compensate for what they perceived as forward or backward ego-motion (motion of the "self" through space) signified by the optic flow. The amount of wall movement was closely related to the amount of postural sway the subjects exhibited, and in some cases young children even fell over. These findings showed why we need to understand perception and action as functionally intertwined. Since that early work, the ideas have been developed to such an extent that modeling now exemplifies a prospective control strategy for continuously regulating action through information. We highlight this development next by discussing the required velocity model.

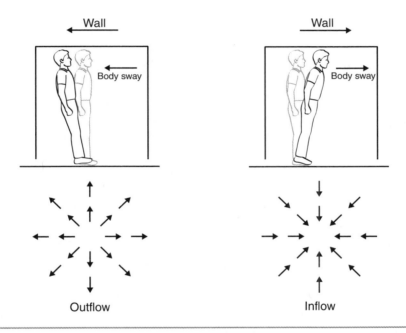

FIGURE 3.3 Unaware that the walls were moving, subjects in the "moving room" experiment unconsciously corrected posture to compensate for what they perceived as forward or backward ego-motion signified by the optic flow.

Required Velocity Model: Prospective Control

Perceiving affordances allows actors to prospectively control their behavior (Fajen et al., 2009). Studies on **prospective control** of catching, for example, show that movements are guided on the basis of information about future states of affairs; e.g., information about whether or not the ball will be caught if current conditions (hand and ball velocity) persist. More generally, prospective control refers to the means by which actors adapt behavior in advance to the physical and informational constraints in the environment.

Perception thus plays a preparatory role in action as well as an online role in tuning action as it unfolds.

Bootsma and Peper examined other potential sources of visual information for the regulation of interceptive actions (e.g., Bootsma, 1998; Peper, Bootsma, Mestre, and Bakker, 1994). According to their required velocity model, catching a ball requires individuals to control the position of their hands. This is the difference between the catching hand's current position relative to the ball and the acceleration of the hand needed to intercept the moving ball, based on an optically specified velocity differential (Peper et al., 1994). Their model specifies that a person can use information continuously to control the hand's acceleration and match the required velocity to intercept a projectile. For example, the current hand velocity at any given instant can be increased or decreased for the hand to move at the required velocity needed to catch a ball. To explain the performance of interceptive actions, predictive strategies traditionally have been designated in information-processing models. In these models, the target's future location and the required kinematics of the limbs are both estimated, by mental computation, in advance of the movement (e.g., Jeannerod, 1981). Access to the spatiotemporal properties of the interception point with the moving object, which is required if using a predictive control strategy, is never necessary with the required velocity model. Rather, by modulating limb acceleration with optical information to achieve and maintain the required velocity, the limb will move to the right place at the right time to catch the approaching ball. Therefore, the required velocity model is a welcomed and elegant means of explaining how interceptive actions are controlled.

In summary, many of the research findings on visual information for interceptive actions are consistent with performers detecting information from the invariants and variants in the optic array and using it to guide their interaction with their environment. They can detect this information according to key properties of each individual's movement system, such as limb length. It is important for practitioners to understand that the coupling between perception and action can be enhanced with practice.

Perceptual Learning and Attunement

Now we can consider Gibson's (1979) notions of information and affordances to understand how decision-making, movement performance, and learning may occur. Performers are remarkably flexible in their ability to adapt to changes in task constraints, criteria for success, and the availability of information. Some degree of flexibility can be achieved by attunement to different informational variables as conditions change. In the theory of direct perception, the learner is not burdened with the task of developing symbolic memory structures through training, observational modeling, and competitive performance; rather, the perceptual systems become progressively more attuned to specifying information available in environments through direct experience in practice and performance contexts. With task-specific experience, the information that the learner detects becomes more subtle and precise.

The notion of perceptual **attunement** implies that differences between experts and novices reflect, in part, differences in the informational variables on which each type of performer relies (Fajen et al., 2009). Therefore, one important element of skill acquisition and training is the process of becoming better *attuned* to relevant variables under specific movement contexts. The perceptual attunement to affordances that many experts develop can be subtle in high-level performance contexts. For example, anecdotal evidence from professional basketball shows that skilled ball handlers become attuned to information on the movements of teammates who are directly behind them. Do they grow eyes in the back of their heads? Not quite. To pick up this sophisticated information, they simply learn to detect the pursuit eye movements (tracking runs of teammates) of the opposition forwards in front of them.

The affordance landscape may change with movements of the performer even though the surfaces and substances in the actor's environment remain static, or as changes occur in the performer's environment while the performer remains static. The world of behavioral opportunities is dynamic (Fajen et al., 2009). Action possibilities can evolve and dissolve in milliseconds in sport, and also over longer timescales, as when a fatigued player late in a match cannot accelerate quickly enough to catch a pass that would have been possible to catch earlier. Action capabilities change over *short* timescales as a result of other factors such as injury and changes in load, and across *longer* timescales as a result of learning, development, and training. When body dimensions and action capabilities change, actions that were once possible may become impossible (or vice versa). Some form of learning must be involved in the perception of affordances to allow actors to adapt to such changes. **Calibration** makes it possible for actors to perceive the world in intrinsic units even after changes in body dimensions and action capabilities (Fajen et al., 2009). The process of calibration involves a scaling between current action capabilities and the demands of the task. For a calibrated actor, affordances can be directly and reliably perceived by simply detecting the relevant information. Although recalibration occurs quite rapidly, it is likely that further experience in a given task leads to further improvements in calibration.

So far, we have focused on how invariants are detected in the *optic flow* that surrounds a person. However, there are additional energy flows that support actions. For example, a driver may use acoustic information from the constant revving of the engine to guide the pressure change needed on the accelerator pedal. A tennis player may pick up and shake a racket to check how it feels before taking to the court. A runner may sense the uneven nature of a trail by perceiving haptic information from the soles of the feet and hearing her own heavy foot falls. In the remainder of this chapter we examine the important roles of haptic (touch) and acoustic information.

Haptic Constraints on Movement

A significant field of research has examined the role of haptic information in constraining movements. When a person holds an implement such as a pen, paintbrush, or baseball bat, information regarding its shape, size, texture, and structure is haptically provided when muscles, ligaments, tendons, and skin are stretched or compressed. Using this perceptual system, a blind person walking along a street and sweeping a cane in order to prospectively regulate gait can generate haptic flow. Gibson (1979) proposed that haptic information is most useful in its dynamic form when people actively generate complex sources of information through manipulation and touch. Numerous experiments have found parallels between the systems for detecting information from the optic and haptic flows, supporting the power of perception through the latter (Gibson, 1979). Indeed, the prevalence of manipulative movements in daily life led Turvey, Burton, Amazeen, Butwill, and Carello (1998) to argue that "the role of dynamic touch in the control of manipulatory activity may be both more continuous and fundamental than that of vision" (p. 35).

People can also use haptic information from the mass of an implement through active manipulation. For example, an athlete typically does not hold an implement such as a racket, bat, club, or stick in a static manner, but tends to wield it (Beak, Davids, and Bennett, 2002). The athlete twists and turns the implement in different directions to exploit information from its significant properties. A wielded object has a resistance to rotation in different directions that is defined by **moment of inertia.** Moment of inertia is a product of the mass of an implement and the radius of rotation (i.e., $I = mr^2$) and can be invariant for different combinations of these variables. Solomon and Turvey (1988) have shown that the perception of the spatial characteristics of handheld rods is not affected by the density of the rods, the direction of wielding relative to body coordinates, or the rate of wielding. Rather, without vision of the rod during wielding, perceived reaching distance was specified by a haptic invariant, the principal moment of inertia of the hand–rod system about the axis of rotation (see also Beak et al., 2002; Carello, Thuot, and Turvey, 2000; Turvey, 1996).

The haptic system participates both in perception and in action, as apparent in the case of dynamic touch. Dynamic touch is the label given to the particular kind of inquiry into the nonvisual perception of spatial and other properties of grasped and manually wielded rigid objects that involve a nonspatial input from muscles and tendons (Turvey, 2007). Successful handheld tool use requires exerting muscular forces to overcome the translational and rotational inertia of such a system (Wagman and Carello, 2001). Doing so requires detection of information relevant to the control of that system—that is, how much force is necessary and how it should be directed (Shockley, Grocki, Carello, and Turvey, 2001).

Kim and colleagues (2013) researched the golf swing using a full-body model rather than the movement of specific segments such as the wrist. By testing the inertia tensor of the golf swing, haptically perceived to control the movement of limbs, they characterized the perception–action coupling of golf swing performance (figure 3.4). This illustrative analysis indicates a close connection of haptic perception (inertia tensor) and action (joints implied in moving the club) during the downswing for a skilled golfer (Kim et al., 2013).

The inertia tensor reflects the mass distribution of the body–object system (i.e., the orientation of the mass distribution of that system with respect to rotation axes) (Riley, Shaw, and Pagano, 2005). Research has suggested that

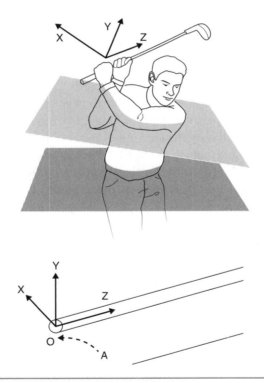

FIGURE 3.4 The grip reference frame was attached to the center of the end of the club shaft from which the spatial inertia tensor was computed. Its decomposition matrix contains the principal axes and moments of inertia, represented at O. The same is applied for the decomposition at a point, for example, along the wrist joint axis, A. But at any joint, the same eigenvectors form the basis of the decomposition, represented at A.

Reprinted by permission from V. Kim, Wangdo et al. "Haptic Perception-Action Coupling Manifold of Effective Golf Swing," *International Journal of Golf Science* 2, no. 1 (2013): 10-32.

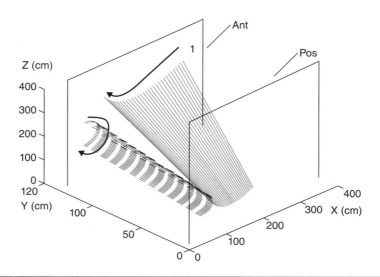

FIGURE 3.5 A three-dimensional spatiotemporal projection of the posteromedial side of the player represented in figure 3.4.

Reprinted by permission from V. Kim, Wangdo et al. "Haptic Perception-Action Coupling Manifold of Effective Golf Swing," *International Journal of Golf Science* 2, no. 1 (2013): 10-32.

perceived properties of handheld objects are constrained by the inertia tensor in a lawful and predictable manner.

In a sport like golf, such evidence suggests a much more important role for taking a practice swing rather than simply rehearsing an upcoming movement. In this way people can attune themselves to the characteristics of the implements they are using when playing with unfamiliar equipment or switching between clubs. Numerous examples exist in sport to suggest how athletes might gain haptic information from an object, such as juggling a soccer ball before taking a free kick, wielding a javelin before throwing, and manipulating a pole before vaulting. More research is needed to examine practice strategies that sensitize learners to haptic information (Teques, Araújo, Seifert, Del Campo, and Davids, 2017).

Acoustic Constraints on Movement

Evidence suggests that humans can also use acoustic information flows to regulate many functional movements (Button and Davids, 2004; Camponogara, Rodger, Craig, and Cesari, 2017). Indeed, Keele and Summers (1976) suggested many years ago that in regard to the temporal organization of movements, the acoustic perceptual system might be superior to the visual system. For example, percussionists must learn to time and sequence complex bimanual movements with acoustic information in order to play effectively. In sport, an abundance of anecdotal evidence highlights the role of acoustic information as a constraint on movement coordination. For example, the runner's reaction to the starting gun is a crucial element of sprinting because the difference between winning or losing can be just a few milliseconds.

The role of acoustic information is not limited to initiating movements; it can also be used in decision-making processes such as stroke selection in racket sports. In table tennis, for example, the particular sound of paddle–ball contact can give the experienced player important information about the speed and spin of the approaching ball. In volleyball, many coaches believe that information about an opposing setter's intentions to produce a short overhead or a long set to an outside hitter can be obtained from acoustic information during ball–finger contact. Some swimmers now train with mini-pacers placed by their ear to regulate the rhythm of a stroke. In many sports in which locations of opponents or teammates are not always visible (e.g., cycling, ice hockey, basketball), auditory information is useful for helping to locate the position and movement of others.

Although there is a large amount of anecdotal evidence, few empirical attempts have been made to investigate how acoustic information acts as a constraint during skill acquisition. Some evidence has shown that acoustic information may be obtained from a bouncing ball in perception of its elastic properties (e.g., Warren, Kim, and Husney, 1987). Typically, research has examined the role of acoustic information in coordinating and timing actions in relation to environmental events. For example, Shaw, McGowan, and Turvey (1991) modeled an acoustic variable that specifies Tc with an approaching object, given certain boundary conditions. They pointed out that early research on acoustic information focused on the localization of static sound sources rather than attempting to ascertain how actions could be acoustically guided. They identified the latter task under the framework of ecological acoustics and considered the convergence between a performer and an acoustic source. Their data supported the idea that the intensity of sound can be used to locomote directly toward a target in the environment, especially if the time difference between the person and the acoustic source is minimal.

Experimental support exists for the use of the acoustic array to support actions (e.g., Schiff and Oldak, 1990; Rosenblum, Carello, and Pastore, 1987). Schiff and Oldak found that sighted individuals were able to make reasonable acoustic judgments about the time to pass of approaching objects using audition alone. Congenitally blind participants were more accurate than sighted participants in their acoustic judgments and matched the accuracy of sighted participants who used visual judgments. Moreover, Rosenblum and colleagues found that the rising change in intensity of an acoustic information source was the most effective invariant for specifying the time to arrival of a looming object.

Summary

According to ecological psychology, changes to the energy in surrounding perceptual arrays that are generated following self or object motion can provide information that humans can directly perceive to regulate action (see Gibson, 1979; Turvey, 1990; Withagen and Chemero, 2009). This conceptualization of the cyclical relationship between perception and movement stands in stark contrast to the traditional mediated view of perception advanced in the information-processing approach (see Schmidt et al., 2018). A consequence of an ecological interpretation is that perception and movement should not be viewed as separate processes to be studied independently. In an effort to establish laws of control for this cyclical relationship, ecological research has examined the nature of the information that regulates movement (i.e., *what* information), rather than the minimal amount of information necessary to successfully complete a task (typical of an information-processing approach).

Depending on the nature of the task constraints, it seems that humans may use various informational variables. Task constraints, such as the time window for task performance, and the nature of the required response, such as rapid movement or verbal or manual judgment, determine the strategy people use and, hence, the information they use to support action. The examples from research that we have presented here show that humans are adept at acquiring different types of information and harnessing these sources to coordinate the degrees of freedom of the motor system. These ideas on the close relationship between action and perception are most important for the design of experiments on the study of skill performance and learning, and of practice tasks that aim to enhance skill acquisition in learners.

Self-Test Questions

1. List some of the informational flows available to ice hockey players as they skate with the puck.
2. Explain why information is conceived of as rich and meaningful in ecological psychology.
3. Discuss why an interceptive action such as hammering a nail is unlikely to be performed using optical tau alone.
4. Describe the concept of information–movement coupling and its importance to a coach.

CHAPTER 4

Intentionality, Cognition, and Decision Making in Sport

CHAPTER OBJECTIVES

After completing this chapter, you will be able to do the following:

- Acknowledge the intertwined relations between cognitions, decision making, and actions and how this relationship underpins sport performance
- Distinguish between knowledge *of* and *about* the environment
- Describe an ecological view of agency and the central nervous system's role in voluntary action
- Understand the nature of decision making as an emergent feature of performer–environment interactions expressed at individual and group levels
- Explain how practice can develop "intelligent athletes" based on the roles of informational constraints and perception to regulate actions

Thus far we have described how athletes can be conceived of as complex systems that are sensitively attuned to information that supports their behavior. However, it is important to acknowledge how factors such as experience and decision making play an important role in athletic performance. As the quote below from James Gibson (1979) indicates, the regulation of behavior as an expression of a cognitive process should not be attributed to one part of the individual–environment system (i.e., a commander or a part of the commander such as the brain). Decision making in activities such as sports exemplifies cognitive processes that are embodied, situated, and dynamic. The selection of action modes or the choice of what to do in changing (dynamic) sport activities is embodied and situated, or embedded, because of the reciprocal and mutually interdependent relationship between flow and force fields that characterizes the link between action and perception in sport.

> The rules that govern behavior are not like laws enforced by an authority or decisions made by a commander; behavior is regular without being regulated. The question is how this can be. (Gibson, 1979, p. 225)

In ecological dynamics, decision-making behavior is defined as transitions in a course of action (figure 4.1) and is a central issue for intelligent performance. An intelligent performer in work, education, sport, and military contexts is a highly adaptive individual who has developed the capacity to make decisions in complex and dynamic situations. The dynamical interactions of an athlete with a performance environment help her detect information from different modalities and guide decision making and actions. In this chapter we will discuss how **athlete intelligence** can be reconceived and influenced by the skill acquisition process.

Intelligent Behavior

The ecological dynamics approach stresses the primacy of individual–environment relations in understanding skill acquisition. Studying the couplings formed between a performer and performance environment helps us to understand complex aspects of human behavior in the actual world such as (1) moving about, (2) selecting routes, (3) deciding with whom to cooperate, and (4) competing with adversaries. In this view, any system capable of successfully engaging in such feats is a cognitive system. These problems can range from activities derived from biology (e.g., goal-path decisions in a school of fish) to abstract reasoning (e.g., deciding on the next move in a chess match) as long as it involves making a decision that solves the problem in an intelligent (adaptive) way (Turvey and Carello, 2012). In the traditional view, the behavioral expression of those decisions is not at the heart of cognition because behavior is assumed to be a simple implementation of a mental (internalized) plan. In this traditional view, as athletes become more skillful, their internalized plans become more refined and sophisticated.

Cognition is embodied and embedded so that perceiving event information related to temporal, spatial, and amplitude characteristics specifies body forces and torques required in goal-directed action. If cognition is understood as something separated from the body and from the environment, it denies that major influences operating on most cognitive systems are from the social and physical environment (e.g., Araújo et al., 2010), as well as from their own action-perception skills (van der Kamp and Renshaw, 2015).

Cognitive processes expressed in intelligent performance behaviors are understood and necessarily constrained by the evolving environment–individual system (figure 4.1). The current state of this system is the result of a history of interactions that constrains the immediate action. In this way, current performance is shaped by retrospective tendencies (including memory and past experience, see Gibson, 1994). An individual's behavioral history channels action to a landscape of possibilities for behavior (affordances). The precise place in the affordance landscape that a performer is guided toward emerges according to the idiosyncratic history of each individual and the context. The affordance landscape reflects the multiple possibilities for action that stand out as relevant for each individual in a particular situation because of specific training, skills, and experience in related tasks. This means that the behavioral landscape is also constrained by goals, desires, or needs toward which actions may be directed as well as the environment that draws the individuals into it and solicits actions (termed prospectivity, see figure 4.1). An important point for sport practitioners to understand when designing practice tasks for each athlete concerns her previous learning, background, and experience as well as her future goals and aspirations.

Actions, therefore, are a direct expression of cognition, contrasting with indirect expressions of behavior such as eye movements or neurophysiological or verbal correlates. As intelligent behavior is constrained both by its retrospectivity (history) and its prospectivity (future), action is an ecologically flexible process (self-organized, emergent). External (e.g., coach feedback or instructions) or internal (e.g., the brain) processes do not cause self-organization. Action modes (e.g., breaststroke in swimming, gripping a hold in climbing, a lateral pass in basketball) that emerge are different from the components that make up the system (e.g., the water, the vertical surface, the field, the ball, the limbs of the performer) and cannot be predicted solely from the

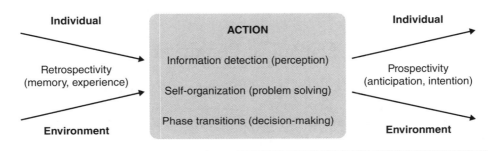

FIGURE 4.1 Cognitive processes sustained or constrained by the dynamics of the individual–environment system.

© Chris Button

FIGURE 4.2 Attunement to affordances in the aquatic environment encourages swimmers to adopt a streamlined position in the water to reduce resistance to motion (drag).

characteristics of those components. For instance, it is well known that water is approximately 800 times denser than air and allows human body buoyancy thanks to the **Archimedes force**. However, the physical characteristics of the water do not tell the performers how to swim. By interacting with the water, swimmers learn simultaneously to generate propulsion, to minimize active drag (by streamlining the limbs, the head, and the body), and to regulate their breathing in order to buoy, to satisfy energetic demand, and to move forward. Consequently, many sorts of solutions to a motor problem can emerge given the many ways its elements can interact under the same constraints. But instead of being a random process, or in the other extreme, a process that is internally programmed (determined) in advance, performers are perceptively attuned to affordances (by deterministically detecting information) that guide self-organizing action toward achieving a task goal (Davids and Araújo, 2010). Following the previous example in swimming, learners become attuned to propel and to breathe in a hydrodynamic manner by feeling aquatic resistance when their body exhibits a more or less streamlined position and their limbs perform various paths, speeds, and orientations (figure 4.2).

Ecological Cognition

A major challenge for learners and movement practitioners is to understand how an individual learns to perceive the surrounding layout of the performance environment in the scale of her body and action capabilities (Fajen, Riley, and Turvey, 2009). As a performer moves with respect to her surroundings, opportunities for action emerge, persist, and dissolve, even if the surrounding environment remains stable. Subtle changes of action can give rise to multiple and marked variations in opportunities for subsequent actions. The dynamic process implied in the perception of affordances provides the basis by which a performer can control her behavior prospectively (see chapter 3). Cognitive processes, therefore, should be understood, not in terms of discrete mental operations, but in terms of the relationship that emerges between individuals and their environment in striving to achieve a task goal (Araújo, Davids, and Hristovski, 2006). However, cognition has traditionally been defined as the information processing that produces mental representations, even though there are no direct experimental observations of internal representations. The definition of cognition proposed by Stepp, Chemero, and Turvey (2011) best captures the embodied–embedded nature of the ecological dynamics perspective: "Cognition is the ongoing, active maintenance of a robust organism–environment system, achieved by closely coordinated perception and action" (p.432). From this ecological perspective, characteristic cognitive capabilities are what they are by virtue of laws and general principles (Profeta and Turvey, 2018), where dynamics (involving laws of motion and change) and dynamical systems (involving time evolution of observable quantities according to law) can offer tools to understand cognitive processes.

For example, in swimming, a variable reflecting the individual–environment coupling is the angle between a limb and the water. The relevance of this measure is that when this angle is 0°, the limb is in hydrodynamic position because it is aligned with the axis of displacement (Guignard et al., 2017). In a team sport example, research on attacker–defender groupings (or dyads) has revealed that the interactions between competing players could also be described in terms of the order parameter dynamics. A relevant variable in this respect might be the distance of the middle point of the two players to the projection of the basket on the floor. With this ecophysical variable it is possible to examine whether the dyadic system interactions are emerging as advantageous for the attacker or for the defender (Araújo et al., 2006). Individual cooperating and competing players do not share a common neuronal system and so emergent coordination phases and transition phases are solely based on the task constraints present in specific performance environments. Part of the attractiveness of these dynamic models is derived from the fact that they can explain different decisions made by performers by means of the same underlying process of originating and decaying attractors (see chapter 1) and without the need to use mental representations (Silva, Araújo, Davids, and Aguiar, 2013).

Agency and the Role of Mental Representations

Traditionally in psychology, agency is defined as the capacity to exercise control over one's own thought processes and actions. Because thoughts and actions are partly self-determined, people can effect change in behaviors through their own efforts (e.g., I feel thirsty, so I drink water). The common explanation for this control is by means of internal mental representations. The following is a commonly used definition of representation (Haugeland, 1991, p. 65):

> A sophisticated system (organism) designated to maximize end (e.g., survival) must in general adjust its behavior to specific features, structures, of configurations of its environment in ways that could not have been fully prearranged in its design. . . . But if the relevant features are not always present (detectable), then they can, at least in some cases, be represented; that is, something else can stand in for them, with the power to guide behavior in their stead. That which stands in for something else in this way is a *representation*; that which it stands for is its *content*; and its standing in for that content is *representing* it.

Two features should be highlighted from this definition: (1) A representation *replaces* (stands in for) something that is not present, and (2) the individual uses the representation to guide behavior (Chemero, 2009). Therefore, in psychological explanations of human behavior, representations have a dual function: They contain knowledge, and they cause behavior. The problem is that if the performer is conceptually separated from the environment, then the partial system (the performer) has to represent the total system (performer–environment system). This explains the traditional tendency to understand behavior through variables that are beyond direct observation (inferred, covert variables) (Schmidt et al., 2018).

Key Concept

A Dynamical Model of the Agent–Environment Relationship

Mental representations are not needed to explain behavior in an ecological dynamics approach. Withagen, Araújo, and de Poel (2017) sketched a dynamical model of the agent–environment relationship, where agency is conceptualized as the capacity to modulate the coupling strength with the environment. This model explained how the performer could shape how he is influenced by available affordances. By modulating coupling strength, the performer simply alters the dynamics of the performer–environment system and thus the behavior that emerges. To modulate action, performers have available extra degrees of freedom that may or may not be used to modulate external forces by internal forces.

The Role of Knowledge in Performance

It is well understood that knowledge constrains (i.e., channels) athlete behavior in sport performance and training, allowing individuals to express agency. Different perspectives exist on how this may occur, including cognitivist theories and ecological theories (Araújo, Davids, Cordovil, Ribeiro, and Fernandes, 2009). Cognitivist theories propose, for instance, that skilled athletes can outperform novices because of the huge knowledge base they have accumulated in their minds during the process of learning. It is proposed that the enrichment of the mind allows skilled performers to express agency by mentally processing information to make more-accurate decisions for actions (e.g., Tenenbaum and Land, 2009). Ecological theories, in contrast, hold that learning entails changes in the perception of key properties of the environment (Jacobs and Michaels, 2007; Savelsbergh, van der Kamp, Oudejans, and Scott, 2004; Ibáñez-Gijón and Jacobs, 2012). In the ecological view, the sophistication of expert performance derives from the improved fit of experts with their environments rather than from an increased complexity of computational and mental processes (see Davids and Araújo, 2010). Put simply, because of their knowledge of the environment, experts are better adapted to specific performance environments than less-able performers.

Gibson (1966) distinguished between knowledge *of* the environment (perception based on information to control action, which constrains actual action) and knowledge *about* the environment (perception mediated by language, pictures, and other symbols that may constrain future action). For example, in tennis, responding to a slice serve would be knowledge of the environment, whereas instructions from a coach telling a player where to focus against an opponent during a baseline rally would be knowledge about the environment. This distinction has profound implications for understanding sport performance (see Araújo et al., 2009). The perception of affordances is what Gibson means by **knowledge of** the environment. It is not formulated in pictures or words, because it is this knowledge that makes the formulation of pictures and words possible. Information is available in the environment, and it can be detected by many observers. In our example, a skilled tennis player can perceive an opportunity from a slice serve to move out wide and create a better angle for a crosscourt return winner.

On the other hand, images, pictures, and words afford a mediated, indirect knowledge, that is, **knowledge about** the world (Gibson, 1979). This kind of knowledge is intrinsically shared, because it involves displayed communication of information in specific formats to others. Verbal instructions or feedback from a coach exemplify how knowledge about the environment is acquired by learners. The value of verbalizations with selected samples of information about the performance environment does not lie in the words themselves, but in what they refer to in the circumstances they are expressed. Thus, to say that expert basketball players "know" what needs to be done in a match means that a highly skilled player is perceptually attuned to events that convey information for achieving task goals at any instance of the game (e.g., she understands how to find a path through opponents toward the basket or how to get a shot off despite the close attention of a defender). Through training, the player does not have to rely on constructing special mental representations about the game, but she has to learn how to act on affordances that inform how she can be successful. For example, does a space on the court immediately afford shooting at the basket or dribbling through a gap between two defenders to a different space that affords shooting? The development of this perceptual attunement to information in the competitive context occurs mainly through practice and training.

Awareness of the performance environment is based on the adjustment of the performer's entire perceptual system (via the body's haptic, visual, proprioceptive, and acoustic subsystems) to the information surrounding him. For instance, in ice climbing, the ice thickness has an impact on the safe anchorage of the ice axes and can be perceived by the sound of the blade struck against the ice, the vibration of the stick and handle in the hand of the climbers, the depth of the blade anchorage, and also the color and the humidity of the ice that can indicate its properties (Adé, Seifert, Gal-Petitfaux, and Poizat, 2017). This adjustment includes a range of processes, all of which may be described as the simultaneous detection of persisting and changing properties of stimulation, invariants despite disturbances of the array of information. As we discussed in chapter 3, the patterned energy flow changes in some ways, but not in all. This means, for example, that performers can use optical changes (variants) and nonchanges (invariants) in the surrounding array to control their movements relative to the environment. The fundamental hypothesis of Gibson's ecological approach to perception and action is that when information about environmental objects, places, events, and people is available and detected, performers will perceive these entities to support their actions (Gibson, 1979). This is what Gibson meant by the term *direct perception*, or knowledge of, the environment.

Intentionality

Ecological dynamics recognizes the powerful roles played by knowledge, cognitions, and intentions and how these processes are deeply intertwined and integrated. It is a fundamental misconception to suggest that ecological dynamics has no role for cognition in human behavior. It is worth noting that Kelso (1995) viewed *intentions* as a most important source of constraint: a specific informational constraint that could be used to stabilize or destabilize existing system organization, depending on needs or desires of an individual. In sport, **intentionality** can frame interactions of athletes with task and environmental constraints to facilitate changes between or refinement of different functional patterns of behavior.

This theoretical idea was demonstrated in a study examining how properties of gait emerged during the run-up to place a foot on a target. Bradshaw and Sparrow (2002) showed how gait during a run-up was adapted by individuals, depending on target size and participant intentionality (to make a hard impact with the foot or a soft impact). No specific instructions were provided to participants on how to regulate gait behaviors, only broad aims of *soft* and *hard impact* with the target were highlighted. The hard impact was likened to a long jump approach, where the intention is to strike the takeoff board and launch into the air to achieve maximum projected distance. The soft impact exemplified the case in which an individual approaches a target in order to stop forward progression and remain within the boundary of the approach (e.g., when approaching the end of a takeoff board in diving but braking to avoid the launch into the aerial phase, known as balking, or when running to intercept a ball without leaving the playing area in a team sport). Runners approaching a target with intentions of a soft impact reduced approach velocity and increased the amount of braking during gait. When the intention was a hard impact, approach velocity increased during the approach phase and there was a decreased amount of braking observed. These findings elegantly exemplified the complex, interwoven relations that emerge during performance between perception (vision of the target), action (gait), and intentions (what happens next at the target area).

This conceptualization of how intentionality frames perception and action contrasts with representational notions of an intention. Intentions are not *causes* of action, but specific constraints on action (e.g., to make a soft or hard impact with a surface after a run-up). Intentions are captured in the continuous interactions of performers with their environments during goal-directed activity and are embodied by the kinds of behaviors typically observed in performers. These intentional patterns of behavioral reorganization emerge in situations in which different affordances can be used to enhance performance in contexts like sport. For instance, Seifert, Wattebled, and colleagues (2013) showed that although ice climbers attempt to determine their own climbing paths, skilled motor coordination emerges from the interaction of the performer with the specific properties of the icefall (e.g., shape, steepness, temperature, thickness, and ice density) *during* ascent. This is because specific motor coordination patterns and the condition of the ice are not completely predictable from ground level before climbing. Rather they vary somewhat randomly through the ascent because they are created by specific weather patterns, the ambient temperature throughout the climb (when a part of the icefall switches from the dark side to sunny side), altitude, etc. These environmental properties are not completely under the control of the climber, which probes the skills of each individual. Thus, the performer–environment basis of conceptualizing behavior indicates that affordances can be used, soliciting an organism to act, but they are not to be viewed as *causes* of behavior because a person may decide not to act on a perceived affordance.

Creativity

This ecological dynamics rationale extends to understanding creativity as grounded in action (e.g., Glaveanu et al., 2013). Because behavior is not pre-planned in the mind, but instead emerges out of the interplay of movement and information, creativity does not so much exist in the head but in the unfolding of action (see Hristovski, Davids, Araújo, and Passos, 2011; Orth, van der Kamp, Memmert, and Savelsbergh, 2017; Withagen and van der Kamp, 2017). **Creativity** can be conceived of as the discovery and emergence, through exploratory behaviors, of unconventional affordances (Withagen and van der Kamp, 2018) of objects and materials. For example, when a soccer player attempts an overhead bicycle kick, this inventive action can only happen successfully given certain ball trajectory characteristics and configuration of players around him. As Withagen and van der Kamp argue, creative ideas like these do not originate in an isolated brain, but they emerge in the practical engagement with the environment. Ideas are not the starting point of performance and by no means instruct the body. Instead, ideas are better thought of as constraints that originate in the correspondence of each performer and a performance environment.

These ideas about creativity were demonstrated in an experiment by Seifert, Komar, and colleagues (2014) who manipulated task constraints for individuals swimming 200 meters in a freestyle form by constraining glide duration (e.g., implementing a freely chosen condition versus maximal and minimal glide conditions imposed on performers) during stroke performance. They observed that swimmers were able to increase their kicking pattern (using 10-beat kicking, whereas 2-, 4-, and 6-beats are the normal patterns) to functionally adapt their behaviors when required to increase the glide phase with their arms. These findings revealed how swimmers were able to adapt their actions to overcome effects of an atypical constraint on their stable movement patterns in order to satisfy an imposed task requirement.

Consciousness

The role of consciousness in action facilitates the detection and use of information, as well as making movement control more flexible and coordinated over a wider range of tasks. Consciousness contributes to individual agency through the adaptive value of being aware of one's needs, preferences, and intentions with respect to actual or potential performance situations. The greater the *ecological significance* of what one needs to be aware of, the more likely it will be attended to. Perceiving is a process of keeping in touch with the world, experiencing things rather than having experiences. It involves awareness *of* instead of just awareness (Gibson, 1979). For example, the experience of observing a basketball free throw when a ball describes a parabolic trajectory through the air implies a particular way of throwing the ball by a basketball player at a specific position related to the basket and to the specific viewing angle of the observer. These physical relations are needed for this experience to emerge. Consciousness is a relation that exists at the level of the individual–environment system. If one subtracts such relations, only material components exist (Shaw and Kinsella-Shaw, 2007b). Individuals can directly perceive their situation and themselves in that situation without needing a "consciousness copy" of it. Grounded situational awareness emerges when the performer notices what surrounds her, what is changing, and what is emerging. For example, a climber can become aware of a favorable hold and perceive how to overcome gravitational force by swinging her body to perform a "dyno" (i.e., a dynamic move that allows her to grasp a hold just out of her current reach).

To be aware of an affordance requires more than collecting information about the environment. Informed awareness involves not only taking in information about the surrounding environment but also considering one's place in that environment (Shaw and Kinsella-Shaw, 2007b). For example, swimmers can raise awareness of the **Archimedes force** by immersing more or less of their body and limbs in the water; they can perceive water density by profiling their body and their limbs differently, either to obtain a streamlined position when gliding or to catch the water to increase propulsion (figure 4.2).

The Brain Is a Participant, Not a Commander, in Cognitive Function

In ecological dynamics, the brain and nervous system are seen as integral components of the person–environment system, which underpins behavioral interactions in performance contexts like sport. Fernand Gobet (2015) argued that studying the nervous system at the level of brain regions or structures is the wrong level of analysis for understanding cognitive processes. Ecological dynamics is aligned with this argument, contrasting with the traditional view of the brain as the "producer" of cognition. This type of reductionist explanation of cognition, as an internalized neurophysiological process, seems to endorse psychological attributes as specific anatomical substrates and not as emerging from interactions of the individual–environment system. This is an organism-centered view of behavior and misses a central point: the reciprocity between an organism and environment (Davids and Araújo, 2010). Since the late 17th century, the brain has been thought of as the control system of the body (e.g., Martensen, 2004). However, if action is guided by information, as Gibson argued, the brain should no longer be conceived as an organ that controls the body, but rather as a contributing component in the dynamical interactions of an individual in a performance environment.

This traditional neurophysiological perspective is predicated on a conceptualization of a nervous system that perceives, executes, conceives, and constructs an action for a performer. However, it is the performer who actually perceives and acts during dynamical interactions with sport environments, not separate parts of the body (e.g., components of a nervous system) (Araújo and Kirlik, 2008). Athletes act to perceive and perceive to act (after Gibson, 1979), with many more subsystems engaged in the emergence of behaviors than simply the nervous system. Perceptual subsystems are constituted by both nonneural (e.g., mechanical, hormonal) and neural (e.g., lateral geniculate nucleus, visual cortex) anatomical structures that are temporarily assembled to establish a functional relationship with the environment. Evidence for this view is abundant in the literature and can be traced back to Dewey (1896) (but see reviews of empirical evidence from de Wit, de Vries, van der Kamp, and Withagen, 2017). Sport performers are active performers engaged in dynamical transactions with their functionally defined environments. Thus, motor performance is not possessed by the brain of a performer, but rather it is best captured as an ongoing, dynamically varying relationship that has emerged (and continues to emerge) between the constraints imposed by the environment and the capabilities of a performer.

This conceptualization does not mean that the role of neurophysiological systems in these continuous interactions should not be considered (Teques, Araújo, Seifert, Del Campo, and Davids, 2017). Gibson proposed that "the brain is a self-tuning resonator" (Gibson, 1966, p. 146). What this means is that in achieving resonance, the perceiver learns to become "tuned" to specific patterns of ambient energy (e.g., light reflected from an approaching ball). Resonance is not something that a brain achieves in isolation, but uses all the body systems and subsystems involved in perceiving and acting in the environment (Teques et al., 2017). In short, brain regions are parts of perceptual and action subsystems that provide performers with the capacity to directly perceive and use affordances in a performance environment. Perceiving is not something that occurs simply in a region of a brain, connected to a set of sensors. This traditional view of the brain as a central system controller is too electromechanical. Rather, many parts of the body (as a highly integrated ecophysical and biophysical system) are involved in actively exploring the richly structured ambient energy array (de Wit et al., 2017). Gibson (1966) argued that there is no one-to-one mapping between structure and function in the brain as is commonly assumed in standard cognitive neuroscience (see Anderson, 2014, for a critical review). Context defines the relationship between structure and function of biological system components. As de Wit and colleagues (2017) summarized, "the function of a neuron depends on the context in which it is operating" (p. 626).

A key point is that the embeddedness of a performer within a performance environment during performance is the phenomenon of interest (see figure 4.3). Why study the behavior of the neurons if what one really wants to study is the exploratory behaviors of a player? Why not move directly to the study of actions and how they reveal the performer's exploration, problem solving, or reasoning in performing a task?

Because action is an expression of cognitive processes, it is possible to look at organizational and functional aspects of contextualized action in testing hypotheses about cognitive processes, captured by ecophysical variables (Araújo et al., 2017).

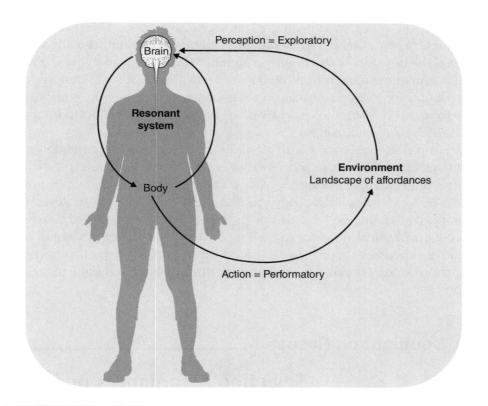

FIGURE 4.3 The embodiment and embeddedness that link the brain, body, and environment.

Reprinted by permission from P. Teques, D. Araújo, L. Seifert, V.L. del Campo, and K. Davids, The Resonant System: Linking Brain-Body-Environment in Sport Performance, in *Progress in Brain Research,* Vol. 234 (Amsterdam, Netherlands, 2017), 33-52.

Cognitive Processes Are Captured by Ecophysical Variables

Ecological dynamics construe that goal-directed behavior in sports emanates from the hard-assembled (physical) and soft-assembled (informational) links between performers and their performance environments (Kugler and Turvey, 1987). This idea implies that cognitive processes can be modeled by ecophysical variables (Araújo, Diniz, Passos, and Davids, 2014). These are variables that express the fit between the physics of the environment and the performer's adaptations. As mentioned before, environmental properties may directly inform what an individual can and cannot do (Withagen, de Poel, Araújo, and Pepping, 2012). For example, Fink, Foo, and Warren (2009) demonstrated (by manipulating the trajectories of fly balls in a virtual environment) that how a performer gets to the right place at the right time to catch the ball is solved by relying on a strategy of canceling optical acceleration (of the image of the ball on the catcher's eyes). The strategy of moving in order to cancel the ball's optical acceleration exemplifies how each player's change in movement can be defined intrinsically by the player's relationship with the environment (Harrison, Turvey, and Frank, 2016, for mathematical formalisms). The vertical optical acceleration of an approaching object can provide time-to-collision information without the need to mentally compute either distance or speed of the object to intercept it (Michaels and Zaal, 2002).

An emphasis on ecophysical variables avoids a traditional tendency to search for variables that are processed internally by the brain to cause behavior. An in situ example is the ecophysical variable goal-directed displacement (GDD) index developed to study tennis rallies (see Spotlight on Research). An important challenge for researchers and practitioners is to explore and observe ecophysical variables in their work to enable understanding of how cognitive processes might be predicated on the links between perception and action during continuous, emergent, performer–environment interactions in sports.

Spotlight on Research

Selecting Affordances in Tennis

João Carvalho and colleagues (2014) sought to investigate how tennis players link affordances, stroke after stroke, to gain advantage over an adversary. Racket sports like tennis are characterized by the continuous coadaptations of players to each other's action, resulting in the availability of simultaneous and successive (known as conditionally coupled) affordances. Carvalho and colleagues (2014) studied how dynamic decision-making behavior of coadapting tennis players was based on nested affordances by investigating an ecophysical variable that captured the interactions of a player–environment system. This variable was the *goal-directed displacement (GDD) index*, a measure that simultaneously considered the distance of the players in relation to two on-court reference points—the central line of the court and the net—during each rally. During one of the exemplar rallies of expert players competing in the Estoril Open tournament, in the sixth shot, player 1 made a parallel variation with a backhand down the line that pressured player 2 to make a major move from the left-hand side to the right-hand side of the court (see figure 4.4). After this, when player 1 hit the next shot, he was closer to the center of the court in a position to win the point. This is the circumstance in which a point may be scored because, in addition to the difficulty of returning a ball after a large displacement, an empty space is created on the other side of the court that can be exploited by the opponent to win the point. Whenever the players were moving away from the more stable and intertwined courses of action, a system transition (a rally break) could emerge, as captured by the values of the GDD index.

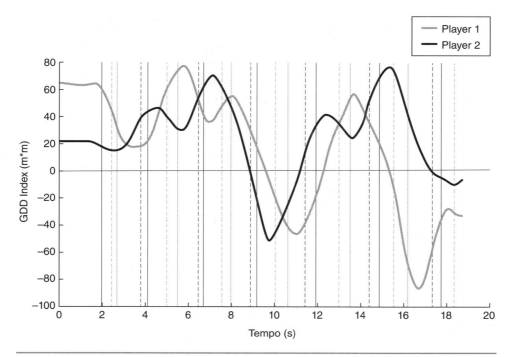

FIGURE 4.4 Example of a rally break involving parallel variation. The vertical lines represent the instants of the strokes (thick line) and of the bounces of the ball (dotted). If the players' lines are on the same side, both players are positioned on the same side of the court playing a crosscourt rally. If the lines are on different sides, the players are positioned facing each other (i.e., one on the right-hand side and the other on the left-hand side of their court).

Reprinted by permission from J. Carvalho, D. Araújo, B. Travassos, O. Fernandes, F. Pereira, and K. Davids, "Interpersonal Dynamics in Baseline Rallies in Tennis," *International Journal of Sports Science & Coaching* 9, no. 5 (2014): 1043-1056.

Therefore, the advantage in a rally is a process that is developed though successive actions, where nested affordances are dynamically assembled and imply perceptual attunement of skilled players to information for the next affordance. This study showed that different courses of action (i.e., dynamic decision-making behavior) could be established between expert players attuned, open, and responsive to match affordances (Kiverstein and Rietveld, 2015). The findings also signify that a player with an advantage is perceiving and creating affordances for the opponent (see Fajen et al., 2009), who is invited (pressured) to act on such affordances. On the other hand, the stability of the interactions between players is highly constrained by the copositioning on court (near or away from the central line of the court or from the net) and the pattern of interactions developed during play (crosscourt or down-the-line rallies). In this landscape of affordances (Kiverstein and Rietveld, 2015), a player with an advantage tries to create a successively more unstable situation for the other player, stroke after stoke, in an effort to destabilize the strength of the codependence of their courses of action.

Decision-Making Behavior Emerges From Performer–Environment Interaction

Decision-making behaviors can be sustained by perception and use of simultaneous and successive affordances and not necessarily by a hierarchical plan or representation capturing a sequence of performance operations (Araújo, Hristovski, Seifert, Carvalho, and Davids, 2017). Affordances favor certain behaviors and select against others (see Spotlight on Research). This notion indicates that the everyday environment offers a range of more or less inviting affordances (Withagen et al., 2012). However, these affordances are only accessible to individuals with the necessary skills to act on them. That is why the characteristics of a performer, such as skill level and repertoire, are important.

Kiverstein and Rietveld (2015) define *skilled intentionality* as "the individual's selective openness and responsiveness to a rich landscape of affordances" (p.701). During the act of perceiving, the hands, legs, ears, or eyes (for example) of a performer can explore the available information in an environment, searching the surrounding, structured energy fields. These fields (i.e., information) are an environmental resource to be exploited by active players (Reed, 1993). For example, where one tennis player with an excellent backhand stroke may perceive an opportunity to force a winning shot when using it, another player who is highly skilled at volleying (the tennis ball) may perceive every ball as an opportunity to approach the net. Thus, athletes interact with a surrounding environment through skilled engagement with the affordances that a performance environment offers them because of their unique skill set.

From this viewpoint, the process of perceptual attunement brings a readiness to affordances that without skill would not be accessible because it is skill that opens possibilities for action to an individual. What this implies is that, while affordances may exist in a performance or practice context, an athlete's skills facilitate their use of specific affordances (which invite actions). Successive actions are modulated by the individual, exerting her agency by intentionally driving the performer–environment system dynamics at appropriate points to yield a trajectory (Withagen et al., 2017). Modulation of actions means that performers

> are capable of a delayed reaction in addition to the immediate reaction to external forces which they can modulate by self-generation of counter-forces. To interact meaningfully with the environment, biological movement systems must have complex interiors, an on-board (metabolic) potential capable of biogenic forces that may be used to cancel, modulate, or delay their immediate reaction to an external force. (Araújo et al., 2006, p. 659)

In turn, these dynamical interactions between players (e.g., tennis) are coupled to larger-scale dynamics, guiding the formation of the behavioral trajectory over longer timescales (such as the tennis example in the Spotlight on Research). Reciprocally, the longer-term dynamics could influence the short-term interactions (and thus highlight specific affordances), for example, by altering environmental conditions. Because a behavioral trajectory is assembled anew on each occasion, the action sequence is historically contingent and variable, allowing for the flexibility observed in ordinary action sequences.

In a performance environment, decision-making behavior patterns emerge under constraints as less functional states of organization are dissipated. Changes in performance constraints can lead a system toward bifurcation points where choices emerge as more specific information becomes available, constraining the environment–athlete system to switch to a more functional path of behavior (such as running into a larger gap on court rather than another that is smaller) (Araújo et al., 2006, 2017).

For example, in team sports, when a performer changes from one action mode (running with the ball) to another (passing the ball when a defender is approaching), a transition in the course of action emerges. Transitions among stable behavioral states (i.e., action modes) emerge as a result of instability of a performer behaving in a performance context, providing a universal decision-making process for switching between distinct behavioral patterns (Kelso, 1995). These stabilities and instabilities do not occur independently but are codetermined by the confluence of the constraints and emerging information. Control lies in the performer-environment system.

From this viewpoint, **decision making** emerges as athletes search in a landscape of attractors (performance possibilities) to arrive at a stable, functional solution. A viable option selected is the *strongest* attractor for an individual at a given moment, with other options having less strength of attraction. This selection only emerges from the continuous interactions of an individual and a performance environment. Ignoring other options is a dynamical consequence because if an individual–environment system relaxes to one attractor, it concomitantly ignores remaining options (attractors). The fact that there is a stronger attractor does not eliminate the influence of other attractors in the dynamic landscape of action possibilities (e.g., Araújo, Diniz, Passos, and Davids, 2014). Under dynamic performance conditions, other attractors (i.e., other options) may emerge and exert their attraction in the dynamics of the system, emphasizing the performer–environment reciprocity.

Team Decision Making

This understanding of decision making can be extended to team cognition and decision making. During competitive performance, the organization of action by perceiving surrounding informational constraints is expressed in knowledge of the environment. This idea emphasizes that the perception of socially shared affordances underpins the main communication channel between team members during team coordination tasks (Araújo and Davids,

2016). Ecological dynamics predicts that the presence of others extends action possibilities that are realizable by individuals to action possibilities realizable by groups. In chapter 9, we highlight in more detail the suggestion that affordances can be perceived by a group of individuals trained to become perceptually attuned to them (Silva et al., 2013). Through practice, players can become perceptually attuned to affordances *of* others and affordances *for* others during competitive performance and can refine their actions (Fajen et al., 2009) by adjusting behaviors to functionally adapt to those of other teammates and opponents. Moreover, individuals on a team can act in a way to create competitive circumstances (the affordances) that are favorable to them. For example, by pressuring opponents to play more in one zone of the playing area, this strategy can create affordances for attacking play by freeing other areas of the field. These processes enable a group of players to act synergistically with respect to specific match circumstances.

The decisions and actions of players forming a synergy should not be viewed as independent acts of individuals, but instead can be explained as the activities of multiple players synchronized in accordance with dynamic performance environments in fractions of a second (Silva et al., 2016). For example, it has been observed that soccer teams tend to be tightly synchronized in their lateral and longitudinal movements (Vilar, Araújo, Davids, and Bar-Yam, 2013). The coordination patterns observed showed compensatory behaviors within the team, an essential characteristic of a synergy (Riley et al., 2011). In chapter 9, we explore how shared affordances (affordances of and for others in a social collective or team) may be harnessed through practice.

Summary

This chapter focused on the intertwined relations between cognitions, decision making, and actions in athletes and how this key relationship underpins sport performance. We discussed what we might mean by athlete intelligence and the links with the embedded–embodied dimension of cognition, exploring distinction between knowledge *of* and *about* the environment that James Gibson (1966) proposed in his seminal paper. An ecological view of agency and mental representations, intentionality, creativity, and consciousness were presented as well as the role of the central nervous system. Decision-making behavior as emerging from the interaction of the performer and the environment was discussed at the individual and group levels. From a practical perspective, this distinction involves understanding the influential roles of intentional constraints, perception, and the nature of information used to regulate actions.

Self-Test Questions

1. List examples of how athlete intelligence can be expressed.
2. Explain why cognition is expressed through actions.
3. Describe the concept of agency using examples from any activity of preference.
4. How would creativity be expressed in solving a problem posed by a sport task?
5. Describe the concept of emergent decision making and its importance to a coach.

CHAPTER 5

Understanding the Dynamics of Skill Acquisition

CHAPTER OBJECTIVES

After completing this chapter, you will be able to do the following:

- Discuss how the perceptual-motor landscape acts as a metaphor for the learning process
- Describe techniques that researchers and practitioners can use to monitor movement pattern stability during learning
- Understand the concept of functional equivalence to explain how human neurobiological systems can be adaptable and creative
- Explain the concepts of degeneracy (or multistability) and pluripotentiality (or multifunctionality) in relation to human movement
- Provide examples of the different forms of degeneracy that humans manifest when they move

---

It is intriguing to consider which processes are occurring when an individual learns a new skill. What underlies the perceptual and motor modifications that differentiate early and advanced learners? How do past and current learning experiences of the individual influence learning? Specifically, does an existing repertoire of movement behaviors facilitate or hinder the dynamics of skill acquisition? What should practitioners look for in terms of evidence that learning is taking place? These questions are relevant in helping us better understand the dynamics of skill acquisition.

This chapter highlights the capacity of humans as complex biological systems to exhibit evolution, innovation, and creativity in their behaviors. In this chapter, we describe empirical research that further illustrates the dynamics of skill acquisition (e.g., Kostrubiec, Fuchs, and Kelso, 2012; Zanone and Kelso, 1992, 1997). We also discuss how to assess skill acquisition from a constraints-led approach, which is a critical concern from both a researcher's and a practitioner's perspective. The concepts of degeneracy and pluripotentiality are discussed with reference to an understanding of how coordination emerges as a consequence of the dynamic interactions among constraints. Finally, we consider in more detail how coaches, physical education teachers, and therapists can use knowledge of the dynamics of skill acquisition to inform their practice.

© Human Kinetics

FIGURE 5.1 The fact that novice jugglers may be able to catch and throw a ball independently but struggle to combine these elements initially indicates the adaptation that the perceptual-motor landscape must experience.

Constructing the Perceptual-Motor Landscape

In chapter 2, we explained how coordinated human behavior results from the movement system settling into specific attractor states within a landscape of available states. The landscape represents all of the possible perceptual-motor behaviors that a system can adopt. Think of different bipedal locomotor activities such as walking, running, and jumping as forming part of a landscape. This landscape, or pattern of dynamic attractors, must be gradually altered and combined to allow the performer to integrate movement patterns simultaneously and in a functional manner. For example, novice jugglers may be able to catch and throw a ball independently but struggle to combine these elements initially, which indicates the adaptation that the landscape must experience (figure 5.1). For learning to occur, the performer must use the task to be learned as a specific form of information to remold the landscape. In other words, "once learning is achieved, the memorized pattern constitutes an attractor, a stable state of the (now modified) pattern dynamics" (Kelso, 1995, p. 163).

Before we provide empirical evidence for the landscape metaphor, we must understand several key concepts. First, we need to understand how the relative match between how the learner currently prefers to move and how he would like to move influences learning. This is relevant because "the extent to which specific behavioral information cooperates or competes with spontaneous self-organizing tendencies determines the resulting patterns and their relative stability" (Kelso, 1995, p. 169). If the initial behavioral tendencies do not conform to what is required of the performer, learning will be more difficult than if there is a close match. By way of an example, consider a young child learning how to write. Because of strengthening preferences to use the dominant limb, writing is likely to take longer to learn with the nondominant hand than with the dominant hand. Undoubtedly, if the learner's range of intrinsic dynamics and the task dynamics are markedly similar or different, the path of learning can take very different routes.

Routes to learning can take the form of **bifurcations** or **shifts** (Kostrubiec et al., 2012: see Spotlight on Research). For example, changes caused by learning can take the form of a totally new movement pattern (bifurcation) or one that is only slightly modified from an existing pattern (shifts). Take the instance of when a skilled golfer may not necessarily need to completely reconfigure his swing, but only needs to make slight adjustments to his current coordination pattern (i.e., his setup position) to enhance his performance (and learning during this process). This process represents a shift rather than a bifurcation.

Note that different learning phases can include continuous improvement; sudden improvement; progression and regression; and no improvement of performance, otherwise known as performance plateaus (Newell, Liu, and Mayer-Kress, 2001; Liu, Mayer-Kress, and Newell, 2006; Pacheco, Hsieh, and Newell, 2017). It is normal for these learning features to persist for many years. Construction of the **perceptual-motor landscape** doesn't happen overnight. As such, it becomes clear that practitioners should expect to see great differences in the rates at which learners acquire movement skills over time (see chapter 8) (Chow, Davids, Button, and Rein, 2008).

Another important point is that the process of learning a new task involves not just one feature of the landscape changing, but potentially the whole attractor layout. An attractor well is a stable region of a dynamical system that is resistant to external perturbations (see chapter 2). As one attractor well is being carved out, nearby attractors can become less stable. Picture a child sitting comfortably on the surface of a trampoline. If another child were to jump onto the trampoline near the first child, the deformation in the trampoline bed would perturb the first child's stability. We can expect a similar reaction from a fluid, interconnected, dynamical movement system. Therefore, when planning programs for skill acquisition, practitioners should take care to reduce the perturbing effects of constructing one attractor on the stability of existing attractors or skills (if that is not a desirable effect of such perturbations). It is critical for practitioners to account for the dynamics of the practice activity so that appropriate manipulation of constraints (typically task constraints) can be undertaken to shape the exploratory behavior of the learners (Chow, 2013).

Spotlight on Research

Different Routes of Learning: Bifurcation versus Shift

In this spotlight we take a closer look at the research of Kostrubiec and colleagues (2012) in explaining how changes in the dynamical landscape as a consequence of learning can be underpinned by two pathways, namely a *bifurcation* and a *shift* route. Data from Kostrubiec and colleagues (2012), via the classic bimanual coordination finger waggling task (see HKB model in chapter 2) was used to exemplify learners with different intrinsic dynamics: (1) bifurcation: two stable coordination patterns at 0° and 180° or (2) shift: three coordination patterns at 0°, 90 °, and 180°. Recall that the phase angle corresponds to the extent to which one finger leads the other in their relative oscillations (i.e., 0° is synchronous finger waggling, whereas at 180° there is a half cycle difference between the fingers). Figure 5.2 provides a visual representation of learners with bistable movement patterns (left column) and learners with tristable movement patterns in the shift route (right column). In panel a, notice the presence of two attractor wells in the left column and three attractor wells in the right column (under "before"). Both groups of learners undertook a practice phase (panel b) in which they learned a new movement pattern that lies between those that are present in the preexisting repertoire of the respective learners. Thus, for the bistable learners, it was 90° relative phase and 135° for the tristable learners. One critical consideration for the selection of these new movement patterns was to ensure that the relational properties of the pattern to be learned falls within the prelearning landscape and that there is competition between the learning task and the learner's intrinsic dynamics that exist before practice (Kostrubiec et al., 2012).

After practice (panel c), a new well was present at 90° in the left column and that learning qualitatively reorganized the attractor landscape (i.e., a clear change from bistable to multistable patterns). This reorganization was considered a bifurcation in terms of a route to learning. However, for the shift learners, there was no change qualitatively in terms of the overall attractor landscape. Three attractor wells are still present, but the original minimum at 90° has moved toward 135°. This is still an indication that learning has occurred with multistability being preserved. Such a quantitative change in one of the attractor wells (rather than a qualitative change in attractor landscape) is considered a shift route to learning (see figure 5.2). The work by Kostrubiec and colleagues (2012) provides meaningful insight into how the existing intrinsic dynamics of different learners can affect the routes of learning.

Application

A recent application of this idea that the intrinsic dynamics might influence the rate and nature of learning has been shown in climbing (Orth, Davids, Chow,

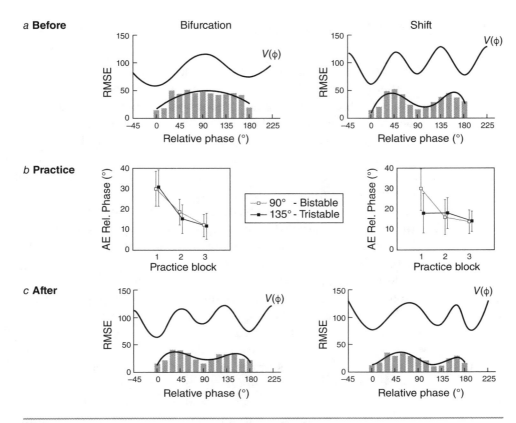

FIGURE 5.2 Learning can take the form of a pattern bifurcation (left panel) or a pattern shift (right panel).

Reprinted from V. Kostrubiec et al, "Beyond the Blank Slate: Routes to Learning New Coordination Patterns Depend on the Intrinsic Dynamics of the Learner-Experimental Evidence and Theoretical Model," *Frontiers in Human Neuroscience* 6, no. 222 (2012). This is an open-access article distributed under the terms of the Creative Commons Attribution License 3.0.

Brymer, and Seifert, 2018). In this study, all climbers practiced for 7 weeks (42 trials) in the absence of instruction, and they showed several means of improving. Individuals showing sudden improvement appeared to develop a new pattern of coordination (in terms of body–wall orientation) that reflected a transition between monostability (i.e., body mainly facing the wall during the climb) before practice to multistability (i.e., body alternating between face and side orientation to the wall) after practice. Those showing continuous improvement did not; they simply improved performance (Orth et al., 2018). The individuals who did not improve in terms of fluency only improved the distance climbed before falling. The implication for skill acquisition is that a learner should not be considered a blank slate and that preexisting movement coordination can affect how the coordination dynamics alter with practice.

Scanning for Changes Over Time

Changes to the perceptual-motor landscape represent the learner's struggle to establish stable movement patterns for new task demands. Accordingly, it is important for theorists and practitioners of motor learning to find a way to monitor changes to the layout of the landscape over time. In research studies, one effective way of probing the entire perceptual-motor landscape during learning has been to use a **scanning procedure** (Zanone and Kelso, 1992). This empirical technique requires the participant to intentionally vary an order parameter (see chapter 1), such as relative phase, in steps. As the behavior of the order parameter is monitored, the observer is effectively scanning the perceptual-motor landscape for stable and unstable regions (differing in levels of variability of selected measures). This scanning technique can result in snapshots of the attractor layout as it is evolving, revealing the relative stability of regions over time (Button, Bennett, and Davids, 2001).

Zanone and Kelso (1992) used a scanning procedure to examine the dynamics of motor learning while participants were acquiring a bimanual coordination task. In five daily sessions, participants sat in front of a visual metronome and were instructed to flex each finger in temporal coincidence with the onset of two lights. A typical session comprised three blocks of five learning trials in which participants practiced a new required relative phase (RP) of 90° between the finger flexions. On the metronome, the movement frequency was set at 1.75 hertz. Knowledge of results in the form of actual RP was provided after each trial. At the beginning and end of each daily session, as well as between training blocks, a scanning run was carried out where the RP was progressively increased from 0° to 180° by 12 discrete steps of 15°. To assess pattern stability over time, recall that trials were administered 7 days later in which participants had to reproduce the 90° condition for 1 minute.

At the end of day 1, the RP variability was still lowest at 0° and 180°, increasing markedly at intermediate values. The low values of RP variability indicated regions of stability in the landscape. As expected, in-phase and anti-phase patterns were most stable, with the latter more variable than the former. In addition, between-participant variability was smallest at these required phasings. By the end of day 5, however, RP variability was also low at 90°. Attraction toward the 90° region was evident by the negative slope of curves on either side of 90°, indicating a switch from bistable to tristable dynamics in the landscape. Recall that data also suggested that this change to the perceptual-motor landscape was relatively permanent. Subsequent analysis of the 0° and 180° patterns revealed that the initial attractors became less stable (and less attractive) as the 90° phase was learned. As we noted in chapter 2, this latter finding clearly shows the metastability that characterizes the tendencies of a movement system that is changing with learning (see Kelso, 1981b).

In figure 5.3, we can observe how the shape of attractor wells changed during Zanone and Kelso's (1992) experiment. Figure 5.3*a* shows how the stability of relative phase fluctuates across the attractor layout, with antiphase and in-phase patterns exhibiting stable states (a bistable regime). As discussed previously, these states are thought to represent the intrinsic dynamics for this task in the absence of behavioral information. In figure 5.3*b*, the three lines show what happens to the landscape when 0°, 90°, or 180° patterns are learned (i.e., when specific parametric influences are added). Note that when 0° or 180° patterns are learned, the width of the associated attractor well has increased. This indicates that learning can enhance the attractiveness

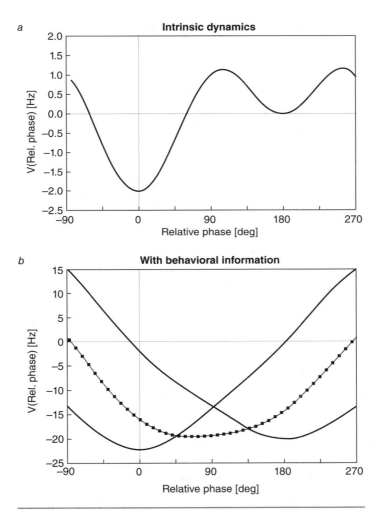

FIGURE 5.3 *(a)* The stability of relative phase fluctuates across the attractor layout, with antiphase and in-phase patterns exhibiting stable states. *(b)* The three lines show what happens to the landscape when 0°, 90°, or 180° patterns are learned.

Reprinted by permission from P.G. Zanone and J.A.S. Kelso, "Evolution of Behavioral Attractors With Learning: Nonequilibrium Phase Transitions," *Journal of Experimental Psychology: Human Perception and Performance* 18, no. 2 (1992): 403-421. Copyright © American Psychological Association.

to the movement system of these states. However, when the 90° pattern is learned, the potential is deformed and the competition between behavioral information and intrinsic dynamics pulls the minima toward 90°. A new, wider attractor well has been created in which increased flexibility arises due to the influence of the underlying intrinsic dynamics. As learning continues at 90°, the shape of this attractor well narrows and deepens as the pattern becomes memorized and increases in stability at the expense of the 0° and 180° patterns (see Wenderoth and Bock, 2001).

In the Zanone and Kelso (1992) study, the rate of learning for the 90° pattern differed among participants. Some people showed evidence of attraction to this pattern after just 2 days, whereas others needed up to 5 days. Of course, differences among learners are a feature that many coaches and teachers recognize, albeit one that is vaguely articulated. A dynamical systems interpretation of motor learning suggests that interindividual variability may be inherent in the learning process because learners begin with differences in intrinsic dynamics.

Nevertheless, this distinction between attractors for more complex movements that involve greater degrees of freedom (dfs) is probably less obvious as compared with the tightly constrained movement of the finger waggling task (i.e., bimanual coordination). Rein, Davids, and Button (2010) clearly highlighted the possibility that in a multiarticular action like shooting a basketball, when shooting distances are progressively scaled, there may be no clear transition from one movement behavior to another (i.e., a stable preferred movement pattern to a new preferred movement). In this study, it was found that only two out of eight participants demonstrated a clear transition between movement patterns (using cluster analysis to determine the presence of different movement patterns). It was observed that participants were more likely to use a single movement pattern and with some variations to achieve the task goal. This provided evidence that for multiarticular movement involving numerous degrees of freedom, there is greater room for exploration and exploitation of possible movement solutions. Indeed, it is highly functional for the human movement system to display such degenerate behaviors. Nevertheless, using a systematic process like the scanning procedure can allow a practitioner to explore the adaptability of a learner.

Symmetry and Functional Equivalence

In a later study, Zanone and Kelso (1997) again used a bimanual finger-waggling task to demonstrate two other interesting characteristics of learners seeking to stabilize a new motor pattern. First, they demonstrated that learners were able to produce symmetrical partners of the patterns that they were practicing. For example, when participants learned a 90° phasing (i.e., the left finger lagging the right by one-quarter of a cycle), they also could execute a

270° or 90° phasing pattern (i.e., the left finger leading the right by the same amount), even though they had never practiced the latter pattern. The authors suggested that practicing the 90° pattern gave rise to a new, stable pattern emerging in the perceptual-motor landscape at 270°. This remarkable finding showed that learning can result in global changes to the perceptual-motor landscape and can affect the stability of other movement patterns even when they are not the subject of specific practice. The finding also seems to indicate a form of *symmetry* across the perceptual-motor landscape, which preserves a global structure even when local practice alters the stability in a specific part of the landscape.

A second result of Zanone and Kelso's 1997 study was that participants could perform the newly learned phase relationship in different ways. Although the task requirement was always met, the different solutions ranged from a smooth, quasi-sinusoidal motion of both end effectors (fingers) to jagged, discontinuous movements. Zanone and Kelso interpreted these findings as the learners demonstrating *functional equivalence*, in which learning occurs at the abstract level of the coordination dynamics regardless of the end effector (limb segment) used to bring about the end result. Kelso and Zanone (2002) later verified this concept by showing that regardless of whether participants practiced a bimanual phasing pattern with their arms or with their legs, they were able to transfer the learned pattern to a different end-effector system. This could be suggested from the experiment on basketball shooting by Rein and colleagues (2010) that revealed the possibility of different movement solutions to achieve the same outcome. These demonstrations of functional equivalence indicate how abstract and universal the learned coordination dynamics can be.

Role of Degeneracy and Pluripotentiality in the Emergence of Coordination

The coordination and control processes in human neurobiological systems are underpinned by the presence of an emergent and intertwined relationship between the specific intentions, perceptions, and actions of each learner (chapter 4). Motor learning continuously constrains the relationship between movement pattern stability and flexibility in each individual. Biological structures have evolved to exploit **degeneracy** across these different forms, and humans are no exception. The remarkable adaptability of humans to move around different environments in a variety of ways (e.g., walking, jumping, crawling, swimming, climbing) is just one obvious example of this capacity. The implications of degeneracy highlight how learners can individually and functionally adapt their motor coordination patterns while consistently achieving a task goal (Seifert, Komar, Araújo, and Davids, 2016). This is significant because it exemplifies the critical role that interacting constraints play in shaping adaptation and function seen in coordination pattern variability (Komar, Chow, Chollet, and Seifert, 2015).

Forms of Degeneracy

As suggested by Mason (2010), degeneracy can take four forms: redundancy, parcellation, synergies, or convergence (see table 5.1). *Redundancy* can create the opportunity for degeneracy to arise because the function of the original structure is maintained by one copy, while any other copy is free to diverge functionally. Human muscles exploit this property when skeletal muscles generate tension across joints and create motion, while other muscles perform different functions (e.g., to brace, protect, pump). Degeneracy can also occur through *parcellation*, which is when an initial structure is subdivided into smaller units so that it can still perform the initial function and can also be functionally redeployed (for instance a grasping action could be subdivided in reaching and then grasping, showing how grasping is entangled with locomotion). Consider the range of functions the human hand can achieve through parcellation either as a collective unit of fingers (e.g., to grasp, punch, stroke) or as individual units of digits (e.g., to type, feed, groom). Degeneracy may also manifest as the assembly of a coordinative structure or *synergy* composed of relevant system components for a specific function. When multiple limbs act in concert to achieve a unified outcome, as in running, jumping, swimming, or cycling, humans are exhibiting degeneracy. This capacity supports the potential interchange of structures because synergies can reorganize to respond to changes in the independent components that form them. For example, humans can choose to jump two footed or from either foot depending on the task goal and circumstances. The final form of degeneracy exists when two or more independent structures *converge* on the same function. This capacity is obvious in most multiarticular tasks (like

Table 5.1 Different Forms of Human Movement Degeneracy

Forms of degeneracy	Example
Redundancy	While playing tennis, one arm swings the racket while the other arm provides balance to maintain posture (same structures, different functions).
Parcellation	In team sports, subgroups of the team fluidly act together to accomplish a task (e.g., to pressure the opponents, to defend a goal).
Synergies	Jumping over a hurdle can be done from one foot or from two feet, depending on factors such as speed of the approach and height of the hurdle.
Convergence	In a dance routine, the independent members of a troupe can coordinate their actions to move synchronously.

opening a door with the right or left hand or with the elbow when the hands are carrying objects) in which numerous body parts contribute to moving the body in accordance with environmental features.

It is important to consider how the presence of degeneracy in complex perception–action systems provides the basis for myriad actions to complete task goals in an information-rich and dynamic environment (Seifert, Komar, Araújo, and Davids, 2016). Degeneracy provides a high level of robustness in neurobiological systems where various synergies can achieve similar functions under certain conditions yet perform distinct functions under other conditions (Riley et al., 2011; Whitacre, 2011). In this sense, degeneracy is able to support stability and flexibility in neurobiological systems. Critically, degeneracy can provide the basis for pluripotentiality in the performer or learner (Seifert, Komar, Araújo, and Davids, 2016). **Pluripotentiality** can be defined as the ability of one structure to perform many functions within complex systems (Mason, 2010; Noppeney, Friston, and Price, 2004; Price and Friston, 2002). Consider the example of the overhead throwing action that is exhibited in other movement skills such as the badminton clear, volleyball serve, and cricket bowling action.

With reference to the role of constraints shaping behaviors, Komar and colleagues (2015) pointed out that pluripotentiality is exhibited when structures that are slightly mobilized under one set of constraints can potentially become more mobilized under another set of constraints. For instance, in breaststroke swimming, swimmers can adapt the same arm–leg coordination pattern at different swimming speeds by generating higher levels of velocity and acceleration with their limbs during propulsion (Komar et al., 2015). In particular, pluripotentiality was exhibited through a stable kinematic pattern of arm–leg coordination between high- and low-speed conditions during propulsion, which generated higher velocity and acceleration in high-speed conditions. The adaptations reside mainly in the time spent gliding with the lower and upper limbs fully extended (meaning that coordination between arms and legs did not change during this phase because the limbs remained immobile in a streamlined position). Further investigations of arm–leg coordination in breaststroke swimming have emphasized that degeneracy can also support pluripotentiality because it reflects greater flexibility of a coordination pattern (i.e., higher range of functions, such as coping with a larger range of aquatic resistance in order to swim faster) (Komar et al., 2015) and to optimize the glide by minimizing active drag (Seifert, Komar, Crettenand, et al., 2014). We can see these spontaneous responses sometimes from skilled athletes when they creatively outmaneuver an opponent or exhibit previously unseen moves to get a shot on target. In simpler terms, degeneracy involves combining many synergetic structures into one function, which is in contrast to pluripotentiality, in which one synergetic structure can be mapped to many functions.

Key Concept

Can a Movement Be Both Stable and Flexible?

Is it possible for a movement to be both stable and flexible at the same time? The theoretical ideas presented earlier and emerging evidence suggest that it is possible. In their study examining ice climbing, Seifert, Orth, Boulanger, and colleagues (2014) exemplify how stability (i.e., robustness against perturbation) and flexibility (i.e., functional variability to constraint) can coexist depending on the presence of specific environmental constraints in the climbing task. A climber can demonstrate functional stability by swinging ice axes against the icefall to create specific anchorages. Functional flexibility is present when the climber can hook the blade of the ice axes into existing holes in the the icefall, which provides some form of support. Adaptive behaviors such as this may surface because system degeneracy can be exploited for exploration as a consequence of the interaction between the task, environment, and learner.

Assessment of Learning

The scanning procedure described earlier would be difficult to implement in realistic learning environments without sophisticated measurement tools. However, regularly assessing a learner's progress is critical for the practitioner to help guide ongoing practice. In the past, movement variability has been typically associated with error, and many practitioners believed that minimizing performance errors would indicate improvement. However, we are now beginning to appreciate that movement variability may be viewed in a more positive light. In the motor system, variability is omnipresent and unavoidable and might even provide a useful signpost for exploratory behavior in learners; in fact, a change in constraints can act as a catalyst for a new movement pattern by helping to induce more variability in the learner. Zanone and Kelso (1992) argued that the movement system must experience critical fluctuations before it can relocate itself in a new attractor state. Further, in order to widen the attractor base that learners currently occupy, they must practice under a range of constraints. Take for example the work by Chow, Davids, Button, and Rein (2008) that determined that participants demonstrate a higher level of movement pattern variability before a transition to a new preferred stable pattern in a soccer chipping task. This is in line with the earlier concepts (degeneracy and pluripotentiality) because adaptation, innovation, and evolvability are inherent traits seen in such systems.

Manipulating constraints is a natural way to learn skills and to assess skill development. For example, task constraints represent a direct route to changing behavior and might produce sudden transitions in technique at the beginning of practice (see figure 5.4). Later in practice, the changes may be less abrupt, and the pattern variability may reflect refinements and adaptations by learners (Liu et al., 2006).

It can often take longer to alter organismic or personal constraints, and we may expect to see slower and more permanent adaptations in coordination as a result of, for example, prolonged flexibility or endurance training. In terms of environmental constraints, cultural and social constraints also have a slower and more subtle impact on behavior, although it has been argued that these constraints emerge and decay more rapidly than some organismic constraints, such as effects of genetic constraints on population variation (Ehrlich, 2000). In a busy traffic environment, for instance, drivers need to adapt their actions quickly, but their typical driving style is less rapidly affected by societal views of safe driving as dictated by changing cultural perspectives (see chapter 6).

When considering how the perceptual-motor landscape changes over time, it is necessary to acknowledge the different timescales in which influ-

© Chris Button

FIGURE 5.4 A soccer coach asks the learner to practice chipping a different type of ball (rugby ball). A change in constraints such as this can act as a catalyst for a new movement pattern by helping to induce more variability. Practitioners should view movement variability more positively because it might provide a useful signpost for exploratory behavior in learners.

ential constraints operate. According to Newell (1986), constraints may be relatively time dependent or time independent; that is, "the rate with which constraints may change over time varies considerably with the level of analysis and parameter under consideration" (p. 347). Newell and colleagues (2001) have pointed out that

> timescales in motor learning and development would include the influence of the timescales of phylogeny and ontogeny in motor learning and the related impact of culture and society on the development of human action. This broader context serves to highlight and emphasize the central role that some scales play in the study of motor learning and development. (p. 64)

The issue of different constraints operating on different timescales has implications for the practitioner's judgment of the learner's rate of progress. When learning a new coordination pattern, more permanent behavioral changes take longer to appear than immediate adaptations to task constraints during practice. Therefore, practitioners should understand that some behaviors might represent transient adaptations to immediate task constraints imposed during practice, and these constraints interact with organismic constraints related to developmental status. Important constraints here include the effects of the specific equipment, location, and instructions that a learner experiences at a given state of development. Practitioners need to observe with care to ensure that emergent behavior under constraints is not due to transient effects but reflects a stable characteristic of each learner's current level of performance. Referring back to figure 5.4, the learner may well learn how to chip the rugby ball in the air, but the coach must also ensure that improvement transfers to chipping a standard soccer ball.

Assessment of learning requires nonlinear pedagogists to be familiar with the influential constraints that shape behavior. In structuring an effective learning environment, these constraints should be manipulated to facilitate the learner's search for more effective coordination patterns. The following four-step plan may help practitioners systematically approach assessment within their learning environments:

1. **Identify** significant constraints that limit behavior within each movement task that the practitioner is teaching (e.g., task, individual, environment).

2. **Examine** the reaction of a few learners at different developmental stages to subtle changes in the constraint, monitoring the learners' initial and short-term reaction.

3. **Modify** the degree and frequency of constraint changes to suit the individual learner.

4. **Using** movement variability as an indicator of attractor stability, continue to evaluate the learner's skill retention and transfer.

When the Learner Gets Stuck in a Rut: Take a Giant Step

Another common concern practitioners often face is how to make experienced performers alter well-established coordination patterns. Despite long periods of repetitive practice, the learner may get stuck in a rut, showing little progress. Although practitioners sometimes call this a *performance plateauing effect,* the movement system actually has become temporarily trapped in a deep, stable attractor state that may not be as effective as other, nearby states. In other words, some motor patterns can become too stable. In addition, the formation of the established pattern has weakened the stability of nearby attractors, making it less likely that the learner can use an alternative coordination pattern. Could the plateau indicate that some change in coordination is needed to stimulate further improvement?

The practitioner can consider two potential approaches to this problem. For simplicity, we will use the example of a tennis player who relies heavily on a two-handed backhand stroke. How can a practitioner help the tennis player explore alternative shots on the backhand side? The first useful strategy involves gradually weakening the stability of the existing attractor state by trying to induce movement pattern variability. This is a counterintuitive notion because traditionally, the aim of practice has been to make movement patterns more stable (and therefore less prone to error) over time. To achieve this aim, the practitioner should encourage the tennis player to keep practicing with the usual technique, but the practitioner must find ways to gradually alter potential control parameters such as ball speed or height of ball bounce to encourage more variability.

For example, during practice the tennis practitioner could use an adjustable ball machine or a range of new and used tennis balls to change the flight characteristics of the ball. In these situations the two-handed technique should become more variable as a function of the altered task constraints, and the player will begin to find it difficult to play a customary shot. For example, forcing the player to strike the ball earlier if it bounces too high, reducing the backlift of the racket for quicker returns, or taking one hand off the racket to release additional dfs may begin to destabilize an existing motor pattern and provide valuable exploratory practice time for the player. It may take some time for this approach to lead to long-term changes in behavior, but given the amount of time invested in stabilizing the original technique, this should come as no surprise.

An alternative approach to changing well-established techniques would be to perturb the system from an existing attractor toward a more functional movement pattern (Newell, 1996). In other words, the practitioner can try a more radical manipulation of constraints to push the performer out of the customary technique. Returning to the tennis player, the practitioner can immediately prevent the two-handed solution from emerging by artificially constraining the nondominant arm by asking the player to hold a ball or a racket in the nondominant hand. Now the player will be quickly forced into practicing the one-handed shot as a consequence of the altered task constraints. This drill also could have the added benefit of helping the player develop balance during the shot by counteracting the position of the playing arm with the nondominant limb (figure 5.5).

In each of these approaches, both the learner and practitioner should understand that there will be a temporary increase in errors as the new movement pattern evolves and the old attractor state is weakened. Although the transition into a new, shallow attractor state is quick in the second approach, it may

FIGURE 5.5 A practitioner can prevent the two-handed solution from emerging by asking the tennis player to hold a ball or a racket in the nondominant hand.

take some time to develop the consistency associated with the two-handed shot. Adding variability to a movement pattern can thus benefit long-term changes in movement behavior. Neither the practitioner nor the learner should interpret this initial rise in movement variability as negative. Instead, sometimes you need to take two steps backward to move one giant step forward. Also note that sometimes we may not see a totally new movement pattern (a bifurcation) but perhaps just refinements (a shift). Nevertheless, the need to perturb the system provides the stimulus for such changes.

Summary

Motor skills practitioners play a valuable role in learners' development. Under the constraints-led approach, their role emphasizes different aspects compared with elements emphasized in other theoretical approaches. Traditionally, practitioners have taught learners to consistently replicate a prescribed idealized technique toward which all learners should aspire. These strategies include high frequencies of evaluation and feedback, practice that focuses on basic skills removed from the performance context, and modeling with advanced performers. However, such practices may lead to poor retention and transfer of a technique that may not even be appropriate for the learner. Conversely, from the constraints-led approach, it has been suggested that practitioners should adopt a hands-off role by allowing learners enough time and space to explore and discover appropriate movement solutions for themselves. The emphasis is on monitoring, guiding, and facilitating the learner's progress. Key pedagogical principles (or design principles) that (1) pertain to the need for learning to be representative, (2) focus on constraints manipulation, (3) are cognizant of the implications of using informational constraints that emphasize either movement effect or movement form, (4) value the role of functional variability, and (5) ensure strong coupling between information and movement (and thus task simplification) could be adopted (see Chow, Davids, Button, and Renshaw, 2016). These pedagogical principles are underpinned by our understanding of the role of degeneracy and pluripotentiality present in neurobiological systems in which adaptability, innovation, and evolvability can be encouraged in learning contexts. Striking a balance between insightful input and discovery learning is essential for optimal skills retention and transfer. Tools such as feedback, modeling, and hands-on instruction still exist within the constraints-led framework; however, knowing when to be hands off is equally important.

In the early stages of learning, it is important that practitioners recognize initial movement tendencies and the subsequent implications for practice. For example, the greater the mismatch between a learner's current movement tendencies and those required by the task, the longer it may take for the learner to progress. We now know a lot more about how the practitioner can manipulate constraints to help limit or promote learning at different rates. Further, we have described how movement variability can be viewed positively as a medium or platform through which transitions from one action to another lead to the emergence of a more functional pattern. Practitioners can emphasize movement variability during practice to weaken stable states of coordination that are mildly dysfunctional and that learners can use to seek alternative and more appropriate solutions.

The changing role of the practitioner does not mean that coaching, teaching, and physiotherapy are likely to become less important or any easier. Indeed, supervising the learning or rehabilitation environment will always remain a challenging and time-consuming art. However, if practitioners can develop their understanding of the dynamics of skill acquisition, they are likely to become more effective at promoting long-term changes in behavior.

Self-Test Questions

1. Explain how to use coordination dynamics to describe the process of skill acquisition for a learner. (Tip: Try to use terms such as *intrinsic dynamics, perceptual-motor landscape, attractor, stability, symmetry, degeneracy, and pluripotentiality*.)

2. Can you offer examples of when you might have learned a motor task through functional equivalence?
3. How might a practitioner assess the initial coordination tendencies of a novice skier?
4. What alternative strategies in nonlinear pedagogy could you use to help a learner who has reached a performance plateau?

Laboratory Activity

Degeneracy in Action

Using a laboratory activity, we can better highlight how degeneracy can be present in the completion of a task.

Experimental Problems

- First identify a discrete motor task (e.g., kicking a ball to a fixed target).
- Thereafter, rules (or constraints) can be progressively included (e.g., kick only with nondominant foot, change the size of the ball, do not allow a run-up).
- As the learner, attempt to complete the task goal of kicking the ball to hit the target while using different movement solutions to achieve the same task goal. How many different solutions can you come up with?

Equipment and Resources

- Selection of equipment for a discrete movement task
- Open laboratory space or gymnasium
- Video camera

Use the video camera to capture the demonstration of different movement solutions to attempt to achieve the task goal. Viewing the recording, can you describe whether these movement solutions were effective?

CHAPTER 6

How Interacting Constraints Support a Nonlinear Pedagogy

CHAPTER OBJECTIVES

After completing this chapter, you will be able to do the following:

- Identify and describe influential personal, task, and environmental constraints on a learner
- List the levels of analysis that form the bioecological model of human development
- Describe nonlinear pedagogy and why this approach is helpful for understanding the interaction between constraints surrounding the learner
- Explain key design principles that underpin the nonlinear pedagogy approach

---

Physical education and sports coaching practitioners are confronted daily with learners whose personal experiences and attributes have been shaped by the sociocultural constraints that surround them. These include historical and traditional practices that dominate a society, group, or team. Movement preferences, individual differences, and nonlinear rates of development are as much a function of the social milieu in which learners have developed as they are of an individual's physiology, anatomy, or psychology. In this chapter, we highlight the importance of sociocultural constraints during learning and argue that practitioners and researchers benefit from greater awareness of their influence. Understanding the interaction of constraints forces one to reconceptualize the learning process as emergent and nonlinear. Consequently, we discuss the implications for practitioners of what has been termed a *non-linear pedagogy* (Chow, Davids, Button, Shuttleworth, Renshaw, and Araújo, 2007; Chow, Davids, Button, and Renshaw, 2016).

Ecological Scale of Behavioral Analysis

When scientists attempt to understand an organism's behavior—such as how they learn new skills—it is important that they adopt an appropriate scale of analysis. Prominent psychologists such as Gibson, Brunswik, and Reed recognized this fact in developing the ecological approach. Ecology is defined as "a branch of science concerned with the interrelationship of organisms and their environments" (Merriam-Webster.com: Online Dictionary). Hence, from an ecological perspective, human behavior, for example, can only be understood in the context of the environments that humans have partly designed and in which they operate (see chapter 3). Arguably, research and practice in sport and exercise psychology have been dominated by an organismic-centric methodology and theorizing (i.e., characterized by a narrow focus on describing internal mental states and processes of individual performers) (Araújo and Davids, 2009). For too long, important elements in the environment, such as cultural norms, traditional practices, and the influence of significant others, have been conveniently ignored, yet we intuitively know that they have considerable influence on motor learning. For example, children may not feel comfortable tackling new learning challenges if their parents or caregivers have shielded them from risky situations from an early age. Let us consider sociocultural constraints in more detail.

Sociocultural Constraints

The acquisition of perceptual-motor expertise in different performance domains (e.g., clinical, physical education, music, sport coaching) is a complex, contextualized process. Theoretically, the constraints-led approach to motor learning has provided major insights, mainly from empirical research on individual and task constraints. However, as Clark (1995) suggests, there is a need to further explore the sociocultural environmental constraints of this model: "Culture also acts as environmental constraints that shape movements. Although these constraints may be more subtle than the physical ones, they are nonetheless ever-present surrounds to the actor" (Clark, 1995, p.175).

The environments in which humans learn and practice skills are flavored by sociocultural factors. For example, the presence of an evaluative coach or audience may (or may not) have a significant impact on the performer. Similarly, the culture of different clubs, regions, or countries leaves footprints that can shape the ways in which people move and act. Sociocultural constraints have always had a significant impact on sport and physical activity participation. For example, the obesity crisis that plagues the developed world may be further accentuated by societal expectations of body image, forcing more and more people away from physical activity and toward sedentary lifestyles (Lewis and Van Puymbroeck, 2008). How comfortable people are with their body shape is affected indirectly by culture and the broad set of values that society may have concerning body shape (Swami, 2015). Another obvious example is that until relatively recent times, women were not encouraged to compete in certain sports (such as soccer, tennis, rugby, and track and field) because their participation was not deemed appropriate through social norms. While recent decades have seen such gender-biased attitudes relaxing, idealistic attitudes concerning the human body are arguably strengthening, particularly in Western and modernized countries.

It is important to note that sociocultural influences, like other types of constraint, can both *disable* and *enable* skill acquisition. For example, Uehara, Button, Falcous, and Davids (2014) identified numerous factors common to Brazilian society (e.g., street soccer; capoeira, a style of martial art; and samba, a form of dance and music) that have a positive impact on the highly skillful soccer players this country historically produces (see Spotlight on Research). Also Rothwell, Davids, and Stone (2018) discussed how historical industrial working practices influenced professional coaching in team sports like the rugby league in the United Kingdom. Some of these practices in sport can be traced to militaristic training that provided the backdrop to physical education syllabi until recent decades (Moy et al., 2015). These fascinating studies underline that working practices in sport and physical education do not exist in a vacuum, but are very much continually constrained by sociocultural and historical tendencies and traditions. Indeed, one can readily identify how cultural practices and traditions present in different countries, such as dance, rituals, and other popular pastimes, enable opportunities for skill acquisition that may not exist to the same extent in other countries. Moreover, sociocultural constraints have often persisted over many generations, and their lasting influence cannot be underestimated (Rothwell et al., 2018).

Environmental constraints that impinge on a learner's development are multiple, intangible, intertwined, and dynamic (Davids, Araújo, Hristovski, and colleagues, 2013). Consequently, an ecological scale of analysis will demand a range of research methodologies to improve our understanding of human behavioral adaptation. Motor learning research has traditionally persevered with a relatively narrow range of research tools emanating from a long history of a positivistic, laboratory-based research paradigm (Uehara et al., 2014). Such tools seem suitable for investigating how unique *personal constraints* interact with task-related factors in the skill acquisition process (Araújo and Davids, 2011). However, for the study of far-reaching *sociocultural* and *historical constraints*, other methodologies may be more functional. Indeed, several

Spotlight on Research

How "Naked Soccer" Nurtures Brazil's Star Players

As a Brazilian himself, Luiz Uehara has always been passionate about soccer and keen to explore how his homeland has become synonymous with the development of talented, highly skilled soccer players. His doctoral degree covered this topic, and he has published several articles considering the various sociocultural constraints particular to Brazil. One article published in the *Journal of Expertise* (Uehara et al., 2018) recognizes the practice activity of **pelada** as an influential factor in many players' backgrounds. Pelada is a form of pickup soccer without coaching, supervision, or referees. Literally translated, pelada means *naked* and it could refer to the barefooted play (and perhaps also the bare surroundings in which pelada is often played). In Brazil, pelada games are highly competitive despite the fact that they may be played in streets or wastelands rather than manicured soccer fields. The fact that many Brazilian soccer legends (including Ronaldinho and Neymar Jr.) report that they spent many hours in their youth playing pelada is suggestive that it may be an ideal vehicle for developing talent. In their article, Uehara and colleagues (2018) link several elements of pelada to skill acquisition principles and conclude that "naked soccer" can be a powerful enabling constraint on perceptual-motor skill development. Using a rich variety of research methodologies, including historiography, case studies, and observational notes, the authors illustrate the typical sociocultural environments through which many Brazilian soccer players have learned to master the "beautiful game."

recent studies have begun to illustrate such approaches, including interviews and observational analysis (Uehara et al., 2014), document and biographical analysis (Rees et al., 2016; Anderson and Maivorsdotter, 2016), and interpretive, phenomenological analysis of practice structure (de Bruin, 2018).

Bioecological Model of Human Development

Urie Bronfenbrenner was a developmental psychologist who truly appreciated the profound influence of environment and sociocultural constraints. In general terms, the bioecological model conceives human development as a function of the interaction between nature and nurture (Bronfenbrenner, 1995). The mutual interactions between performers and context create an ecological dynamic that can eliminate the organismic asymmetry (bias toward the person) typical of traditional research approaches in the behavioral sciences (Davids and Araújo, 2010).

While the bioecological model serves as both a theoretical and methodological framework to investigate sociocultural constraints on expertise development, it cannot serve as a general explanatory theory of skill acquisition. Indeed, as Araújo and colleagues explain, "this model is more a framework for organizing knowledge than a [general] theory of sport expertise" (2010, p. 174). Thus, as we will describe later, the bioecological model should be used to provide methodological guidance for identifying relevant constraints that affect human development. To our knowledge, the bioecological model is unique in offering a holistic, longitudinal, and contextual overview of human development. Bronfenbrenner's model is predicated on the interaction of four key elements that constrain human development. These elements are the process, person, context, and time (PPCT) (see Krebs, 2009). The *process* is recognized as a principal constraint on human development (Krebs, 2009). Bronfenbrenner and Morris (2006) stated, "this construct encompasses particular forms of interaction between organism and environment, called proximal processes, that operate over time and are posited as the primary mechanisms producing human development" (p. 795). Proximal processes can generate both positive and negative effects on a developing individual. For example, young athletes attending an elite sports academy may thrive in that process or may find the experience traumatic without the requisite psychobehavioral attributes and drop out altogether (Abbott, Button, Pepping, and Collins, 2005). Clearly, each individual has the capacity to influence proximal processes through her unique experience and attributes.

The second component of the bioecological model is the *person*, analyzed by means of his biopsychological characteristics developed during person–environment interactions (Bronfenbrenner and Morris, 1998). As a specific example, Stattin and Magnusson (1990) illustrate person–environment interactions by assessing the implications of the biological maturation rate for the developmental process of females. They showed that the behavioral patterns (social adaptation) of postpubescent girls were related to factors such as age of menarche and association with older, working boys. The authors acknowledge that to understand the role of biological factors on personal development, one must also consider mental factors and environmental factors simultaneously.

The third component of the model is *context*. In human development, context is emphasized as a joint function of characteristics of the person and the environment. It encompasses the physical, social, and cultural features of the immediate settings in which human beings live (e.g., family, school, and neighborhood), as well as the broader contemporary and historical context in which an individual is born (Moen, Elder, and Lüscher, 1995). Steinberg, Darling, Fletcher, Brown, and Dornbusch (1995) recognized the importance of context in analyzing parenting style on youngsters' development. They suggest that although authoritative parenting works, in that adolescents typically fare better when their parents behave this way, it works better in some contexts than others. In certain ecologies, proximal processes outside the control of parents may entirely overwhelm the benefits of authoritative parenting (Steinberg et al., 1995). For example, in neighborhoods experiencing poverty and crime, the broader societal factors that developing children must contend with may subsume any particular style of parenting.

The final component of the bioecological system is *time*, which permits an analysis of both "the historical period through which a person lives [and the] timing of biological and social transitions as they relate to the culturally-defined age, role expectations, and opportunities occurring throughout the life course" (Bronfenbrenner, 1995, p. 641). Bronfenbrenner and Morris (2006) classified time into three levels: micro-time, meso-time, and macro-time (figure 6.1). These timescales distinguish between the rapid discontinuity associated with certain momentary proximal processes (micro); the regular periodicity of other interactions over days, weeks, and months (meso); and the more gradual evolution of other episodes that may occur over a life span (macro).

The bioecological model conceptualizes the environment in terms of four nested subsystems: **microsystem** (e.g., family support), **mesosystem** (e.g., training facility), **exosystem** (e.g., demography), and **macrosystem** (e.g., national historical context) (see Krebs, 2009). These subsystems can be conceived of as fitting into a concentric structure with the individual at the center and each subsystem building on and influencing the others to form the ecological environment (see figure 6.1). The microsystem is the innermost level

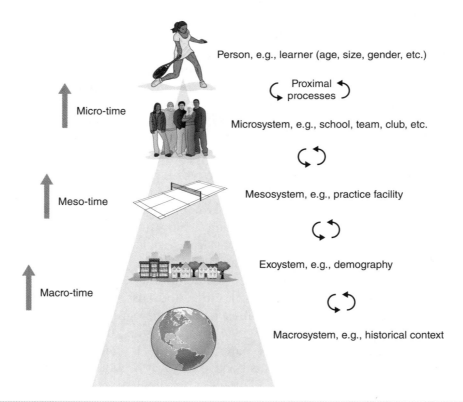

FIGURE 6.1   A diagram of the bioecological model of human development.

in which the developing person is directly involved in activities, roles, and interpersonal relationships with the immediate physical, social, and symbolic features of her environment. The mesosystem is a system of microsystems. When a person transits from one microsystem to another, a mesosystem is created. A mesosystem entails interrelations emerging between two or more settings containing the developing person. In other words, a person's interactions in one place, (e.g., workplace) are influenced by interaction with other contexts, such as the family (see Bronfenbrenner, 1979; Krebs, 2009). The exosystem comprises the settings in which the developing person participates, including at least one that does not contain that person, but in which events occur that indirectly influence the person's development (Bronfenbrenner, 1979; Krebs, 2009). Three important exosystems that are likely to indirectly affect the development of children and youth are the parents' workplace, the family social network, and the neighborhood community. In line with these ideas, it's worth noting that previous researchers in skill acquisition have reported that certain characteristics of a neighborhood community, such as population size of a city, may influence the inhabitants' expertise acquisition in sport (see Côté, Macdonald, Baker, and Abernethy, 2006).

The last level of the nested system is the macrosystem that embraces all the possible links among microsystems, mesosystems, and exosystems. This system was defined by Bronfenbrenner as "the overarching pattern of micro-, meso-, and exosystems characteristics of a given culture, subculture or other broader social context" (2005, p. 150). As such, the macrosystem level includes a range of putative influences (such as political, historical, economic, and sociocultural) on the developing individual that are undeniably present, but rarely considered, within the context of motor learning. For example, the broad macrosystem dimension may help us to describe and interpret historical playing styles, cultures, and stratifications that characterize and bind together certain sports and nations (e.g., New Zealand rugby union, Brazilian soccer, Australian-rules football, Indian cricket, American basketball, Russian gymnastics, Nordic winter sports, Northeast African endurance running, Jamaican sprinting).

Nonlinear Nature of Learning

Although many scholars have attempted to apply the bioecological model in research designs (see Moen et al., 1995), it has seldom been used to examine skill acquisition processes (Krebs, 2009). It is possible that a lack of familiarity with qualitative research methods has hindered application of Bronfenbrenner's model, particularly in sports science (Mullineaux, Bartlett, and Bennett, 2001). However, according to Krebs (2009, p. 123) "[the] bioecological model offers a possibility to use new research designs to conduct better investigations to assess the athlete's personal attributes." As we have suggested throughout this book, human development is a complex process influenced by many interacting factors. This complexity inevitably brings the potential for nonlinearity in system outputs. Indeed, within the parameters of contextualization, ecological analysis cannot be maintained with a linear deterministic focus. For this reason, Bronfenbrenner advocated that environmental properties cannot be "distinguished by reference to linear variables but analyzed in systems terms" (Krebs, 2009, p. 117). As explained in chapter 1, nonlinear systems do not develop in a gradual or predictable way, but instead they can experience sudden jumps, pauses, or setbacks that may be difficult to predict. Sociocultural and historical events and traditions can provide a form of life that underpins ways of acquiring skills, experience, and knowledge in sport contexts (Rothwell et al., 2018). A major challenge for practitioners is to understand how environmental constraints interact with task and personal constraints in enhancing skill and expertise in sport. Next, we examine how the three categories of interacting constraints can provide a pedagogical methodology for enhancing skill in humans as nonlinear dynamical systems: a nonlinear pedagogy.

What Is Nonlinear Pedagogy? Key Design Principles

Ample evidence supports the view that human learning is nonlinear in nature and, therefore, teaching and coaching methodologies should account for such nonlinearity (see Chow and Atencio, 2012). According to Renshaw, Chow, Davids, and Hammond (2010), an embodied model of motor learning (Port and van Gelder, 1995) such as the constraints-led approach (CLA) views mind, body, and the environment as continuously influencing each other to shape emergent behaviors. From this perspective, motor learning is a process of acquiring movement patterns that satisfy the key constraints acting on each individual (Renshaw, Davids, Shuttleworth, and Chow, 2009).

However, CLA only promotes the understanding of how skills are acquired from a motor learning domain. It does not provide a principled pedagogical framework for *designing* motor learning programs considered as nonlinear dynamical systems for humans. A *nonlinear pedagogy* approach, based on nonlinear and complexity phenomena, has been increasingly advocated in recent years to provide practitioners with key principles to underpin teaching and coaching with CLA (Chow et al., 2016). Pertinent information on how to assess performance, how to structure practices, and how best to deliver instructions and provide feedback are particularly relevant (see Chow, Renshaw, Button, Davids, and Tan, 2013; Ovens, Hopper, and Butler, 2013). Nonlinear pedagogy emphasizes the need to design representative and facilitative learning experiences for individuals, supported by principles framed by understanding the nonlinearity in human learning (figure 6.2). Recent work in nonlinear pedagogy has demonstrated that its underlying theoretical principles can be adopted to address the key question: What design principles can be used to support teaching and learning (see Chow et al., 2009)?

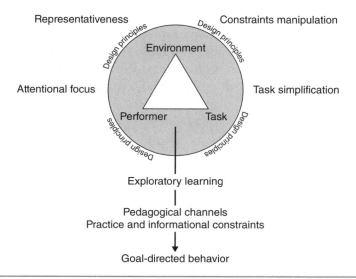

FIGURE 6.2 Pedogogical principles of nonlinear pedagogy.

Adapted from J.Y. Chow, "Nonlinear Learning Underpinning Pedagogy: Evidence, Challenges, and Implications," *Quest* 65, no. 4 (2013): 469-484.

Situated for Representative Learning Design

Nonlinear pedagogy provides a framework in which learning is situated in realistic contexts (Chow, 2010). The acquisition of knowledge occurs as a consequence of the interactions between the learner and the environment. Barab and Roth (2006) further stressed this ecological scale of analysis in providing sources of information in the form of material content, patterns, and invariant properties that invite learners to construct meaningful relations. Davis and Sumara (2006) even suggested that pupil learning should occur in a "bottom up" manner, reflecting higher levels of situated and authentic learning with the focus on students.

Fajen, Riley, and Turvey (2009) point out that athletes need to be placed in realistic learning environments so that they can attune to information that will enable them to make *intelligent* and informed decisions based on their own action capabilities and those of their teammates and opponents (see chapter 4). By way of example, consider how golfers spend many hours of practice time on a driving range working to develop their swing. One might question to what extent this activity is representative of the environment in which golfers actually play. Representative learning design advocates that golfers need to continually experience the natural challenges they face while navigating a course. In golf, such challenges include different setup positions, light and weather influences, decisions about which club to use, how best to approach the green and putting strategies, and so on (Stöckl, Lamb, and Lames, 2011). Repeatedly swinging at a ball on a tee may seem beneficial for the highly precise task demands of striking a golf ball, but the sport of golf involves much more than this activity. An *intelligent* golfer will understand how important the context of each shot she plays is and this awareness is certainly not reproduced within the confines of a driving range!

Task Simplification

The need to establish functional information–movement couplings in learning movement skills is one of the cornerstones of a nonlinear pedagogical approach (see chapter 3). The circular relationship between information and movement is key to understanding the concept of *affordances* and its role in movement control. The focus is on the *individual* and how opportunities for action are pegged to the individual as he operates within an environment (social or physical). Nonlinear pedagogy is based on the importance of establishing functional affordances, and these opportunities for action can be meaningfully created when the learners are placed in representative in situ learning contexts. Modifying task demands systematically in order to maintain informational–movement couplings is called **task simplification** (figure 6.2). This typically involves making a challenging performance task simpler to achieve in a practice session but without modifying the key affordances that guide behavior.

Körner and Staller (2018) recognized the value of task simplification in advocating for a nonlinear pedagogy of self-defense training for police officers. For example, they note that training scenarios need to embed factors such as surprise attacks, high-aggression dynamics, and psychological pressure so that in a nonlinear pedagogy of self-defense "crisis becomes normal" (Körner and Staller, 2018, p. 653). Within simulated attack scenarios, police officers must learn to recognize key sources of environmental information (e.g., body language of potential offenders, presence of a weapon, their own levels of arousal) and learn to couple appropriate responses to such information.

Manipulation of Constraints

The role of constraints manipulation is an important aspect of nonlinear pedagogy. Much has been written about the CLA and its role in skill acquisition (see Renshaw, Chappell, Fitzgerald, Davison, and McFadyen, 2010), which provides an understanding of how coaches actively can shape specific learning opportunities for athletes. It is a major component of nonlinear pedagogy that contains principles of learning design underpinned by a deep understanding of how key constraints interact with each other to use cognition, perception, and action to support performance and learning in sport. Typically, task constraints are adjusted by practitioners to prompt learners to explore and acquire different movement behaviors (Chow and Atencio, 2012). Numerous examples have been investigated in papers (e.g., see Tan et al., 2012; Lee, Chow, Komar, Tan, and Button, 2014) concerning how constraint manipulation can channel learners to exhibit varied movement behaviors, for example, encouraging short and long play in tennis by altering the dimensions of the playing area (e.g., Fitzpatrick, Davids, and Stone, 2018). The manipulation of constraints by the coach or teacher is a powerful aspect of nonlinear pedagogy for encouraging transitions toward, and acquisition of, new preferred stable movement behaviors in learning systems.

Exploratory Learning: Leveraging Functional Variability

An important aspect of nonlinear pedagogy is associated with the role of functional movement variability in enhancing acquisition of coordination because movement variability is seen as a feature of nonlinearity in human learning (see chapter 5; Chow, Davids, Hristovski, Araújo, and Passos, 2011). "Noise" amplifies exploratory activity and may guide the learner to discover individualized functional solutions to a specific task goal (Newell et al., 2008; Schöllhorn, Mayer-Kress, Newell, and Michelbrink, 2009). Nonlinear pedagogy incorporates and recognizes the critical role of infusing perturbations (e.g., in the form of encouraging variability in practice conditions) in a learning environment to support exploratory learning and extensive search of the perceptual-motor workspace in individual athletes. This is especially relevant when a learner is stuck in a rut and remains on a skill plateau (chapter 5). To encourage a transition to new modes of behavior, a coach can incorporate a perturbation to practice by altering task constraints, such as instructions or equipment, to challenge the learner to try new coordination patterns (see figure 6.3). For example, swim coaches often use devices such as flippers, paddles, and even parachutes to induce exploratory technique changes from learners (Schnitzler, Brazier, Button, Seifert, and Chollet, 2011). Relatedly, Baker and colleagues (2003) noted that highly skilled performers modify task difficulty for themselves as a strategy to prevent skill plateaus from forming.

Enhancing Attentional Focus

Another aspect of nonlinear pedagogy involves the impact of instructions based on an external focus of attention that seems to reduce conscious and explicit control of movement. An external focus of attention is "where the performer's attention is directed to the effect of the action," compared to an internal focus of attention, "where attention is directed to the action itself" (Wulf, 2007). Instructions to learners can be varied by guiding them to focus attention on either the effects of a movement on the environment (i.e., the outcomes of an action) or on body movements (i.e., limb segments) involved in producing an action, respectively (see Wulf and Lewthwaite, 2016, for a review). However, it should also be noted that many of the previous findings on the impact of different attentional focus of attention instructions seem to have greater relevance to *skilled participants*. Novices and children may respond

FIGURE 6.3 A runner training with the added resistance of a parachute.

differently to external focus of attention instructions, and the perceived benefits of these instructions may not be as convincing. Beilock, Carr, MacMahon, and Starkes (2002) proposed an explicit monitoring hypothesis stating that pressure causes increased attention to a skill-focused process that disrupts performance of proceduralized skill. This hypothesis suggests that performance outcome could be better for novices when using an internal focus of attention. For example, a novice tennis player may benefit from a simple instruction (e.g., focus on sending the ball over the net) whereas an experienced player might need to focus on a particular element of skill execution (e.g., foot placement, backswing). Thus, the benefits of external focus of attention instructions can also be task constraint or even learner dependent (Peh, Chow, and Davids, 2011). Regardless of the locus of attentional focus, it can be a potent tool for developing skill from a nonlinear pedagogy perspective.

What Does This Mean for the Teacher and Learner?

In brief, the focus of nonlinear pedagogy is on the individual and is clearly a learner-centric approach. The recognition is that learners should be presented with opportunities to acquire movement solutions that are individualized, based on the learning and performing context. Each individual learner needs to satisfy unique interacting task and environmental constraints impinging on him at any moment. Encapsulating these constraints, practitioners need to develop design principles that incorporate representativeness, manipulation of constraints, attentional focus, functional variability, and the maintenance of pertinent information–movement couplings. These design principles can then be delivered through the key pedagogical channels of practice design, constraints manipulation, modeling, instructions, and feedback (used sparingly) to allow functional goal-directed behaviors to emerge. Nonlinear pedagogy provides the design principles and mechanisms that underpin learning activities that simulate competitive performance contexts and that are suitably catered to the individual learner.

Representative Learning Designs in Practice

Teachers must try to design learning activities based on in situ contexts that are representative of how the game skills will be used on actual or modified game settings. Passing in soccer should be practiced in the presence of defenders and under conditions that simulate important aspects of performance, for example, using field markings and goal areas. The same philosophy is true in individual sports. Surfers need to practice the art of getting up onto the board while in waves. There is little to be gained by practicing jumping up to a crouched position on the board on dry land when the performance scenario requires such an intricate coupling between action and environment. Springboard diving practice should mainly take place in a pool rather than a dryland practice area so that takeoff and aerial movements can be interlinked with affordances of entry into the water with the hands (not feetfirst into a foam pit).

The case for establishing representative learning design is clearly supported by motor learning investigations outside of school settings (see Pinder, Renshaw, and Araújo, 2011). Using ideas of task simplification (preserving links between information and movement) rather than task decomposition (breaking down tasks into microcomponents for ease of practice) can further enhance representation (Davids, Button, and Bennett, 2008). This idea implies that long jumpers should not be encouraged to practice run-throughs without hitting the takeoff board to jump, although less-demanding pop-offs (simulated mini-jumps) are better than run-throughs if an athlete is in danger of overtraining. Practice task constraints devoid of other performers (i.e., defenders) or structured in a contrived, artificial manner will render inappropriate affordances acquired by the learners that are not functional.

From a practitioner point of view, modifying practice tasks enables learners to access key perceptual information available in the performance context

Representative Learning Design

The pedagogical principle of representation ensures that the information–movement coupling of the structured practice environment is relevant and representative of the performance context. What this means is that relevant information sources and affordances of the to-be-learned performance context should be present in a practice task simulation.

and couple it with appropriate actions. Tan and colleagues (2012) found that the aim of representation is for learners to experience opportunities for developing tactical awareness, make appropriate decisions, and practice skills in manageable practice environments. These skills are clearly evident in a sound representative learning design in which situated learning is encouraged.

Creating an Intrinsically Motivating Learning Environment

It is paramount that practitioners provide a learning environment that is intrinsically motivating for learners. Chow, Davids, Renshaw, and Button (2013) found that a nonlinear pedagogical approach can provide a context in which learners are motivated to learn. Underpinned by the self-determination theory (Deci and Ryan, 2000), it has been suggested that a key requirement for a curriculum that aims to educate children through the medium of physical activity and sport is to ensure that chosen activities and pedagogical approaches support the basic psychological needs of autonomy, competence, and relatedness (see Chow et al., 2013). The key question is how do you create such an intrinsically motivating learning environment within the framework of nonlinear pedagogy?

Chow and colleagues (2013) also stressed that teaching methods should facilitate opportunities to pursue **autonomy**, **competence**, and **relatedness**, which will result in intrinsically motivated behaviors such as effort, persistence, and problem solving with respect to task goals. By manipulating suitable and relevant task constraints, practitioners can design learning activities situated in performance settings that cater to individual learning needs. When these individual differences are catered to, the opportunities for the learners to fulfill their psychological needs will be greater. Working in *smaller groups* (e.g., small-sided games), presents problem-solving opportunities through appropriate manipulation of constraints and *questioning*. With such a focus on learner–task interaction, a sense of autonomy (e.g., through making decisions on his own), competence (e.g., through being successful at meeting task goals from modified activities), and relatedness (e.g., through opportunities for interaction among peers in small-sided games) can be attained more readily (also see Renshaw, Oldham, and Bawden, 2012, for a discussion on how nonlinear pedagogy underpins intrinsic motivation).

Summary

Humans perform and learn skills within complex, multilayered environments that affect how movements are constructed. Social and cultural factors exert subtle but enduring influence on skill acquisition, and their important role must be acknowledged. Because constraints are multiple, dynamic, and interacting, it may seem overwhelming to identify them in any given situation. Bronfenbrenner's bioecological model (figure 6.1) provides a useful framework for identifying and modeling the interacting constraints on a learner or group of learners.

Advances in the literature of human movement science over the last decade have provided strong evidence to underpin pedagogical approaches that account for the dynamism and complexity that are inherent in learning movement skills (see Chow et al., 2016; Ovens et al., 2013; Renshaw, Araújo, Button et al., 2015). There is increasing recognition that individual differences among learners need to be accounted for when practitioners plan teaching interventions in learning contexts (Chow and Atencio, 2012). The focus on the individual and pedagogical practices will have to cater to the dynamic and complex interactions that occur between learners, the task, and the environmental constraints. The study of how the individual learner adapts behavior is nested in a situated environment (Chow, 2010; Jess, Atencio, and Thorburn, 2011). When we examine the learner as being situated within the environment, important insights into how learners establish important information–movement couplings can be better understood.

Complexities present in behavioral changes encourage us to view learning as a nonlinear process in which sudden transitions between various movement patterns and emergence of new coordination are typical rather than atypical in learning contexts (see Chow et al., 2011; Liu and Newell, 2015). Nonlinear pedagogy provides practitioners with key principles that can inform the design of practice in a systematic and theoretically grounded fashion (Davids et al., 2008).

Self-Test Questions

1. How do sociocultural constraints differ from organismic and task constraints?

2. Describe the key elements of the bioecological model in relation to your own development within a sport or physical activity.

3. Explain the concept of representative learning design to a practitioner.

4. How might a coach use nonlinear pedagogy principles to develop the intrinsic motivation of a learner?

CHAPTER 7

Redefining Learning: Practical Issues for Representative Learning Design

---

CHAPTER OBJECTIVES

After completing this chapter, you will be able to do the following:

- Identify the stage of motor learning of an individual according to Newell's model
- Describe the refined three-stage model offered from an ecological dynamics approach
- Understand skill transfer in terms of representative learning design
- Understand how to assess learning through retention, transfer, and technique variation

---

In chapters 1 to 4, we discussed the theoretical ideas of ecological dynamics and how practitioners can better understand key concepts like information–movement coupling and cognition. Then in chapter 5, we explained that these theories underpin the constraints-led approach to motor learning and enable us to redefine skill acquisition as skill adaptation (Araújo and Davids, 2011). These ideas lie in stark contrast to traditional approaches to motor learning. For much of the 20th century, researchers preferred to conceive of learning as a relatively permanent process in which an individual's perceptual and motoric abilities were gradually altered through neurophysiological adaptations (Davids, Button, and Bennett, 2008). The emphasis was on the creation and storage of representations of movement patterns via memory structures. Assuming an individual could construct an optimal representation of a movement and adjust it when required, learning could be considered successful (Schmidt, 1975).

While not denying the existence of neural structures that support movement (Araújo and Davids, 2011), the ecological dynamics approach places more emphasis on the process by which individuals learn to adapt to constraints. Skill adaptation that underlies the transfer of skills from one context to another is a key aspect of practice and could be achieved through the constraints-led approach, variable practice, and, more globally, nonlinear pedagogy. In this chapter, we explain how the perceptual-motor landscape evolves according to a classic model of motor learning originally proposed by Karl Newell (1985). While of considerable value and based on Bernstein's insights, Newell's model can be updated to include emerging ideas about information regulation from ecological psychology (Jacobs and Michaels, 2007). Thus, we propose a reconceptualization of the three-stage model of learning for the 21st century.

In the final section of the chapter we further illustrate the dynamics of skill acquisition by discussing retention and transfer effects. In particular, we explain various transfer dimensions (far versus near, specific versus general, lateral versus vertical) and, more important, the reason to consider the *specificity* of transfer rather than the distinction between *near* and *far* transfer tasks.

Newell's Model of Motor Learning

Let's first consider and describe the three stages that learners navigate to find adaptive behaviors. How can we characterize the differences between performers at different skill levels? Newell (1985) formulated a model based on Bernstein's (1967) insights on the mechanical degrees of freedom (dfs) of the body. This model provides a good framework for understanding the relationship between coordination and control, and it is useful for understanding how motor system dfs can reorganize over time as people adapt to changing constraints. We will use the overhand (otherwise known as the overarm or overhead) volleyball serve as a vehicle for understanding Newell's model.

Assembling a Coordination Pattern: Stage 1

The first stage of Newell's (1985) model concerns the assembly of a suitable coordination pattern from the large number of available motor system dfs. To create a **coordinative structure**, the learner assembles the appropriate relative motions among relevant body parts, such as legs, hips, trunk, and arms. For example, a novice volleyball player needs to explore the perceptual-motor landscape that is created by interactions with important objects (the volleyball held in the nonserving hand), surfaces (the court), obstacles (the net), and strategic goals (serving the ball over the net and into a specific area of the opponent's court). In the absence of intervention from a practitioner, learners may explore many different areas of the landscape as they seek a relatively stable movement pattern to achieve the task goal.

A volleyball player attempts to coordinate an action in which the ball is thrown into the air and struck with the hitting hand. Through practice, a basic coordination pattern may emerge from the available motor system components, particularly the throwing arm, the hitting arm, and the legs. Early in learning, this basic pattern may emerge and disappear quite suddenly as the learner tries to coordinate throwing, hitting, and stepping subcomponents of the movement into a successful serving action. Gradually, a reasonably successful coordination pattern begins to appear regularly during practice. Under the specific task constraints of the volleyball serve, the attractor (composed of the throwing, hitting, and stepping subcomponents) becomes more stable. As the player develops and acquires other movement patterns during practice, a range of attractors or functional coordination patterns are gradually formed into a larger landscape to serve the performance of related skills such as spikes, digs, and serves with various ball trajectory.

As mentioned in chapter 5, a **shift** between the existing pattern and the to-be-learned pattern might occur. In other words, a positive transfer occurs when a functional coordination pattern (attractor) that already exists in the landscape is functionally adapted for another task, rather like a multipurpose tool. A good example of this process occurs when a tennis player's basic overhand movement pattern (attractor) for serving a tennis ball can be refined to support the action of overhand serving in volleyball. A close match between motor system intrinsic dynamics and those of the task may exist in many vocations with similar task demands that require similar tools and equipment. Typically, a more continual adaptation occurs as an existing attractor is destabilized during a struggle with a nearby attractor in the landscape and is assembled into the new, more functional system organization.

Alternatively, very early in learning, or when more mature adults try to take up new activities, completely new attractor states may develop, thereby increasing the number of stable states and causing a sudden **bifurcation** (see chapter 5) in movement patterns (Kostrubiec, Fuchs, and Kelso, 2012; Zanone and Kelso, 1992). Thus, if a novice volleyball player is a young child who has not played tennis and has done very little overhand throwing, the child needs to construct a new attractor in the rather empty perceptual-motor landscape. However, after a short period of practice, a learner's intrinsic dynamics typically contain at least the trace of a suitable attractor that can be adapted. This is particularly true for older children and young adults. After all, most complex movement routines involve some elements of *foundational movement patterns* that are explored early in infancy, including grasping, gripping, hitting, intercepting, stepping, postural control, balance, buoyancy, and locomotion (Hulteen, Morgan, Barnett, Stodden, and Lubans, 2018).

Once a reasonably successful solution to the search problem has been discovered in the coordination stage, it is not uncommon for learners to try to couple multiple dfs in an attempt to reduce the control problem to a smaller number of larger coordinative structures (or subspaces of the total number of dfs). The learner, who might need consistency, often seizes on a basic but fixed motor pattern. This is exactly what Bernstein (1967) observed as a performer attempts to compress the abundance of motor system dfs into more manageable components. Volleyball serving can occur successfully as long as the learner is not required to move too much, little strategic variation is required, and the performance context does not change.

Liu and Newell (2015) found that learning a new pattern of movement coordination is a different process from learning to scale an already producible coordination mode to new task demands. Their detailed kinematic analyses of individual learners revealed that practice of a new pattern of movement coordination can be accompanied by higher variability during the transition between patterns. In contrast, subtle scaling of an existing pattern does not typically elicit such behavior (Liu and Newell, 2015). With regards to the volleyball serve, such variability may reveal itself in switches between a flat-footed serve and a serve with a step or a jump. These switches (or bifurcations) are the early signs of a more functional coordination pattern emerging.

Gaining Control of a Coordinative Structure: Stage 2

The second stage of Newell's (1985) model is the control stage. Once the relationships among body parts and the basic coordination of the serving action have been established, the individual is faced with the challenge of gaining a tighter fit between the assembled coordinative structure and the performance environment. Most obviously, placing the serve in a location difficult for opponents to return the ball is crucial. Less obvious factors may include specific variations of courts, such as ceiling height, floor surface (e.g., uneven sand in the case of beach volleyball), and ambient lighting. To gain control, the learner needs to explore the coordinative structure for serving in order to function adaptively in different situations. During this exploration, players probe an assembled movement pattern by varying the values for important parameters of the coordinative structure in relation to environmental demands. In chapter 2, we noted that variability in the movement system is unavoidable and omnipresent. According to Liu, Mayer-Kress, and Newell (2006), this stage of learning is typically characterized by subtle, refined variations in movement patterning as attractor stability is probed to strengthen its adaptability in different circumstances.

Exploring the perceptual-motor landscape leads to generating and acquiring perceptual feedback, a process that directly tunes a coordinative structure until the learner attains desired kinematic outcomes and satisfies the set of task constraints (Fitch, Tuller, and Turvey, 1982). In volleyball serving, players can use information, such as the mass of the ball and the position of opposing players, to tune their basic patterns of coordination. In learning to ride a bicycle, a child can pick up haptic (touch) information from the stiffness of the handlebars and the rate of change in direction of the front wheel to tune the coordinative structure for steering. Perceptual search is necessary for acquiring these information sources, and as we explained in chapter 3, Gibson (1979) argued that exploratory behavior in practice is important for revealing relevant information sources to guide actions.

During the control stage, exploration and search processes are facilitated if previously assembled coordinative structures are flexible enough to be progressively released and are allowed to re-form into slightly different configurations over practice trials. In the case of a novice volleyball player, both coordinative structures regulating the movement of the arms and legs eventually are reconstructed into one larger unit. The control stage is characterized by the reconfiguration of motor system dfs so that coordinative structures become more open to being reconstrained by an environmental information source or by the performer's intention.

The requirement for adaptive behavior in many human movement contexts is enhanced by the metastability of the movement system (Kelso and Engström, 2006). Recall from chapter 2 that *metastability* refers to a dynamic form of stability in neurobiological systems in which system parts adhere together specifically to achieve functional movement goals while maintaining their own separate identities and flexibility of operation (see Spotlight on Research in chapter 2 for an example in climbing). By exploiting metastability tendencies, the advanced learner gradually copes with subtle variations in performance conditions caused by unplanned changes such as trajectory of the ball toss, competitive stress, and fatigue. Depending on the tactical requirements of a game, an advanced learner can vary movements intentionally. For example, a short ball toss can be allied to a power strike, or a long toss can be accompanied with less forceful ball–hand contact. Perceptual information generated by environmental movement becomes critical as the player attempts to control the newly released dfs. As learners become increasingly tuned to the perceptual consequences associated with stable attractor regions, greater control over dfs is temporarily surrendered to environmental information such as optic or acoustic variables.

This process is exemplified by coordination of the ball toss by skilled volleyball players with and without a striking action. Figure 7.1 shows how the ball toss is adapted for striking. When not required to strike the ball, the toss is configured in a different way. Various information sources acting as constraints facilitate the self-organization of task-specific coordinative structures. This is what is implied by the formation of a strong information–movement coupling, which can be tuned to operate in different contexts.

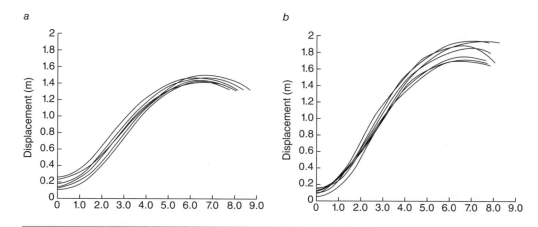

FIGURE 7.1 Time-displacement profiles for ball placement during *(a)* serving conditions (placement and hitting the ball) and *(b)* ball placement–only conditions for one representative subject. Displacement data on the y-axis are calibrated in meters.

Spotlight on Research

Free(z)ing Coordinative Structures

The classic learning study of Vereijken, van Emmerik, Whiting, and Newell (1992) provided an initial impetus to investigate motor system reorganization with practice. The research team asked five novice skiers to learn to produce slalom-like movements on a ski-simulator machine over 7 days. During this period, 140 trials lasting 60 seconds each were undertaken. The researchers gave no specific task instructions and recorded the amplitude and frequency of movements by using joint markers on the ski platform and the joints of the upper and lower body. The authors argued that if joints were not actively involved in task performance, the variability around the mean of recorded joint angles (in degrees) would be low, as would the ranges of the angular motion of the joints. Moreover, relationships between joints would be high as learners constructed strong couplings between key joints.

The data showed that, early in learning, the variability around the mean of joint angles over the period of the movement (estimated by the standard deviation, or SD) was low. The range of angular motion of the joints was also low and the values for cross-correlations between joints were high. These are exactly the type of findings that one would expect if learners were freezing dfs in order to control a multiple-dfs action. However, there was evidence that learners were attempting to unfreeze these strong couplings in order to permit joints to become more actively engaged in the movement.

With practice, the magnitude of the angles for the hip, knee, and ankle increased, and there was a decrease in the cross-correlations between the hip and knee and the hip and ankle. The rapidity of learning effects on coordination is underscored by the fact that the biggest change in the SD of mean joint angles occurred between trials 1 and 8 of the total number of trials (*n* = 140) (see figure 7.2). The SD of the

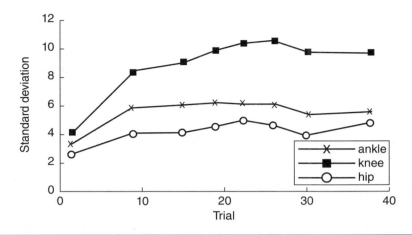

FIGURE 7.2 The biggest change in the SD of mean joint angles occurred between trials 1 and 8 of the total number of trials ($n = 140$).

Reprinted by permission from B. Vereijken et al., "Free(z)ing Degrees of Freedom in Skill Acquisition," *Journal of Motor Behavior* 24 (1992): 133-42.

knee joint demonstrated the biggest increase over trials, which suggested that the knee joint was most influential in learners gaining control of the slalom movement during practice.

Application

Think of situations in which performers free or release dfs to satisfy temporary task constraints. For example, what coordination patterns would you expect from a beginning skier who has to negotiate a steep black run? How do advanced skiers deal with the constraints of a bumpy mogul field or deep, powdery snow?

Skilled Optimization of Control: Stage 3

The final stage of Newell's (1985) model refers to the skilled optimization of a coordinative structure that the performer has gradually made more flexible and open to exploit environmental information sources, thus enhancing efficiency and control. At this performance level, players become adept at exploiting forces from the movement to ensure flexible and efficient actions. For example, experimenting with control of the volleyball serve can help to optimize performance. As players seek an optimal solution to the challenge of serving under different task constraints, they can alter the force, duration, and amplitude of the movement pattern. For instance, in a serve-reception task, Paulo, Zaal, Seifert, Fonseca, and Araújo (2018) investigated *how* and *who* received the serve in volleyball. These authors showed that initial velocity of the ball, height of the ball trajectory, and distance between the ball and receiver led to various reception patterns in expert volleyball players. In particular, higher initial velocities accompanied by higher maximum height of the serve and smaller longitudinal distances between the receiver and intended target of the server increased the chances for the use of the overhand pass. Conversely, decreasing alignment of the receiver with the ball and the target (i.e., when the receiver faces away from the net when intercepting the ball) increased the chances of using the underhand lateral pass. However, the use of the underhand lateral pass was associated with lower-quality receptions, suggesting that training various reception patterns in various conditions of serve would be beneficial (Paulo et al., 2018).

Newell's use of the term *optimal* suggests that energy efficiency is a significant factor that governs the emergence of a movement pattern during performance. According to Newell (1985), energy efficiency is "an a priori organizing principle of coordination and control" (p. 304). Skill, or optimal organization, arises when the components of a coordinative structure are quantitatively scaled so that performers are able to use the reactive forces of the limbs during movement. Passive, inertial, and mechanical properties of limb movements are fully exploited in a skilled movement, which is characterized by smoothness and fluidity. At this stage, coordinative structures become stable as additional dfs are released. This stabilization increases the number of controllable parameters open to constraint by environmental information and results in more flexible movement (Bernstein, 1967).

In the expert volleyball serve, for example, this increased fluency may allow performers to take advantage of elastic energy released by the tendons during muscle stretch-shortening cycles not previously stimulated. Hence, as a result of reflex involvement, the acceleration phase of the hitting hand and arm may be increased and may be combined with torso rotation to generate power in the serving action. With optimization, the serving movement now becomes highly energy efficient. This is why observers often describe the execution of actions by elite athletes as effortless. Similar example of higher fluency and more economic behavior could be observed in expert rock climbers (Cordier, Dietrich, and Pailhous, 1996; Seifert, Orth, Boulanger, et al., 2014) and ice climbers (Seifert, Wattebled, Herault, et al., 2014). In particular, expert climbers further exploit external forces (i.e., gravitational forces) to swing their body as a pendulum and reach and grasp high holds rather than using essentially internal forces (i.e., muscular forces).

Additional characteristics of optimal skilled performance levels include instantaneous *adaptations* to sudden and minute environmental changes (Newell, 1996). Adaptability reflects both *stability* (i.e., persistent behaviors) and *flexibility* (i.e., variable behaviors) under many different constraints. Adaptability means *adapted* and *adaptive* (or adaptable) behaviors: Adapted behavior to a set of constraints reveals stability against perturbations, while adaptive behavior reflects flexibility to guarantee functional solution to constraints that dynamically interact. For instance, if the task goal for an icefall climber is to anchor her ice axes in the ice surface, she can demonstrate functional stability such as swinging ice axes against the icefall to create specific anchorages. But if the icefall already provides support in the form of existing holes in its structure, an ice climber can also demonstrate functional flexibility by hooking the blade of the ice axes into these existing holes in the icefall, affording support on the ice surface (Seifert, Wattebled, Herault, et al., 2014).

Therefore, even at the stage of optimal skill performance, discovery learning plays an important role as people search for creative task solutions (Orth, van der Kamp, Memmert, and Savelsbergh, 2017; Withagen and van der Kamp, 2018) or patterns that are even more energy efficient. At all stages of learning, performers are searching for the most functional solutions for satisfying the constraints placed on them. Exploration and innovation still exist at the expert level, reflecting the process by which individuals increase their action system boundaries (i.e., affordances boundaries). Doing so, they might increase the range of their skills or at least their flexibility.

Is the Stage Model of Learning Universal?

In combination, Newell and Bernstein's insights on motor learning are extremely helpful in understanding how learners cope with coordinating the numerous muscles, joints, and segments of the body during practice of a multiarticular action. However, as an understanding of concepts from dynamical systems theory and ecological psychology has emerged over the years, it has become apparent that this model represents a simplification of the skill acquisition process.

In recent times, researchers have reconsidered Bernstein's (1967) original insights into changes to motor system dfs as a result of learning. Notably, Newell, Liu, and Mayer-Kress (2001) themselves acknowledge that the transition from the coordination stage to the control stage is not a linear and permanent process, as some translations of Bernstein's original writings imply. More recently, it has become clear that motor system dfs become reorganized depending on a range of constraints acting on the system at any one time as learners exploit metastability tendencies in the movement system (see Chow, Davids, Button, and Koh, 2006; Liu et al., 2006; Newell et al., 2005; Orth et al., 2017; Seifert, Boulanger, Orth, and Davids, 2015). Even highly skilled performers may switch back to the coordination stage and exhibit rigid movements (typically characteristic of novices) if this is deemed a functional pattern for satisfying the task constraints under specific performance circumstances (see data on the volleyball serve by Temprado, Della-Grasta, Farrell, and Laurent, 1997).

Newell and Vaillancourt (2001) argued that Bernstein's original conceptualization of the change process in motor systems was probably too narrow in that it failed to recognize that motor system reorganization can result in an increasing and decreasing number of mechanical dfs caused by the changing nature of the constraints that need to be satisfied. Sometimes a reduction in the motor system dfs used in coordination patterns can be functional for expert athletes performing under particular task constraints. In some situations, motor problems become more challenging because of an inordinate emphasis on precision or because unreliable environmental information is present, for example, poor lighting during a cricket or tennis match, a slippery walking or driving surface, or performing in front of a critical audience.

In these types of intense practice contexts and in competition, fluctuations in emotional states such as anxiety and arousal can lead to diminished accuracy of information detection (Bootsma, Bakker, van Snippenberg, and Tdlohreg, 1992). For example, Weinberg and Hunt (1976) reported a reduction of sequential muscle activity in favor of an energy-expensive, inhibitive cocontraction of agonist muscles and antagonist muscles in highly anxious throwers. We can interpret observed increases in muscle tension as efforts to refreeze dfs and to reorganize coordinative structures in an attempt to regain control. Further, because of natural processes such as aging, illness, and disease, changes to the organization of motor system dfs can result in an increase or a decrease in the number used in a particular coordination solution.

Research on soccer kicking has neatly illustrated how learners can adopt different approaches to using motor system dfs to satisfy the task goals of kicking a ball over a height barrier while varying the force control over different distances. Chow, Button, Davids, and Koh (2007) found that some learners increased and decreased involvement of motor system dfs over practice in a nonsequential way as they searched for a functional chipping action in soccer (see chapter 2 for more details on kicking a ball in soccer). Berthouze and Lungarella (2004) have even gone as far as suggesting that a strategy of alternately freezing and freeing motor system dfs might be the most successful way to acquire movement coordination. This idea requires evaluation in further research, but regardless, evidence suggests that increasing or decreasing motor system dfs involvement depends on the constraints of the task and the person's natural state at any one moment (Newell, Broderick, Deutsch, and Slifkin, 2003).

In summary, the three-stage model of learning is a useful guide that contains general characteristics of learners that practitioners can recognize relatively easily. In reality though, each individual learner may progress through the stages in her own unique way, and the task characteristics have a strong influence also. Furthermore, Newell and Bernstein's ideas focus more on how movements are reorganized during learning and less on how information regulates action, which is what we discuss next. Nevertheless, the three-stage model still has value in providing a general topography of the typical learning process.

Learning Redefined From an Ecological Dynamics Approach

As mentioned in chapter 3, the ecological dynamics framework goes further than dynamical system theory and integrates theoretical assumptions from ecological psychology by considering motor learning at the ecological scale (i.e., by understanding how constraints shape perception–action coupling during learning). Therefore, processes such as education to intention, education to attention (attunement), and calibration (Fajen, Riley, and Turvey, 2009; Jacobs and Michaels, 2007) lead to a functional reorganization of the dfs and can be integrated into Newell's model of motor learning (Davids, Araújo, Hristovski, Passos, and Chow, 2012; Renshaw et al., 2015). In such a way, the ecological dynamics framework supports a modified three-stages-of-learning model: search and exploration, discovery and stabilization, and exploitation (see table 7.1).

Table 7.1 A Modified Three-Stage Model of Learning From the Ecological Dynamics Framework

Stage of learning	Skill development characteristics	Perceptual learning characteristics	Behavioral characteristics
1. Search and exploration	Exploration of dfs to achieve a task goal: searches internal and external dfs to achieve a certain task goal	Education of intention: converging task goals with learner's goals	Primary goal usually satisfied, lots of errors, inefficient, not adaptable
2. Discovery and stabilization	Exploring different task solutions and stabilizing them: identifies tentative performance solutions and attempts to reproduce them	Attunement: the appropriate perception and use of sources of information	Multiple goals satisfied, variation in movements followed by increasing consistency, more adaptable to different contexts
3. Exploitation	Exploiting perceptual-motor dfs: immediate adaptation to situational demands	Calibration: scaling action to the information	Effective and efficient goal achievement, optimal performance in different contexts

Adapted from Davids et al. (2012).

Search and Exploration

This stage consists of *exploring the system dfs* (e.g., number of components and subsystems of the human body) *to achieve a task goal*. Because many perceptions and actions are possible in any situation, learners need to *edu-*

cate their intentions to specify what needs to be achieved in a performance context (Jacobs and Michaels, 2007). Much like a search engine for browsing the Internet (e.g., Google), learners need information to filter and direct their search toward fit-for-purpose solutions. Indeed, in certain situations, particular perceptions and actions are more functional than others, and with experience, learners improve at choosing perceptions and actions to achieve task goals. Thus, learners search how to organize internal and external dfs to find a way to achieve the task goal. As mentioned by Renshaw and colleagues (2015), the education of intention is not just an information-guiding process. Intention directs the attention of a learner to functionally explore (act) and perceive relevant informational variables for further action. The education of intention would result in a convergence of the learner's goals with the task goals through a continuous rearrangement of the system dfs.

Hence, the first stage of learning involves the assembly of a coordinative structure that satisfies the learner's intention to achieve a task goal (as Newell's model suggested). At this early stage of learning, neither the information used to guide movement nor the pattern itself need necessarily be the most efficient or effective way to move. Instead, through search and exploration, the learner can soft-assemble (temporarily use) a solution to get the job done!

Discovery and Stabilization

With practice, the learner discovers task solutions and stabilizes them during goal-directed behavior by reorganizing the previously exaggerated constriction of dfs (Davids et al., 2012; Renshaw et al., 2015). This process consists in *education of attention*. This means, in a sense, that without changing intention, the learner becomes *perceptually attuned* to more useful informational variables. According to Jacobs and Michaels (2007), attention is effectively educated if learners detect an informational variable that specifies the property that they intend to perceive (regardless of whether a nonspecifying variable might specify other properties). In other words, with practice, learners converge from sources of information that may be only partly useful in one situation (i.e., nonspecifying) to sources of information that are more useful (i.e., specifying) under a variety of circumstances. Therefore, this stage includes not only the stabilization of discovered performance solutions but also the exploration of the limits of these solutions and, consequently, the search for new information–movement couplings (Davids et al., 2012).

Hence, at the second stage, the learner's objective is to gain better control of a movement solution. Here, attunement to specifying variables allows learners to regulate how they move in accordance with environmental factors. With better control of movements comes temporary stabilization of preferred information–movement couplings and thus more consistency in achieving the desired task outcome. However, it is relevant to highlight that absolute stabilization is not the goal. Instead, an effective balance between stability and flexibility is desirable. With the discovery of a (stable) solution, the learner can choose between stability and flexibility when appropriate.

Exploitation

With practice, learners become attuned to a wider range of informational variables that more precisely specify how to move effectively (Jacobs and Michaels, 2007). This process is called **calibration** and can be conceived as scaling the perceptual-motor system to information. Withagen and Michaels (2002) hypothesized that calibration of behavior is functionally organized, meaning that calibration is specific not to the anatomical structures used in performing the behavior but to the function that the behavior serves. Therefore, skilled behavior corresponds to the ability to modify actions to perform the same function effectively (referring to the property of degeneracy).

At this final stage, the learner is becoming very efficient in exploiting the system degeneracy for an immediate adaptation to situational demands and effective goal achievement. As defined in chapter 5, degeneracy of the perceptual-motor systems is the ability of many structurally different body components to perform similar function or yield similar output (Edelman and Gally, 2001; Seifert, Komar, Araújo, and Davids, 2016). For instance, Seifert, Wattebled, Herault, and colleagues (2014) showed that both novice and highly experienced ice climbers can hook the blade of their ice axes in the existing holes of the icefall, but only highly experienced climbers are calibrated to useful informational variables (e.g., deep holes, holes orientated downward, holes surrounded by solid ice), and use this information to influence their actions. Therefore, when the hole is deep, climbers just hook into the hole, whereas when the hole looks small and is surrounded

Key Concept

Learning Can Be Considered *Stagelike* but Not *Staged*

Some characteristics of learning are captured well by the three-stage model, but this is not so for others. Learning is not a normative or homogeneous process, and individual differences occur (Newell et al., 2003) across the stages. Therefore, processes like education of intention, perceptual attunement, and calibration can occur and reoccur in all the three stages (Araújo, Davids, Cordovil, Ribeiro, and Fernandes, 2009). Also, exploration is not a strategy only for beginners, but also for experts. Indeed, while novices explore to learn, advanced performers learn to explore, and experts explore efficiently. Hence, an individual's progress through the stages is not predictable nor continuous. In other words, the story of learning has a beginning, a middle, and an end but how we each navigate each stage is very much our own journey.

by fragile ice, climbers swing their ice axes into the hole to establish more anchorage. In short, to achieve a similar function (e.g., anchoring the blade of the ice axe), climbers exploit perceptual-motor systems degeneracy. Experts are better able to exploit the degeneracy property because they are more flexible, attuned, and calibrated than novices to informational variables that can guide their action.

Key Features of Learning: Issues for Representative Learning Design

It is now helpful to readdress a few practical considerations that arose from the preceding discussion of the ecological dynamics framework for motor learning. In this section we examine the implications of these theoretical ideas for representative learning design that confront most practitioners concerned by skill retention and transfer.

Retention

Retention refers to the fact that given particular practice conditions, humans can usually retain some essence of a movement pattern regardless of the type of task they perform (Newell, 1996). This is because there may be a trace of an attractor well that has previously formed in the learner's intrinsic dynamics and can provide a modicum of stability for action (see chapter 2). Recall that an attractor well is a stable region of a dynamical system that is resistant to external perturbations. For example, in human movement systems, the attractor well might be the stable patterning between limbs that characterizes a swimming stroke or perhaps the coordination of the upper and lower body that allows us to ride a bike after many years without practice. This characteristic of motor learning is particularly important in rehabilitation from injury or illness.

In theories of cognitive learning, the inability to retain a skill is attributed to the poor retrieval or the degradation (forgetting) of information for the relevant motor program over time (Schmidt et al., 2018). From the ecological dynamics framework, skills are not forgotten because of a degraded representation; rather, the intrinsic dynamics become unstable because of the lack of practice and performance becomes more variable. It is also possible that the constraints that gave rise to previous motor skills may have changed significantly. For example, the learner's physical characteristics may differ as a result of aging or growth and development. Because of rapid changes in sport technology, such as material composition of equipment, the performance environment may be unfamiliar compared with the original acquisition period. Therefore, skills are more likely to be retained if they are originally acquired across a range of constraints. Of course, other factors such as a reduced practice time, the duration of the retention period, and the activities undertaken during that time will also affect the stability of the original movement pattern. Because the original attractor is further weakened by the formation of other attractors, the likelihood that the performer can reproduce this stable action in the future without extended practice decreases.

Interestingly, renewed interest in skill retention has emerged in recent years with attention directed at activities that consolidate learning (e.g., the timing and quality of postpractice sleep). **Consolidation** is the process of ensuring a skill is learned robustly, especially during postpractice periods when they are prone to disruption or to being lost. Research has begun to demonstrate that the tasks that are undertaken immediately after practice can either interfere or augment what is being learned (Walker, Brakefield, Morgan, Hobson, and Stickgold, 2002). Research on consolidation is at a relatively early phase, and many aspects of the phenomenon are yet to be uncovered. Although the concept of consolidation is somewhat challenging to explain from an ecological dynamics perspective at this time, we choose not to ignore it, but instead to call for further research to examine the mechanisms of skill consolidation.

Transfer

Transfer refers to the influence of previous practice or performance of a skill on the acquisition of a new skill (Magill, 2006). A crucial question concerns the relationships between learning and preexisting skills when to-be-learned skills are induced through exploratory activity (Nourrit, Delignières, Caillou, Deschamps, and Lauriot, 2003; Pacheco and Newell, 2015; Teulier and Delignières, 2007; Chow, Davids, Button, and Rein, 2008) and transfer processes that emerge when task and environmental constraints are manipulated (Zanone and Kelso, 1997; Kelso and Zanone, 2002). Skill transfer occurs when prior experiences under a particular set of constraints influence performance behaviors in a different set of constraints compared with those in which the skills were originally learned (Newell, 1996; Rosalie and Müller, 2012). For this reason, practice task constraints should seek to simulate aspects of the ecological constraints of performance environments. Indeed, practitioners often expect learners to transfer their practice performance into competitive situations. The essence of transfer is being able to adapt an existing movement pattern to a different set of ecological constraints (Issurin, 2013). Preexisting skills serve as a foundation that a learner can use to identify new coordination patterns and information–movement couplings (Newell, 1996; Zanone and Kelso, 1997). In particular, capacity to transfer learning to different performance conditions has been related to opportunities to explore different coordination tendencies and the information–movement couplings that regulate them (Newell, Kugler, Van Emmerik, and McDonald, 1989; Newell and McDonald, 1992).

Positive, Neutral, and Negative Transfer

Exploration during practice can lead to positive, neutral, or negative transfer effect on performance. In rock climbing, positive transfer means that climbers are able to transfer their existing skills when performing on-sight climbing (i.e., climbing a new route). Recently, Seifert and colleagues (2015) and Orth, Davids, Chow, Brymer, and Seifert (2018) examined the rate of learning and the degree of motor exploration and skills transfer (e.g., climbing a new route) when the handhold properties were manipulated. The researchers compared simple tasks over a horizontal-edged hold route with complex tasks over a double-edged hold route that allowed horizontal and vertical grasping patterns. Positive transfer on climbing fluency occurred when climbers trained on the double-edged hold route (versus the horizontal-edged hold route) because introducing choice into handhold properties affords adaptation and problem solving at the level of route finding. This positive transfer specifically occurred in more-skilled climbers who were capable of using existing experience to adapt rapidly to the multiple hold choices in the new climbing route (Orth, Davids, Chow, et al., 2018). This example supports the necessity of maintaining complexity and representativeness when designing learning situations in order to replicate the richness of climbing in outdoor environments, which develops the climber's ability to explore effectively.

Transfer Dimensions

Transfer can occur between *near* transfer tasks, when the degree of similarity to targeted task is high, and *far* transfer tasks, when the conditions and situations are different from the targeted settings (Baldwin and Ford, 1988; Barnett and Ceci, 2002; Issurin, 2013). The issue for practitioners is to determine the degree of similarity between one task and another because the definition of similarity is ambiguous. **Similarity** could relate to the degree of complexity between two tasks (i.e., *lateral* versus *vertical* transfer), but it could also relate to the proximity of a new skill to one already learned. *Horizontal* transfer (domain scaled) refers to two tasks that have the same level of complexity that challenges and involves perceptual, motor, and cognitive domains in different ways. *Vertical* transfer (parameter or constraint scaled) occurs when acquired skills and abilities are exploited for the acquisition of more-complex skills, which allows learners to achieve a higher skill level.

Traditionally, the degree of specificity or generality of the learned skill is a question of whether a *specific* procedure or a more *general* problem-solving principle is involved in achieving the new task. A specific procedure might be characterized as a set of particular steps described in terms of superficial features, whereas a general principle might be characterized as a deeper, structural, or causal understanding (Barnett and Ceci, 2002). Generalization presupposes that knowledge, skills, and abilities acquired in learning can be applied to different settings and situations. From an ecological dynamics framework, specificity or generality of transfer does not refer to information processing, but is considered in terms of how to establish an attractor for a new action in the presence of an old attractor (Seifert, Wattebled, Orth, et al., 2016). **Specific transfer** can emerge under practice task constraints in which existing intrinsic dynamics (i.e., performance disposition or tendencies) of an individual *cooperate* with the dynamics of a new task to be learned, facilitating emergence of successful performance behaviors. On the other hand, **general transfer** can occur when intrinsic and task dynamics do not cooperate closely, and the individual athlete has the potential to further develop only general capacities that exist as part of his current intrinsic dynamics, such as perceptual skills like anticipation and visual search, strength, or postural stability. Thus, general transfer occurs when processes that support performance behaviors are used under a new set of performance constraints. Put another way, general transfer is supported by processes that help learners adapt existing coordination functions to use exploratory or transitional behaviors (Newell, 1996).

In summary, specificity and generality of transfer are influenced by the particularities and commonalities of the environmental and task constraints faced in interacting with the specific intrinsic dynamics of each learner. As mentioned previously, attractors can compete and cooperate within the intrinsic dynamics, and *positive* transfer occurs when an existing attractor provides a basis for learning a new skill. If the new attractor shares elements with an old attractor, a practitioner might expect positive transfer; for example, the attractors for throwing a javelin and throwing a cricket ball are compatible. *Negative* transfer occurs when an existing attractor has too much influence in pulling the system away from the site of a new, emerging attractor in the landscape. For example, competing skills such as the alteration in weight distribution required for skiing and ice-skating could lead to performance decrements in the sport to which one is transferring an initial skill.

The process underlying skills transfer is also apparent in the calibration and recalibration processes. In a grasping task (e.g., grasping a rod in various conditions), Wagman and Van Norman (2011) hypothesized that transfer of recalibration occurred across changes in grasp position (end versus middle of rod) and object property (whole versus partial length of the rod). Instead of recalibrating to one particular property of the wielded objects, recalibration occurred to the properties of the rod set as a whole. If calibration is based on the properties of the rod set as a whole, transfer of calibration occurs across changes in grasp position (Withagen and Michaels, 2002). A similar interpretation was suggested by Seifert, Wattebled, Orth, and colleagues (2016) to explain the skill transfer between indoor wall climbing and ice climbing. The transfer of recalibration seems to have occurred functionally between indoor climbing walls (where fingers and feet are used to support the body weight) and icefall environments in which the ice axes were readily adapted to support and control the body weight and the use of extremities for ascent.

Spotlight on Research

Specificity of Transfer Between Rock and Ice Climbing

Ludovic Seifert and colleagues (Seifert, Wattebled, L'Hermette, et al., 2013; Seifert, Wattebled, Orth, et al., 2016) examined whether the intrinsic dynamics of climbers who practice regularly on an indoor climbing wall cooperate or compete with the constraints of climbing on a frozen waterfall (an icefall). On an indoor climbing wall, routes consist of holds with similar textures, which affords gripping with the fingers in a consistent internal environment (e.g., ambient temperature remains the same during ascent). In ice climbing, properties of an icefall require the use of tools on the feet (crampons) and in the hands (ice axes), and performance conditions (e.g., weather, temperature, surface) can change significantly within and between climbs. One can expect *generality* of transfer between previous experiences on an indoor climbing wall and performance on an icefall to be apparent. This would lead to elementary benefits to performance revealed by emergence of perception–action coupling, management of body weight with respect to the environmental constraint of gravity, and the discovery of surface properties through exploratory finger and feet actions. *Specific* transfer processes enhance the stability of specific perception–action couplings, which are refined through regular practice under dynamic and interacting constraints in icefall climbing by the way climbers use particular tools to ascend the surface. Specific transfer reflects the emergence of a highly coupled performer–environment system, such as the complex system made up of climber, ice tool, and icefall. In indoor climbing, these tools play no part in ascending a surface but are necessary for ice climbers to explore the physical properties specific to the icefall environment (density and thickness) in order to estimate ice fragility.

Application

The design of some practice task constraints simulates properties of a performance environment more *specifically* than others, thus facilitating rates of learning. For instance, when many performers climb an icefall, they make holes and steps that novices can detect, which facilitates the anchoring of ice tools in appropriate locations. In doing so, novice climbers become more attuned to informational variables for actions (e.g., existing holes in the ice), and they functionally exploit environmental properties as they better interact with the ice tools and the icefall (Seifert, Wattebled, Herault, et al., 2014).

Transfer and Representative Learning Design

Brunswik (1956) proposed the term *representative design* as an alternative to *systematic design* to advocate for the study of psychological processes at the level of organism–environment relations. It means that perceptual variables should be sampled from the organism's typical environment so as to be representative of the environmental stimuli from which they have been adapted and to which behavior is intended to be generalized. This definition of representative design emphasizes the need to ensure that experimental task constraints represent the task constraints of the performance or training and learning environment that forms the specific focus of study. Representative design emphasizes the specificity of the relationships between the participant and the environment, which is often neglected in traditional approaches to behavioral sciences.

The ability of performers to use information from the environment to support actions is predicated on an accurate and efficient relationship between perceptual and motor processes, referred to as *perception–action coupling* (Pinder, Davids, Renshaw, and Araújo, 2011). For example, Dicks, Button, and Davids (2010) compared movement and gaze behaviors of soccer goalkeepers in typical video simulation and in situ research designs. These authors showed significant differences between task constraints that required verbal or simulated movements compared with the in situ (representative) interceptive action condition during a penalty kick. These findings suggest that high representativeness of learning and training design would favor *perception–action coupling* and skill transfer between the learning situation and a new situation or between training settings and competition. In another example, Pinder, Renshaw, Davids, and Kerhervé (2011) suggested that the use of ball-projection machines in practice might remove key information sources from the performance environment and significantly affect the timing and control of interceptive actions in cricket batting. In particular, significant differences were observed in the practice task constraints when facing the bowler compared to the bowling machine. When facing a machine, batters exhibited earlier initiation of the backswing, front foot movement, downswing, and front foot placement. Therefore, one could expect specific skill transfer (supported by functional coupling between perception and action processes) when the bowler throws the ball, while general skill transfer would occur when a machine throws the ball.

The importance of representative learning design may have particular significance when we consider the acquisition of potentially life-saving skills. Should children learn to swim in a swimming pool or should they practice in open-water environments where the risk of drowning is greater (Button, 2016)? Guignard, Button, Davids, and Seifert (now in press) suggest lower transfer might be expected when learning in a swimming pool instead of an outdoor aquatic environment. This was partly attributed to practice in a swimming pool involving less decision making relating to risk management. In fact, general transfer of skill could be expected between swimming in a pool and in outdoor aquatic environments. In the pool, water temperature does not fluctuate and the surface remains in a somewhat steady state. In the sea, currents, rip currents, waves, and temperature could fluctuate. These variables could cause swimmers to stop swimming and dive to avoid a wave, float to benefit from the current, or tread water to estimate the time between two waves. Therefore, water safety skills should be considered as foundational movement skills, transferable to various outdoor aquatic environments such as ocean, river, and lake because those environments are dynamic and present variables (e.g., waves, currents, rip currents, obstacles, low visibility) and favor performer–environment coupling (Button, 2016). Indeed, a radical shift has been proposed in the teaching of aquatic skills toward acquiring a range of survival skills transferable between any aquatic environment (both swimming pool and natural environments) (Stallman, Junge, and Blixt, 2008). In particular, Stallman and colleagues (2008) recommend eight aquatic foundational movement skills that are closely linked to common causes of drowning (i.e., did not recognize danger, unintentional immersion, difficulty in returning to the surface, unable to orient in the water, panic, fatigue) and are more representative of swimming in outdoor aquatic environments. When these skills are complemented by an appreciation of the environment and one's action boundaries, the foundational basis for a pedagogy of aquatic skills is created (see figure 7.3).

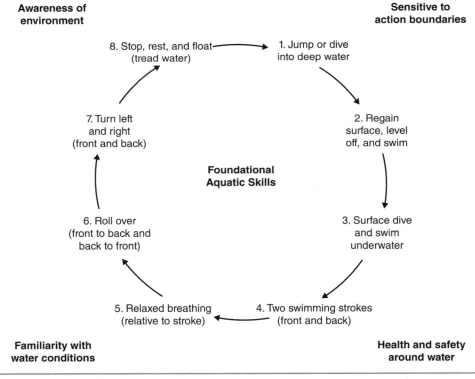

FIGURE 7.3 A model of the eight core foundational aquatic skills based on Stallman's (2008) recommendations. Four key cognitive elements have been added to the model to demonstrate awareness of the context within which aquatic skills must be acquired.

Adapted by permission from C. Button, "Aquatic Locomotion: Forgotten Fundamental Movement Skills?" *New Zealand Physical Educator* 49, No. 1 (2016): 8-10.

In summary, to design representative learning situations, practitioners should consider the following factors carefully. First, what are the interacting constraints on movement behaviors and how are they represented in practice (i.e., action fidelity and realism). Second, it is crucial to adequately sample informational variables from the specific performance environments (i.e., relevant affordances) and thereby ensure the functional coupling between perception and action processes. Finally, is progression toward task goals evident during practice (Araújo and Davids, 2015)? Practice designers should ensure that (1) the degree of success of a performer's actions are controlled for and compared between contexts (supporting skill transfer) and (2) performers are able to achieve specific goals by basing actions in learning contexts (movement responses, decision making) on information comparable to what exists in the performance environment (Pinder, Davids, Renshaw, and Araújo, 2011).

Summary

Using the ecological dynamics framework, we can redefine motor learning as an ongoing dynamic process involving a search for and stabilization of specific, functional movement patterns across the perceptual-motor landscape as each individual adapts to a variety of changing constraints. In this way, different timescales of learning should be considered with a central focus on skill adaptation or transfer (Newell, Mayer-Kress, Hong, and Liu, 2009).

As you progress through the book, it may be useful to take stock and reflect on how some of the information you've been reading relates to skill acquisition in a variety of performance contexts. Here are important pedagogical implications of the ecological dynamics framework:

• Time spent in practice does not necessarily guarantee the acquisition of expertise and skill transfer. What athletes are challenged to do during practice is a more accurate index of skill acquisition than amount of time spent on the training field (Davids, 2000). The microstructure of practice needs to be monitored so that qualitative differences between practice sessions are understood.

• Practitioners could facilitate rapid development, skill acquisition, and transfer by careful identification and manipulation of the major constraints on each learner during practice design. Planned manipulations may cause behavior jumps or sudden transitions in skill level. This is akin to infants who skip motor milestones, exemplified by research observing the appearance or disappearance of stepping in infants. In this respect, behaviors may be waiting in the wings to be brought out from each learner (Thelen and Smith, 1994).

• The smallest unit of analysis is the individual–environment coupling. Variability in movement performance needs to be carefully interpreted. Sometimes high levels of variability help in adapting to the environment, and on other occasions low levels help increase performance stability. In any case, adaptability to constraints must be questioned as well as performance outcome stability or improvement.

• To understand the complexity of sport performance and skill acquisition, practitioners and sport scientists need to recognize the limitations of monodisciplinary perspectives. Teams of scientists need to develop a multidisciplinary approach to analyzing constraints on the different functional levels of performance (e.g., cognitive, social, physiological, biomechanical).

• Nonlinear pedagogy is a practical approach that converts concepts from the ecological dynamics into design principles that inform how to facilitate learning.

Self-Test Questions

1. How does the ecological dynamics framework for skill acquisition differ from traditional approaches in its definition of learning?

2. Reflect on your own learning experiences with a movement activity you participate in and the current repertoire of skills you have available. Map out a hypothetical perceptual-motor landscape, labeling the valleys as attractors for stable actions that are well learned. Sketch the peaks and the rugged terrain to depict the less stable skills that are more open to perturbations. List some of the influential constraints that help to configure the landscape.

3. How might the coordination of young children swimming in a pool differ when practicing in a river or the sea?

4. Explain how retention, specific versus general transfer, and movement variability can be indicative of the learning process from an ecological dynamics framework.

CHAPTER 8

Designing Individualized Practice Environments

CHAPTER OBJECTIVES

After completing this chapter, you will be able to do the following:

- List some of the key sources of individual differences in learners
- Explain how the fit between intrinsic dynamics and task demands influences the rate of learning
- Associate the different factors that contribute to individual differences with the constraints model
- Discuss how influential factors such as emotional engagement and focus of attention can influence the learning process
- Suggest ways that practitioners work with individuals to design learner-centered practice environments

---

Individual differences are one of the most obvious features of the learning process, and yet they are sometimes some of the most neglected aspects of pedagogical practice. People learn at different rates and in different ways. They have different strengths and weaknesses in different dimensions such as skills and experiences and different physical, emotional, psychological, and perceptual capacities. Indeed the fact that people tend to find their own solutions to common motor problems in sport, at work, and at home should come as no surprise to those interested in nonlinear pedagogy. Individual differences are also to be expected as athletes recover from injury or as patients rehabilitate from treatment. This chapter focuses on how and why practitioners should acknowledge individual differences and the implications for designing individualized learning environments.

A range of factors contribute to individual differences in learners. One important source lies in the extent to which the learners are emotionally engaged in the skill acquisition process. In this chapter, we describe how practitioners can channel a learner's emotions productively by designing practice environments in a considered way. We discuss how using a constraints-led approach can enhance the self-regulation skills of a learner that he can harness during performance to adapt to the dynamic variations of competitive performance contexts, or in subelite sport and physical activity to be able to maintain an active lifestyle. We also highlight several practical strategies to direct the learners' attention appropriately while they practice. Finally, we provide suggestions about how practitioners can work *with* individual differences rather than *against* them. The key message from this chapter is to acknowledge that there are inherent differences between learners, and practitioners need to engage learners at an appropriate level to meet individual needs. By closely monitoring and manipulating key constraints, practitioners can encourage learners to search for and exploit individualized adaptive movement solutions within acceptable safety boundaries.

Individual Differences in Skill Acquisition

One of the greatest challenges for many movement practitioners is designing practice activities for groups of learners that accommodate individual differences: in other words, individualizing the learning process. Individualizing the learning process for the learner forms the central aspect of the nonlinear pedagogy in which individuals are sensitive to the continuous, dynamical interactions among constraints. As was discussed in chapters 5 and 7, the task requirements of a new motor skill sometimes provide a close match with preexisting intrinsic dynamics (i.e., when learners have practiced an action that has movement patterns similar to a new action) that lead to immediate and relatively successful performance. Indeed, the close fit between task and intrinsic dynamics may also explain precocious behavior in sport when some athletes perform incredibly well from an early age. In those cases, the genetic constraints (e.g., a propensity for speed endurance) are harmoniously aligned with the task (e.g., capacity to swim long distances without fatiguing) and the other personal constraints (e.g., individual differences in buoyancy) needed to succeed in a specific sport like open-water swimming (Davids and Baker, 2007). Conversely, problems may arise for some learners when there is a conflict between the intrinsic dynamics they bring to a learning situation and the specific task requirements (e.g., driving a ball in squash and tennis). In the case of skill performance, more-stable movement patterns from the past have to be destabilized before a new pattern is acquired. Within the same

A Good Fit for Learning

The reason some learners produce successful movement patterns early in learning and others take a considerably longer time is linked to the fit between the intrinsic dynamics of the movement system and the task demands. Where there is a good fit between the two, positive transfer is more likely to occur. Where the task dynamics and a learner's intrinsic dynamics clash, negative transfer will result. By way of a practical implication, provision of appropriately scaled equipment for practice might enhance the fit between intrinsic and task dynamics and reduce competitive tendencies of other nearby attractors. Additionally, providing demonstrations with similar body scaling of limb segments might convey more accurate relative motion information to learners attempting to reorganize motor system degrees of freedom (dfs) during practice. For example, the gender and expertise level of a model may need to be carefully considered when designing a learning environment in gymnastics or figure skating and indeed in most sports.

sports, consider also how lateral dominance can interfere with a learner's attempts to perform a skill with their nonpreferred hand. As Swinnen (2002) puts it, "the acquisition of new skills is often hampered by the emergence of preferred coupling modes that need to be suppressed to develop differentiated patterns of activity between the limbs" (p. 359).

As we have described in this book, goal-directed movements of a performer emerge as a consequence of the interaction among key constraints in the learning context. That is why it is important that coaches and teachers refrain from having an optimal movement template in mind (e.g., a classic technique for a forehand drive in tennis or an ideal golf swing) to which all learners should aspire. All learners bring different capacities to the learning context and could solve performance problems in different, sometimes unique, ways. In many situations, the emergence of movement behaviors tends to be specific to an individual because the various constraints interact in different ways for different individuals. Differences in the ways we move and learn are perhaps most obvious among children, but they persist into adulthood and throughout the life span. Clearly, a range of factors contribute to individual differences. The following are some of the more obvious.

Contributing Factors to Individual Differences

Numerous sources contribute to individual differences in learning capacity and rate (see table 8.1). Ackerman (2014) suggests that these sources belong to six major categories: (1) physiology, (2) morphology, (3) aptitudes, (4) needs, (5) temperament (personality), and (6) attitudes. Within the confines of this chapter, we cannot detail the broad range of dimensions that contribute to

Table 8.1 Sources of Individual Differences in Learning

Performer	Task	Environmental
Prior experience	Goal	Culture
Genetic attributes	Information	Rituals
Anthropometry	Equipment	Social support
Focus of attention	Feedback	Climate
Motivation	Clothing	Economy

the individualization of learning. Instead, we will discuss examples from these categories that are particularly pertinent to motor skill acquisition: performer, task, and environmental constraints. Then we will discuss the key issue of how practitioners can deal with individual differences.

Performer Constraints: Prior Experience Perhaps the strongest influence on individual differences is prior experience of the movement or of the environment in which the movement is to be performed. Prior experience may provide learners with knowledge of the task goals and also of the task-relevant information on which their movement patterns should be adapted. For example, because of previous experience of a route, a mountain biker can ride assertively, whereas a biker with no experience of the route typically needs to ride a little more cautiously. It is for a similar reason that experienced climbers seek to preview a route to ascend a rock surface from a starting position on the ground. Gaining perceptual information from the preview could help them ascend in an assertive manner by adapting to surface features that have been identified from the perspective of the ground (Button, Orth, Davids, and Seifert, 2018). Indeed, it is known that prior experience of a sensory environment enhances plasticity in the visual cortex of the brain, thereby improving the brain's ability to adapt to that environment on subsequent occasions (Hofer, Mrsic-Flogel, Bonhoeffer, and Hübener, 2006).

Clearly, previous history can result in the generation of memorized information about the task. In ecological dynamics terms, the influence of memorized information can force the phasing of movement patterns toward a required relation and alter the intrinsic dynamics in a relatively robust fashion (Tallet, Kostrubiec, and Zanone, 2008). Memorized information that is strongly patterned in the neural architecture can constrain an individual's capacity to perceive and act in a certain way for many years. Hence, skills that are well learned and easier to perform after significant periods without practice retain strong interconnections between different parts of the brain. This well-known phenomenon is summarized in the common phrase "just like riding a bicycle," which pertains to picking up a skill quickly after a long period without practicing it.

Performer Constraints: Genetic Attributes How can we understand the influence of genetic constraints on individual differences? Humans are born with a relatively small set of inherited and simple action patterns (i.e., reflexes) and a large set of movement capacities that are yet to be developed. Unless you have an identical twin, the genetic information transcribed into your DNA is unique and it contributes to your capacity to learn and perform motor skills. The common description of gifted athletes as naturals implies that their genetic profile appears highly suited to their chosen sport. The increasingly popular field of epigenetics describes how genetic attributes can be either suppressed or unlocked by environmental conditions. For example, some people appear to respond or benefit more when exposed to the same training and practice stimulus than others do (Epstein, 2013). Indeed, how genetic constraints shape variations in human performance is a question of increasing interest in movement science and sports medicine (e.g., Johnston, Wattie, Schorer, and Baker, 2018).

Twin studies have often been used to demonstrate that the rate of learning a skill is largely determined by heritable (i.e., genetic) factors. For example, Fox, Hershberger, and Bouchard (1996) showed that practice reduces twin differences more for monozygotic (genetically identical) twins than it does for dizygotic twins (both groups of twins were brought up apart). Such findings do not diminish the importance of practice but can be used to infer how genotypic factors might contribute to individual differences. More recent work has shown that decreased skill-learning capacity could be related to neurotrophic factors such as dopaminergic transmission, which are heavily influenced by certain gene expressions. For example, genetic polymorphisms of the catechol-O-methyltransferase (COMT) enzyme and dopamine receptor (DRD2) genes have been linked to individual differences in motor learning, although they were task dependent (Reis et al., 2009; Roohi, Sarihi, Shahidi, Zarei, and Haghparast, 2014).

Collectively, the emerging evidence suggests that if your parents and ancestors were proficient learners, then you are more likely to have inherited this positive attribute. However, this field of study is still very much in its infancy and controversy exists over the relative influence of environment versus genetics (Yarrow, Brown, and Krakauer, 2009). This problem is a manifestation of the longstanding nature–nurture debate over the precise proportion of performance variation accounted for by genetic characteristics or environmental influences (e.g., Davids and Baker, 2007). Much has been written about this particular dualism in science, and resolution has proved remarkably difficult over the years because it is clear that both nature and nurture act as constraints on behavior (for excellent analyses, see Ackerman, 2014; Johnston and Edwards, 2002; Ridley, 2004). It is generally accepted that successful performance can be enhanced by both interacting genetic and sociocultural constraints (from a specific environment). Athletes who have a stronger genetic propensity for capacities favored by specific sports and that experience environmental constraints that promote excellent conditions for learning and practice are more likely to succeed (but are not guaranteed) at the highest levels of performance. Overemphasizing each category in isolation from the others is treated with caution by academic researchers (e.g., Davids and Baker, 2007; Moreau, Macnamara, and Hambrick, 2019).

Performer Constraints: Anthropometry An individual's intrinsic dynamics are also partly determined by the structural configuration of his body. Each person must learn to harness his own system architecture effectively in order to produce coordinated movement. Factors such as the length, inertia, and stiffness of limb segments present physical properties that form the foundations of preferred movement patterns. For biomechanical modeling purposes, system architecture has typically been considered as a complex configuration of mechanical springs, struts, and levers. For example, a human leg is subject to the same universal laws of motion that determine the behavior of other physical systems such as a linked pendulum. For an inanimate object, knowing its initial state, physical properties, and external forces acting on it is sufficient to predict its behavior. However, this is not true for biological objects that have onboard sources of energy (i.e., within muscles) that can generate forces to satisfy their needs. The human musculoskeletal system differs in important ways to such mechanical models. For example, the internal energy sources that drive muscle contraction provide both inhibitory and excitatory characteristics that are not easily accounted for by simple models (Waldvogel et al., 2000). Overcoming the internal resistance of joints to produce and maintain movement is largely governed by individualistic factors such as the relative location of tendon attachments to bones. Also, the viscoelasticity of muscle and connective tissue means that the force produced from each contraction depends on its initial state (codetermined by numerous factors such as position, prior stretch, temperature, and metabolite availability for example) (Zajac, 1989). Indeed, the biological complexity of the human movement system recognized by Bernstein (1967) prompted him to argue that a simple one-to-one relationship between neural signaling and motor output could not, and does not, exist (see also Berkinblit, Feldman, and Fukson, 1986).

The various characteristics of system architecture also change on different timescales. After many consecutive contractions, a muscle unit begins to fatigue and its response to stimulation becomes less efficient (Gandevia, Allen, Butler, and Taylor, 1996). Over a considerably longer timeframe, an individual's flexibility and suppleness gradually deteriorate as old age is approached and the resting tone of muscle and connective tissue increases (Berkinblit et al., 1986).

The rapidly evolving science of anthropometry involves the measurement of the human individual and it enables us to determine a person's size, form, and functional capacity. Advances in measuring and tracking technologies such as wearable sensors, 3-D body scanning, and functional MRI (fMRI) are providing increasingly sophisticated insights into the structural differences between individuals. The challenge for scientists is to link anthropometric data to a more comprehensive theory of intrinsic dynamics.

Performer Constraints: Psychological Characteristics   The brain is the most complex and sophisticated biological organ known to humans. Indeed, there is still much to be learned about how the brain operates to regulate our perceptions of the world, our desires and emotions that drive our behaviors, and not least, our personalities that define us as individuals. However, despite the huge amount that we do not know about brain function (Bizzi and Ajemian, 2015), it is still of value to reflect on our current understanding of how perception and emotions impinge on intrinsic dynamics.

Ecological psychology reminds us that perception can involve minimal indirect cognition because information to support action is typically abundant in the properties of our environment (e.g., texture, flow, slant, reflections) (Gibson, 1979). The important consideration for intrinsic dynamics lies in each person's capabilities to detect and recognize these properties. Our perceptual organs are continually developing and maturing throughout our life spans and, therefore, their functionality and integration may differ considerably from one individual to the next. Indeed, delays in the development of visual and vestibular system function have been offered as potential explanatory factors for conditions such as developmental coordination disorder (Wilson, Ruddock, Smits-Engelsman, Polatajko, and Blank, 2013). Furthermore, the richness of the perceptual information that we can use to regulate our actions will help us to become less dependent on individual sources of information (e.g., visual information only) that may be unavailable under certain performance conditions. Effective opponents or adverse environmental conditions can prevent access to the information that athletes have learned to depend on and need in order to regulate actions in functional ways. Adapting actions to different sources of regulatory information will help athletes maintain their flexibility in dynamic performance environments. For example, becoming better attuned to somatosensory information from lower limbs (e.g., haptic and proprioceptive system feedback) can help soccer players become attuned to where they are in space, freeing up their visual system from tracking the approach toward intercepting an object like a ball (Hasan, Davids, Chow, and Kerr, 2016).

It is now well established that our perceptions of the world are shaped by our action capabilities (Gibson, 1979; Proffitt, Stefanucci, Banton, and Epstein, 2003). Physical properties of the world, like the width of a road and the sound of an approaching car, help to shape our experiences, affordances, and decisions that are continually presented to us while navigating the physical environment. A road may be deemed crossable if we have the action capabilities of traversing the required distance before traffic gets close enough to endanger us. Therefore, an older or injured person is more likely to perceive the distance to cross as longer than a fit and healthy individual does (Cordovil, Araújo, Pepping, and Barreiros, 2015). **Embodied cognitions** such as distance estimations are receiving increased attention in recent years and they are helping us to understand why differences in decision making and behavior exist (Withagen and van Mermeskerken, 2009).

Emotions influence perceptions, actions, and intentions during decision making, and the intensity of emotion generated reflects the significance of stimuli to an individual (i.e., shaping the strength of the response on the visual cortex) (Pessoa and Adolphs, 2011). Emotion also strengthens memories (positive or negative) and produces greater engagement in ambiguous, unpredictable, or threatening situations when individual and group goals are influenced (e.g., performing when failure might have significant consequences such as nonselection for a team or losing an important match) (LaBar and Cabeza, 2006). It is worth considering data on how skill-based differences interact with emotions to constrain the cognitions, perceptions, and actions of different individuals. A comparison of the performance of novice ice climbers revealed that the intraindividual movement choices (e.g., kicking, hooking into the ice) and interlimb coordination modes of novices displayed less variability than those of experts (Seifert, Wattebled, Herault, et al., 2014). The novice climbers tended to intentionally adopt an X position with their arms and legs that provided highly stable interactions with the surface of the ice. These coordination patterns were functional for novices because they provided a sense of safety. However, adoption of these highly secure patterns was not functional for the goal of climbing the icefall quickly, as demonstrated by the levels of variability in positioning of the experts. The implication is that energy efficiency and competitive performance were not prioritized in the goals of novice performers, whose specific coordination tendencies emerged as a function of their fear in interacting with the ice surface. This emotion was, understandably, a major constraint on their specific cognitions, perceptions, and actions. We shall return to the important topic of emotional engagement during practice in the next section on affective learning design.

Task Constraints   Task constraints can be considered a form of **behavioral information** onto which an individual's intrinsic dynamics are mapped. Whenever we set out to complete a task, we have already set ourselves a significant task-related goal. For early learners, the task goal may be as simple as achieving a desired outcome safely (e.g., skiing to the bottom of a groomed run without falling over). For advanced learners, task goals are likely to be more sophisticated, numerous, and challenging (e.g., skiing to the bottom efficiently while exploring unfamiliar areas of a route). Primary task goals can be directed toward accomplishment or outcomes, in which case they may be relatively stable (e.g., to win a race), but also secondary task goals may emerge and change throughout an activity (e.g., to help pace another runner through a difficult stage in the race). As we become more skilled, the goals we set ourselves generally alter over time and, of course, may differ considerably from individual to individual.

In setting a task goal, performers typically consider the difficulty of the task demands and the availability of assistance to them. Guadagnoli and Lee (2004) pointed out that there is a curvilinear relationship between these dimensions of the required task. Depending on the learner's skill level, a zone seems to exist in which the challenge of the task is ideal for promoting learning and performance development. If too much or too little augmented information is provided by the practitioner, or if the task is too easy or too hard, the challenge point is not set appropriately for the learner, which may delay her overall progression (Pinder and Renshaw, 2019).

When people make an error, they typically alter the next movement attempt to reflect changes in how their bodies and environment are perceived. Diedrichsen, White, Newman, and Lally (2010) refer to this process as *error-based learning*. However, this approach invites the question of whether learning can occur when no errors are made. In fact *errorless learning* can be beneficial in promoting implicit learning whereby the learner is not required to generate and test hypotheses as they would when employing trial-and-error strategies (e.g., Poolton, Masters, and Maxwell, 2005). Indeed, implicit learning can result in movement patterns that are more robust than those produced under stressful or fatigued situations (Button, MacMahon, and Masters, 2011).

Another significant source of individual differences is embedded within the equipment and clothing that people use while performing movement skills. Subtle differences in the size, weight, and responsiveness of a tennis racket between players, for example, can lead to different outcomes in learning

Spotlight on Research

Changing Task Goals and Individual Differences

The fact that many task goals are transient explains why they may be a significant source of individual differences. Lee, Chow, Komar, Tan, and Button (2014) demonstrated this feature nicely in a school-based experiment in which participants were required to learn a tennis forehand stroke under different instructional constraints. One group of children (linear pedagogy group) learned the skill under a prescriptive regimen in which the task goal was primarily to reproduce a model movement pattern. Another group of children (nonlinear pedagogy group) learned the stroke in minigames in which adaptability and attunement to modified task constraints were emphasized in the lessons. While both groups acquired the same skill level after 120 minutes of practice, the nonlinear pedagogy group showed a greater number of movement patterns and individual differences during the posttest (figure 8.1).

(continued)

Changing Task Goals and Individual Differences *(continued)*

Children taught with a nonlinear pedagogy strategy were encouraged to change their task goals though the manipulation of constraints, which developed more innovation and creativity without a decrement in their overall performance levels. Interindividual differences as a function of task goal variation has been identified in a range of other sport skills such as soccer chipping (Chow, Button, Davids, and Koh, 2007), basketball shooting (Rein, Davids, and Button, 2010), and swimming (Seifert et al., 2011).

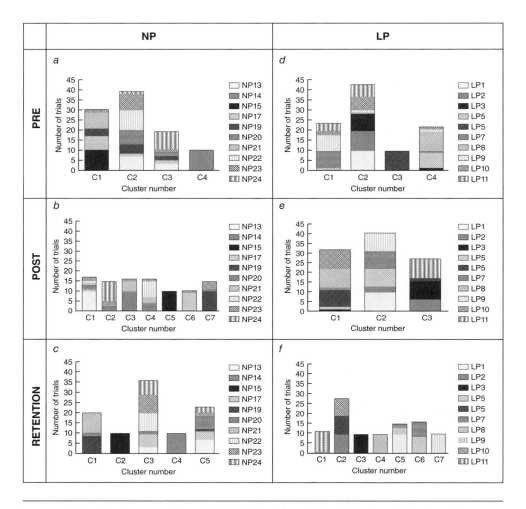

FIGURE 8.1 Number of trials and distribution of participants (LP and NP) in each cluster. Each bar represents the number of trials and distribution of participants found in each movement cluster for specific target trials in the six data sets—NP: pre (*a*), post (*b*), retention (*c*); LP: pre (*d*), post (*e*), retention (*f*). C1 through C7 represent movement clusters.

rates. In particular, equipment that is scaled relative to an individual's physical capacities seems to result in better learning outcomes (Buszard, Farrow, Reid, and Masters, 2014). It is also likely that the relative fit and properties (e.g., thermal protection, cushioning, contrast) of clothing and safety wear can also impinge on movement in different ways. A body of research has recently shown that retroreflective strips strategically attached to the clothing of road workers and cyclists on moving joints significantly improves the conspicuousness of individuals to passing vehicle drivers (Wood, Lacherez, and Tyrrell, 2014) in comparison to other types of clothing.

Environmental Factors

Why is it that certain regions of the planet or countries are synonymous, in some people's eyes, with the highest skill levels in specific sports? For example, Brazil and soccer playing; New Zealand and rugby union; Jamaica and sprinting; Scandinavia and snow sports; United States and basketball, and, within cricket, spin bowling in South Asia. Sometimes sports organizations refer to their DNA, signifying that they like to identify themselves with a specific style of performance (e.g., the soccer club FC Barcelona and a certain style of dominating possession of the ball in play). The environment can interact with task constraints and intrinsic dynamics in subtle but important ways to nurture individuality (see chapter 6). Recall that the environment can be broadly conceived of as the physical conditions for practice and performance (e.g., climatic variations, grounds) as well as sociocultural influences (e.g., family, coach, peer group influences, rituals). The physical environments in which we work and play provide universal factors that impinge on us similarly. For example, physical energy flows such as gravity, ambient temperature, and light are similar across a group of individuals within a geographical locality. However, it is our sensitivity and responsiveness to some of these energy flows that drives differences in how we move. A well-studied example of environmental constraints on variation concerns individual responsiveness to altitude in terms of acclimation and performance (Mazzeo, 2008). For reasons still not entirely clear, some individuals acclimate much more effectively to training at altitude (termed *responders*) than others (*nonresponders*) do, leading to considerable variations in the physiological benefit to be gained by athletes preparing for competition. It is likely that genetic factors, yet to be fully determined, are heavily responsible for differences in the ways individuals respond to environmental features such as temperature and altitude (Jedlickova et al., 2003).

Climatic variations across the world also give rise to different practice environments. For example, Araújo and colleagues (2010) suggested that dry, bumpy, and irregular surfaces typical of Brazil's shantytowns (favelas) may at least partly contribute to the flamboyant and innovative style of playing that is often associated with famous Brazilian soccer players. On the same topic, Uehara, Button, Falcous, and Davids (2014) have recently considered the influence of numerous sociocultural constraints (e.g., samba music and dance; capoiera, a type of martial arts; pelada, a type of informal soccer game; and poverty) on Brazilian soccer player development. When one begins to consider the important social influences of friends, family, and coaches, it becomes clear that each of us has our own unique set of environmental constraints that interactively influence how and why we move the way we do. In summary, the environment can contribute to individual differences in terms of how each person responds to the specific physical and sociocultural mix of variables that form the context within which she performs and practices.

Affective Learning Design

In the previous section, numerous factors were discussed that contribute to individual differences. Perhaps one of the most influential of these factors is the extent to which a performer is emotionally engaged (or not) in a task. This is known as **affective learning**. Ecological dynamics clearly puts the learner at the center of learning. Recent work by Moy, Renshaw, and Davids (2015) has provided a viable starting point for understanding the theoretical and empirical approaches that support meaningful affective learning design. Similar to Deci and Ryan's self-determination theory (SDT) (2000), the concepts and ideas in relation to this theory focus on understanding human basic psychological needs. Later, we share empirical work that attempts to examine the impact of an ecological dynamics approach on addressing the three psychological needs of competence, autonomy, and relatedness as espoused by SDT.

In a study on hurdling, Moy, Renshaw, and Davids (2016) were particularly interested in examining how a nonlinear pedagogy approach could potentially lead to higher self-reported levels of intrinsic motivation. Novice participants (with no hurdling background), intermediate participants (with some hurdling experience), and skilled participants (representation at school level) were taught hurdling lessons either from a nonlinear pedagogy approach or a more traditional style of teaching. The nonlinear pedagogy approach emphasized effective constraints manipulation and provision of instructions that focus on movement preferences (e.g., the only task instruction to the students was to run fast over the hurdles and to try to take three steps between each hurdle). In addition, learners were presented with obvious scaling of constraints: The task constraints of hurdle height or interval distance increased progressively through the lanes (e.g., lane 4: 6-meter intervals and 68-centimeter height, lane 5: 6.5-meter intervals and 68 centimeter height, lane 6: 6.5-meter intervals and 76-centimeter height, and so on), and students were allowed to choose which lane to start practice (high probability for autonomy). Participants reported substantially higher levels of self-determination and intrinsic motivation during the nonlinear pedagogy hurdles lesson in contrast to the traditional teaching approach. This is a significant finding because it is a clear indication that the students presented with the nonlinear pedagogy sessions experienced greater enjoyment and interest in the lessons because the three key psychological needs were met: autonomy, competency, and relatedness.

Headrick, Renshaw, Davids, Pinder, and Araújo (2015) highlighted that it is also critical to consider affective constraints in the representative design of learning experiences. Two key principles stand out: (1) the need to design emotion-laden learning experiences that simulate actual constraints of performance environments, and (2) taking into account how different learning phases or periods can be associated with individualized emotional and coordination tendencies. In practical terms, these principles indicate that the design of practice must be representative of the possible emotions that could be elicited from the athletes. For example, creating real game scenarios in practices, such as chasing an equalizer or a winning goal in soccer, will generate emotions that will likely raise anxiety or even adrenalin levels. In addition, practitioners must be cognizant of the changes to individual athletes (in terms of affective status) as they progress through different learning stages (and even daily or weekly fluctuations in affective constraints). Clearly, novices have different emotional responses to success or failure than skilled athletes do.

Focus of Attention: Remaining in the Moment

Practitioners can use instructions as a task constraint to promote exploration and encourage learners to find individualized solutions. Indeed, Newell and Ranganathan (2010) describe the practice of a movement skill as an exploration process by the learner to search for a functional movement solution. Instead of imposing a movement solution on the learner, instructions act as an informational constraint to direct the search. Recent research in motor learning has investigated the effectiveness of instructions based on their focus of attention (Wulf, 2007, 2013), namely internal focus of attention and external focus of attention. Wulf, Lauterbach, and Toole (1999, p.120) defined an external focus of attention as "directing the performer's attention to the movement effect of the action" performed during learning, as compared with "directing attention to the movement action itself" in an internal focus. Simply put, instructions can be modified to focus the learner's attention on a movement's effects on the environment (the outcomes of an action) or on the body movement (body segments) involved while producing an action.

Wulf, Hoess, and Prinz (1998) examined the effects of providing different types of instructions on complex motor skills. Specifically, the adult participants in the study had to perform slalom-type movements on a ski simulator, and the goal of the task was to make oscillatory movements with the largest amplitude possible. Participants were provided with instructions on how the force should be exerted on the platform they were standing on. The external focus group was asked to exert a force on the outer wheels (right side) of the platform, and the internal focus group was asked to exert a force on their outer foot (right side) as long as the platform moved in the respective direction (right side). In addition, the control group received no instructions other than to try to produce large-amplitude movements. All participants practiced the task for 2 days under their respective informational constraints and they were assessed a day later without instructions. The external group produced the largest amplitudes, while the internal group produced the smallest. The control group performed better than the internal group. The results of the retention test showed that the external group displayed significantly greater amplitude, and there were minimal differences between the internal and control group. Many related studies examining the impact of different attentional focus of instructions followed and found similar results: Instructions with an external focus of attention produced better learning effects. These studies included Wulf and colleagues (1999) for golf; Wulf, Chiviacowsky, Schiller, and Avila (2010) for a throwing task; Schücker, Anheier, Hagemann, Strauss, and Völker (2013) for a running task; and Polskaia, Richer, Dionne, and Lajoie (2015) for a cognitive task on postural control. Andy, Wong, and Masters (2017) found that both young and older adults that were provided with analogies outperformed participants that received explicit instruction.

So, why would instructions with an external focus of attention be advantageous? According to Bernstein's (1967) description of the four levels of control (level 1: tone, level 2: synergies, level 3: space, and level 4: action), responsibility for coordination and control is delegated to the lower levels of the central nervous system when there is an increased sophistication of performance (i.e., levels of tone and synergies). This allows the learners to harness the self-organizing movement–system dynamics that are most functional for the necessary task (see also Profeta and Turvey, 2018). When learners receive instructions with external attentional focus and direct their attention to the effect of the movement, little disruption to the lower levels of control occurs. Whereas focus on the movement form can lead to a more conscious control of the movement, which can result in less functional movement outcomes (Peh, Chow, and Davids, 2011).

Focus of attention instructions can influence the extent to which an individual's intrinsic dynamics can be expressed. For example, badminton learners who were provided instructions with an external focus of attention exhibited more evidence of using their own individualized serving actions than participants who were provided instructions with an internal focus of attention (Peh, 2018). Specifically, many participants using an internal focus of attention produced movement patterns that were similar to a prescribed, effective serving action typically expected in good serves (e.g., an emphasis on the elbow joint as a key cue in the serving action). Notably, the learners using an external attentional focus were still as successful in performance outcome for the serving task. These observations showed that degeneracy exists in learners, and the inherent coordinative behaviors of the participants self-organized into functional movement solutions as they met the demands of the task even though instructions using different attentional focus were provided to them. Perhaps the intrinsic characteristics of complex dynamical systems afforded flexibility and adaptability to the learner in the exploration of a functional movement solution within the learning environment shaped by ongoing interacting constraints from the task, environment, and the learners themselves (Chow, Davids, Button, and Renshaw, 2016).

The collective findings from this body of work relating to focus of attention instructions suggests that practitioners should be sensitive and aware of the impact that different informational constraints can have on skill acquisition. The critical factor in enhancing learning is to understand how affordances can be acquired by learners when different informational constraints are provided. In our view, strengthening information–movement coupling is imperative, and a focus on perceptual information from the environment is crucial to enabling a performer to build affordances that are representative and functional. Thus, the emphasis is on being present and remaining in the moment in order to understand that a performer is not an independent entity but a part of the puzzle in the environment–task–performer system.

How Practitioners Work With Individual Differences

Many counselors, psychotherapists, physiotherapists, life coaches, personal trainers, and sport psychologists have been quick to realize that an individual approach is the only effective way to understand the complex problems that learners present them with, and consequently they spend very little time working with large groups. Despite the arguments for a focus on the individual learner in a nonlinear pedagogy, many practitioners have little choice but to work daily with large groups of learners. For example, it is not uncommon for teachers and coaches to assume sole responsibility for groups of 30 students during a practice session. Given the multiple demands these practitioners must manage, it is not surprising that many question the feasibility of the hands-off approach that this book advocates. However, practitioners can use several simple strategies to shift the focus back to the individual without demotivating other learners in the group.

Abandon a One-Size-Fits-All Philosophy and Move to a Learner-Centered Approach

It's not surprising, we argue, that practitioners must first appreciate that there is no single optimal way for everyone to move nor indeed a "textbook technique." This one-size-fits-all philosophy has dominated traditional pedagogical strategies in the past. Instead, each individual brings unique constraints that will shape the optimal solutions he should adopt. The term *optimal* here refers to the most functional movement solution available to a performer at a particular stage of development and experience based on the intrinsic dynamics of the current system. This conceptualization of the term optimal is referenced to the individual, and by no means implies that a specific mode of coordination exists to which all learners should aspire. A learner-centered approach requires the practitioner to consider how to place each learner at the center of the practice environment. Of course, this might be extremely challenging when working with large groups (for example, 40 children in a school physical education setting or 30 players on a team), but the following suggestions will show that it is not impossible!

CASE STUDY: TENNIS SERVE

Instead of demonstrating the standard serving technique to a group of early learners, present them with a performance problem (e.g., to hit the ball over the net into a target zone) and set activities that help them develop solutions. It is quite likely that many early learners will initially approach this solution with an underhand technique (rather than the traditional overhand action), but is this necessarily the wrong way to begin learning how to serve effectively at this stage? One way to discourage them from stabilizing or relying on an ineffective solution is to require learners to devise three ways to hit the ball to the target area. Another is to modify the size and position of the target area and the height of the net. One could also vary the equipment (e.g., racket length and mass) available to learners, depending on their developmental status.

Provide Opportunities for Exploration and Creativity

The traditional emphasis in many practice activities is on reproduction of a specific movement pattern and a requirement that everyone progress toward the same goal. However, if the emphasis were shifted toward the process of exploration and adaptation to constraints, then individual differences would be naturally observed and could flourish. This does not imply that individuals should be prevented from stabilizing a preferred pattern, but instead that they should be allowed to search for and find it (as well as other possible solutions) before exploiting a functional solution and repeating it.

CASE STUDY: SWIMMING

Historically, swimming has been taught with a strong focus on reproduction of classic strokes: freestyle, backstroke, breaststroke, butterfly. As such, swimming lessons tend to be dominated by direct teaching strategies such as instruction, feedback, demonstrations, and plenty of repetition. Alternatively, playing aquatic games such as water polo, underwater hockey, and even tag provide more opportunities for the learner to create different ways of moving through the water. During these activities and games, other important aquatic skills (such as treading water, diving, and changing direction) are interspersed with requirements to swim, while also adding fun and potentially competitive elements to the practice. Button (2016) reminds us that an important, potentially lifesaving benefit of practicing transferable swimming skills is that individuals will be better equipped to adapt to changing conditions and to other aquatic environments (see chapter 7).

Manipulate Relevant Constraints to Suit Specific Individuals

One obvious strategy that may help individuality to emerge during learning is the manipulation of task constraints. As discussed earlier, task constraints are possibly one of the strongest contributors to individual differences and, therefore, can provide a powerful means through which learners can search for and find their preferred styles. Influential constraints such as task goals, rules, equipment, and the creation of subgroups can each be modified by the practitioner to help learners in a manner appropriate to their skill level.

CASE STUDY: LEARNING A DANCE ROUTINE

While certain types of dance (e.g., contemporary, hip-hop, and improv) encourage individuality, other group dance styles (e.g., Bollywood, line dancing) require performers to synchronize elements of their movements. What are influential task constraints for dancers? In learning a new routine, dancers have to sequence different movements, often in time to music. Modifying the tempo of music offers instructors a way to potentially simplify the task demands (by slowing the music) and make them more challenging (by speeding up the music). Furthermore, silencing parts of the music sequence and requiring dancers to keep going until the music returns is a useful strategy for testing how well participants have learned their roles. As discussed previously, instructors might also modify task goals (e.g., express yourself more, take the lead) to help individuals find preferred styles of movement.

Safety, Space, and Time Considerations

Movement practitioners often excuse a lack of focus on individuals by citing concerns about safety if others are left unsupervised or about restrictions in space or time, so one should be mindful of these important logistical factors.

Therefore, it becomes critical that practitioners develop skill in planning and delegation to ensure that they allocate appropriate attention to these factors. Planning may involve ensuring sufficient spaces for subgroups of learners to practice activities together. Furthermore, putting measures in place (e.g., delegating to group mentors and leaders) that allow all learners to engage in the practice may be necessary, particularly with younger learners. Safety is achieved when individuals are able to judge their own action boundaries and the level of risk in an activity. These are important characteristics of skill acquisition and should not be removed completely from the learner's responsibility, within acceptable limits. Learners need to seek and discover these safety boundaries if they are to be able to exploit opportunities for learning in unstructured play environments, an important part of athlete development (Phillips, Davids, Renshaw, and Portus, 2010).

CASE STUDY: ROCK CLIMBING

As an activity, rock climbing presents numerous inherent dangers and it does not lend itself to instruction of large groups of inexperienced climbers. That said, many components of rock climbing can be practiced in a group while maintaining an emphasis on individuality and safety. For example, comparatively safe aspects can be practiced with minimal risk such as previewing a climb, preparing harnesses and knots, and possibly top roping (where the learning climber is braced at all times by a rope that runs from a belayer at the bottom through an anchor system at the top and back to the climber). Indoor climbing areas typically cater to a range of skill levels while providing a cushioned floor surface should the climber fall. Ultimately, climbing is about testing one's own action capabilities within challenging environments, and there are numerous ways for practitioners to design practice environments that present these challenges without compromising safety. Designing climbing routes on indoor surfaces can allow learners to explore different ways to grip and stand on protrusions in order to traverse a route with fluency, that is safely and quickly (Seifert, Boulanger, Orth, and Davids, 2015).

Consideration of Habituation Effects

Habituation refers to the need for a warm-up period before performance during which people can show poor movement timing and coordination while demonstrating more errors than usual. It occurs when a person practices for a long period (e.g., several weeks or months) and then takes a short break (e.g., several days) from the task. Habituation effects can be observed when a person recovers from a serious injury or illness and performs routine tasks like walking or riding a bicycle. Another example can be observed when professional athletes return to full training after a vacation or an injury. When returning, there is often a need to readjust or habituate to the task, and this need is skill dependent (experts need smaller habituation periods). Habituation effects are sometimes attributed to so-called rustiness. As people readjust to the task context, their initial performances can have a higher level of variability than normal.

Many examples of sport behavior reflect habituation to a specific context in the short term, such as practice swings in golf and baseball, bouncing new balls when preparing to serve in tennis, and getting used to swimming in water of varying density (e.g., when triathletes perform a warm-up swim before starting a triathlon). Task exploration can occur when people face unfamiliar task constraints in the form of a new performance goal or novel conditions (Gauthier, Martin, and Stark, 1986). The latter is a particular problem faced by touring professionals in sports such as motor racing and tennis, where they must perform on different surfaces and circuits (e.g., tennis players who perform on clay courts in one continent before traveling to compete on grass courts in another part of the world). Kelso (1992) recognized the valuable role of movement variability in such circumstances when he argued that "without variability, in this sense, new forms of behavioral organization would be severely limited" (p. 261).

CASE STUDY: RETURNING TO PLAY AFTER INJURY

Athletes rehabilitating from injuries require special consideration in terms of practice scheduling. For example, team sport players typically train together in squads; however, when recovering from injury they are often given individualized training programs. This common practice provides the rehabilitating player additional opportunities to retune their bodies to the more intense demands of competition. As full perceptual and motor abilities gradually return, players can return to group training, although astute coaches realize that the individual focus should be retained.

Assign Responsibility to the Learner

Ultimately, an important challenge for the movement practitioner is to encourage the learner to explore and become autonomous and self-sufficient in remaining engaged with a sport or physical activity. This is a significant aspect of motivating athletes to take control of their lives and work hard during practice and training, as predicated by the tenets of the self-determination theory (Deci and Ryan, 2000) discussed in more detail in chapter 2. Self-control is also an important means by which the practitioner can exploit individual differences in learners. Assigning responsibility to the learners regarding factors in the learning process, such as when they receive feedback (e.g., Chiviacowsky, 2014; Janelle, Barba, Frehlich, Tennant, and Cauraugh, 1997), has been shown to promote motor learning and perceptions of autonomy and competence. If learners are given some control over factors in the learning process, like task difficulty, progression rate, and feedback mode and scheduling, then they are more likely to become attuned to their own needs and requirements during learning than if the practitioner always makes these decisions for them.

CASE STUDY: SIMULATOR TRAINING

Simulator training is a common way to develop motor skills in workplaces such as medicine, aviation, and the emergency services. Simulators are effective environments in which to promote self-control in learning because individuals can typically practice alone, and the environments and tasks can be modified to suit different skill levels. For example, a trainee surgeon practicing suturing techniques within a simulator could be given the freedom to choose how he receives feedback (e.g., how much time it takes to complete the task), when he receives feedback (e.g., after blocks of trials), when he progresses to the next level of difficulty (e.g., on reaching 90% proficiency at each level), and how he schedules his practice (e.g., several skills practiced in random order). Another popular technology-based learning approach concerns the use of virtual reality (VR) systems to digitally simulate the constraints of a task and a learning environment. Indeed, growth has been rapid in the use of new digital technologies that allow individual learners to interact in the more immersive environments of VR with relative ease and at relatively low cost (e.g., Oculus Rift and HTC Vive). In sport, increased accessibility and mobility of VR systems has led to a growing interest in their application to developing athletic performance (Stone, Strafford, North, Toner, and Davids, 2019).

Westend61/Westend61/Getty Images

FIGURE 8.2 An athlete practicing with the help of virtual reality.

The use of these new technologies in training has the potential to become a way to individualize practice tasks and schedules for different learners (figure 8.2), but their future use needs to be supported by a clear theoretical framework (see next section).

An Ecological Dynamics Rationale for Using VR Systems in Sports Training

Adopting an ecological dynamics rationale, a key issue with VR systems in sports training, is providing opportunities for individual athletes *to interact* with key variables in digital performance environments. A significant challenge is to develop the capacity of learners to continuously integrate perception, cognitions, and action during learning while immersed in a virtual world (Stone et al., 2019). Learners in VR training programs should have specific intentions to achieve particular task goals, perceptual variables to perceive and affordances to use, and actions to regulate during practice.

The use of VR systems in sports training offers a great deal of promise and could help facilitate a process of *individual–constraints* coupling (Seifert, Button, and Davids, 2013), enabling each individual to resolve similar performance problems in a uniquely functional way. Indeed, this type of training design could help eradicate a standard one-size-fits-all practice schedule. Sports practitioners could use VR systems to individualize task and environmental constraints away from the physical practice context before athletes engage in physical training. This individualized approach could be considered under the rubric of enrichment training, which is the process of complementing athlete practice with specialized, contextualized training that acts as an adjunct to physical work on skills, conditioning, and strategies in the performance arena.

Enhancing athlete self-regulation (of emotional, psychological, perceptual, and physical subsystems) by exploiting adaptive variability is another important performance area in individualized practice that use of VR systems has the potential to enrich. Aspects of competition and performance that VR could simulate include crowd noises designed to cause adverse effects in performers when putting in golf or taking penalty kicks in soccer. As another example, climbers could be sensitized to the sheer scale of a mountain surface through a close-up, 3-D image of a range as they engage with an instrumented climbing wall. A note of caution is necessary, however. As we have explained, in real-world practice, a lack of representativeness in VR learning designs may also lead to less faithful simulations of performance environments, inhibit acquisition of skills, and weaken (far) transfer to performance in competitive environments.

An ecological dynamics rationale, therefore, proposes that coaches could individualize training designs that can parameterize the continuous, functional interactions of an athlete with a simulated competitive performance environment. Experienced coaches, when surveyed for their experiential knowledge, have identified individualized training schedules as the most important aspect of training. This is because individual athletes respond differently to manipulations of task and environmental constraints (Greenwood, Davids, and Renshaw, 2012). Although individualization of training is important, it can be costly in terms of effort, time, and human resources (effectiveness and efficiency). Indeed sport organizations find it difficult to exploit the full potential of an individualized training approach, typically relying instead on a multitude of group-based sessions. The problem with this group-based approach to practice and learning is that many athletes miss out on the refined, fine-tuning work necessary for improving small aspects of their personal performance. This is why some coaching organizations are now offering an athlete-centered approach (see for example Athlete Centered Skating, an organization that offers individualized coaching programs for ice skaters, https://acskating.com).

VR learning programs should be designed to help individual athletes understand and develop their relatively unique performance solutions by manipulating key interacting constraints to facilitate skill development. This encourages exploration of the virtual environment before engaging with related physical practice tasks. For VR systems to be effectively used in athlete development, they must facilitate unique interactions that draw on physical, physiological, cognitive, and emotional characteristics of individual learners, shaping how they solve performance problems (Araújo, Davids, and Hristovski, 2006). As we have explained in this chapter, individual rates of skill development are likely to progress on different timescales. Therefore, VR training systems can take into account the varying rates of learning, growth, and maturation in different individuals that could affect their skill development. This individualized learning approach could be achieved with specific feedback provided by continuous algorithms that can identify and adapt the digital learning environment for each athlete directly in real time.

A particular focus in developing individualized training programs could involve use of VR in athlete rehabilitation after injury. The use of VR systems may enrich rehabilitation programs and prevent the boredom of the repetitive, muscle-exercising regimens that dominate current methods. For example, overuse and repetitive strain injuries could be reduced by forcing athletes to adapt couplings of cognition, perception, and nuanced subtle movements that involve problem resolution without the need for excessive physical loading on the skeletomuscular system. In professional sport, an injured player becomes expensive overhead for an organization because she may not directly contribute to team performance. This cost can lead to pressure to accelerate meticulous rehabilitation work or rush the player back, which puts her in danger of injury relapse. Although rehabilitation procedures may focus extensively on physical exercises, psychological components such as perceptual, cognitive, and decision-making skills are also important features in performance rehabilitation (chapter 4). VR may enhance functionality of athlete performance by working on perceptual skills, maintaining sharpness of decision making and cognition, as well as self-regulation through simulation of competitive performance scenarios from a first-person perspective (Craig, 2013). In VR system training, reduced **action fidelity** may be beneficial during the rehabilitation period by reducing the risk of reinjury while returning performers to competition speed. Indeed, this aspect of rehabilitation has been called *game conditioning* in team sports, and some performance maintenance or consolidation may be better than no learning at all during this highly specific phase of rehabilitation. VR performance simulations eliminate the possibility of physical contact with other performers, and athletes can carefully adapt their use to noninjured limbs, involving fewer motor system degrees of freedom, and significantly reducing risk of reinjury.

In summary, the use of VR is not meant to replace physical practice but rather to complement it as an adjunct source of specified training. In this way, VR could enrich effectiveness and efficiency of an individualized training program by doing the following:

- Individualizing specific training scenarios identified by coaches and athletes for enriching performance away from the competition or practice arena

- Refining awareness of a team sport player on court or on field by helping him develop visual exploratory activity (scanning behaviors)

- Improving an athlete's self-regulation of performance under digital practice conditions that simulate specific emotional contexts in competition

- Rehabilitating an injured athlete before she returns to practice with other performers

Summary

In this chapter, we discussed how ecological dynamics can be applied by practitioners to focus attention on individual differences, viewing variability of behavior as attempts to satisfy unique constraints on performers within specific contexts. We also discussed the applications of this theoretical perspective within a nonlinear pedagogical approach to practice. Technological advances, such as VR systems, and new analytical methods have helped us to gain a more detailed appreciation of the structure of movement variability, which provides a relevant focus when one is concerned with how motor system dfs are reorganized during practice. These technologies can also help individual athletes develop better perceptual awareness, cognitive activity that defines their intentions in performance contexts, and emotional control through practicing self-regulation in carefully designed digital simulations of the competitive environment. It can also help them recover functional performance capacities while injured.

Because of the potentially unique matching of an individual's intrinsic dynamics with a set of task dynamics, each person may exploit system variability in a slightly different way. The emergence of behavior under interacting constraints is a key theoretical idea that promises to help us understand decision making at many levels of analysis in sport and physical activities. When working with groups, practitioners must allow this fact to inform their instructional methods rather than neglecting individual problems and rates of learning. The question of how to design practice for teams of performers (i.e., sport teams) is where we turn our attention in the next chapter.

Self-Test Questions

1. What are some of the most influential factors that contribute to individual differences between learners?
2. Describe practical implications of the affective learning design concept.
3. Discuss how a physical education teacher might adopt an individual-learner focus within a typical lesson plan.
4. How could VR systems be used to enrich individualized training programs in your sport?

Laboratory Activity

Inducing Individual Differences via Constraints

Using a laboratory activity, you can highlight how individual capabilities are body and action scaled.

Experimental Problems

- Identify a discrete task (e.g., reaching, grasping, or climbing tasks; interceptive tasks) or cyclic task (e.g., swimming, running, cycling).
- Thereafter, progressively include constraints to simulate various anthropometric properties that will affect capabilities:
  - Carrying a heavy backpack will change your reaching perception and reduce jumping capabilities, simulating the experience of obese people.
  - Grasping a foam ball in your hand will constrain your climbing capabilities because you won't be able to use your full hand, just a few fingers. This will help you to understand the differences in action capabilities that occur when children have to act within a similar environmental and task design as adults.
  - Wearing paddles and fins will affect your swimming capabilities because you might experience a higher propelling surface area. This could require more strength to overcome higher active drag, especially in case of ineffective hand orientation and path, or an asymmetric

kicking action. It will show you why women, who often have smaller body dimension and less strength than men, swim with slightly altered technique (e.g., stroke rate and stroke length management, motor co-ordination, glide).

- Find a way to artificially modify your body properties (e.g., by wearing equipment or clothes or holding an object) and attempt to complete the task goal by modifying your movement coordination pattern.

Equipment and Resources

- Selection of equipment, objects, and clothes for a discrete or cyclic movement task
- Open laboratory space or gymnasium or swimming pool
- Video camera, measuring tape, and scale to measure and to compare estimation and action capabilities in initial condition versus in condition for which body properties are artificially modified

CHAPTER 9

Practice for Sports Teams

CHAPTER OBJECTIVES

After completing this chapter, you will be able to do the following:

- Explain how synergies emerge from the self-organizing tendencies of complex systems and how they are manifested in sport teams
- Differentiate between global-to-local, and local-to-global self-organizing tendencies
- Explain what coadaptation is between components of a complex adaptive system (e.g., players in a sport team)
- Explain how different individual performance capacities give rise to team behaviors as a product of coadaptation
- Apply theoretical constructs to derive principles of practice for team sports

---

This chapter provides an overview of how the key theoretical concepts introduced earlier in the book can be used to design practice tasks in team sports, including intrinsic self-organizing tendencies, synergy formation between individual components, emergence, and coadaptation between athletes. Localized interactions between individual organisms belonging to social groupings made up of many separate components are supported by straightforward interaction rules. As we noted earlier, self-organization is the foundation for continuous athlete–environment interactions and does not need to involve a dedicated central controller located in the brain (chapter 2). As constraints change in the environment, self-organizing tendencies can shape system changes expressed in dynamic patterns of coordinated action between individual system components (e.g., the interactions between athletes on a sport team).

Despite the numerous degrees of freedom in complex adaptive systems, rich, coherent patterns of behavior can emerge from interactions. A coach and practice can influence these patterns of behavior to a certain extent by encouraging certain tactical formations to emerge from the teams (e.g., perhaps most obviously in set-play situations such as a face-off in ice hockey: figure 9.1a). However, the intrinsic tendency for person–environment interactions is based on self-organization, which can also be exploited in team sports practice. When the game is in full flow, the organization between players is emergent and difficult to predict, such as in a goalmouth scramble (figure 9.1b).

Synergies are temporary couplings coordinated between many individual degrees of freedom of a complex system to support coherent patterns of behavior. Typically, synergy formation could emerge to achieve a specific *function*, such as forming a pattern between players to achieve a sport task goal (defending a goal or attacking it, see figure 9.1b). It's important to note that synergies are functional and become well adapted to environmental constraints or a performance context with practice. Synergy formation can occur within each individual as elegant coordination patterns are formed to achieve a movement goal such as a jump shot at speed in basketball or a bicycle kick in soccer. Synergy formation can also occur between individuals in team sports as players tactically adapt to changes in the playing area to achieve collective goals during defensive or attacking subphases of play (Araújo and Davids, 2016a). In sport teams, synergies may emerge between players to create a 2v1 overload in one part of the playing area, or when four attacking players coadapt their positioning when faced with two defenders in soccer (Passos et al., 2011; see figure 9.2). Synergies change in strength over time, known as the location effect, meaning that during certain phases in a game, such as approaching the moment of a crucial pass, synergies between players become functionally stronger (Passos, Milho, and Button, 2018).

This chapter examines the relevance of ideas on self-organizing tendencies and synergy formation for understanding practice task designs to enhance skill and expertise of players on sports teams. Synergy formation between many competing and cooperating athletes is based on the tight integration of cognition, action, and perception (see chapter 4). This deeply intertwined relationship can be developed during training and exploited during performance, underpinning exquisite coordination, organization, and rapid adaptation of performers. Ecological dynamics promotes the idea that cognition (implied in many activities like strategic and tactical behaviors in team sports) is an integral part of *athlete–environment interactions*, defined by the capacity to use information that is ecologically specific for the regulation of functional behaviors in achieving intended task goals. Cognition continually frames the

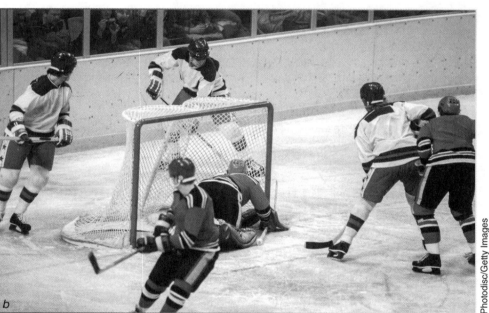

FIGURE 9.1 A comparison of the top and bottom of the figure shows that different patterns of behavior (synergies) ebb and flow throughout a team sport like ice hockey. *(a)* An elevated perspective of ice hockey players in a face-off to restart play. Players on competing sport teams can follow advice from coaches about tactical positioning at set-plays. *(b)* Sometimes no amount of practice on strategic positioning can prepare players for the dynamic constraints of competition. During a game, players exploit self-organizing tendencies and coadapt their positioning with other players to receive a pass, tackle opponents, or contribute to a goalmouth scramble.

Courtesy of Jonathan Monteiro.

FIGURE 9.2 An aerial perspective of a soccer match in which the attacking team has possession of the ball and has created a numerical advantage in a certain area of the field against the defending team.

capacity to actualize affordances (accept opportunities or invitations for action) to achieve intended performance outcomes in competition.

Global-to-Local and Local-to-Global Self-Organizing Tendencies

The tendency to self-organize underpins the synergy formation available to any complex adaptive system, including athletes and sports teams, and is especially prominent when under constraints. The type of constraints that shape synergy formation, maintenance, and dissolution is of particular relevance to coaches, teachers, and other movement educators. Continuous feedback loops play an important role when systems self-organize under constraint. During between-individual component interactions, synergies can be constrained by global-to-local or by local-to-global self-organization tendencies (Riley, Richardson, Shockley, and Ramenzoni, 2011). *Global-to-local* tendencies in organization of system degrees of freedom emerge when an external constraint regulates involvement (or noninvolvement) of separate components in an organized pattern. In team sports, an external agent (e.g., coach, trainer, instructor, or physical therapist) globally constrains the formation of dynamic patterns between the players, relying heavily on *extrinsic feedback loops*. Global-to-local management of system components in sports teams can be constrained by means such as verbal instructions, directions and signals, images, orders, and tactics (figure 9.3). How to deliver this information needs to be managed carefully, and this process is best imposed by members of what we call a **department of methodology** in an elite sports organization, as we shall discuss later in the chapter.

Synergies are also formed between system dfs through exploiting *local-to-global* organizational tendencies. This type of coupling tendency is underrated and not typically emphasized among sport practitioners. In team games, this type of constraint on synergy formation emerges through localized interactions between cooperating and competing players, not from specific instructions of an external controller. It emerges through the continuous interactions between each individual on a sport team (e.g., adjusting distance and orientation to immediately adjacent players). Interactions between performers in sport are predicated on the role of *intrinsic* and *extrinsic feedback loops*, in conjunction with processes of anticipation to adapt ongoing actions. These localized interactions are regulated by information from the environment. They include simple adjustments to copositioning in synchronized movements between teams and subgroups of players and between individual players to provide depth, width, and length in tactical patterns and shapes in a playing area (Duarte et al., 2013).

A large body of evidence suggests that *global-to-local tendencies* for synergy formation between individual players, constrained by extrinsic feedback loops in traditional coaching methods, have a useful role in sports pedagogy and team preparation. But they are often imposed through overused and overrated methods of coordinating the actions of players (as in the Williams and Hodges 2005 study of soccer players and the Reid, Crespo, Lay, and Berry 2007 study of tennis players). Rather, a more efficient and effective way of exploiting self-organizing tendencies in sports teams may be to harness available *local-to-global interaction tendencies* between intelligent team performers (see Key Concept) coached to continually coadapt actions and movements during competition (Passos, Araújo, and Davids, 2016).

Promoting local-to-global interactions and thereby developing intelligent team performers requires innovative and nontraditional ways of designing learning environments. The process of skill adaptation in practice requires exploration of task and environmental constraints by learners as they assemble functional performance solutions. An imperative is for coaches and teachers to develop learner adaptability and attunement to performance-relevant affordances (Davids, Renshaw, Pinder, Greenwood, and Barris, 2016). As a result of this process, several solutions and failures inevitably emerge through self-organization. Performance failures help to identify information sources

Intelligent Team Performers

To facilitate the flexibility and adaptability needed at the highest performance levels in team sports, practice and training processes should be conceptualized as a means to exploit synergy formation in spontaneous interactions among team players. Sports practitioners should implement constraints thoughtfully and with due consideration to help players develop the leadership qualities, autonomy, and coordination necessary to become intelligent team performers. The primary role of sports practitioners is to develop, with the specific group of players, a variety of game models and an acute understanding of the principles of play to harness self-organization tendencies (Button, Lee, Mazumder, Tan, and Chow, 2012). Principles of play represent a set of essential intentions that can continuously guide player interactions during competitive performance and help them find tactical solutions for immediate events, transitions, and challenges that emerge. These events may require rapid reorganization by subgroups of performers because of constraints such as (1) changes in weather, (2) tactical alterations by opponents, and (3) performance contingencies such as fatigue, injuries to players, substitutions and sending-offs, and changes in scores (i.e., needing to manage a lead or chase a game). Intelligent team performers are often the players that anticipate and recognize these moments first in a game and help others on the team to respond to them collectively.

that are not functional, and discovered solutions help to constrain the search for selected affordances to adaptive solutions.

Emergence is an important concept in understanding how self-organization processes underpin the local-to-global interactions of players on sports teams. Emergence can be observed in the spontaneous appearance of synergy as a system property (e.g., an overload of attacking players in a certain part of the playing area) that is not reducible to actions of an individual player. Emergence is predicated on continuous coadaptations of individual system components, framed by surrounding information such as movements of other players and the location of things such as goal, basket, try line, end zone, and field markings. To better understand processes of emergence from the continuous interactions of performers in team games, first we should explain the fundamental concept of coadaptation in evolutionary systems (Passos, Araújo, and Davids, 2013).

Coadaptation in Evolutionary Systems

Coadaptation at the evolutionary scale of analysis refers to how characteristics and behaviors of species change over the timescale of years in response to pressures exerted by other species (e.g., in predator–prey relations) and the environment, perhaps caused by changes in habitat and climate. To successfully function (e.g., breed, feed, defend territory, and avoid predation), individual organisms need to continually adapt to changes in the environment that might hinder their achievement of these goals. In nature, different organisms have developed tools that enhance their fitness within their own species through the process of continuous coadaptation to arising constraints.

The concept of *fitness*, considered in evolutionary terms, explains whether an individual (or group or team) is functionally adapted to an ecological niche, characterized by a particular landscape of affordances. Biological species need to adapt because of continuous interactions with their environment, which, in turn, is modified, originating an everchanging process of coevolution, with its consequences for functional behaviors (Kauffman, 1995). Because of these ongoing system dynamics, coadaptation is the engine of evolution and change. The process of coadaptation drives an organism's relations with its environment in different directions, some of which may enhance its fitness in a performance environment (provide a performance solution), and others may lead to performance decrements and extinction caused by a lack of fitness or functionality (performance failures). In this sense, one can understand the essential coadaptive functions of a biological organism as *competing* with other species and environmental changes and *cooperating* with individuals in a collective to enhance the capacity to survive. To coadapt successfully, biological organisms need to interact with the informational constraints of their environment.

Sports teams as complex systems must also demonstrate continuous coadaptation in order to gain advantage over other teams. The most successful sports teams are those that identify and respond quickly to environmental pressures that may threaten their status. For example, they are attuned to the changing strengths and weaknesses of rival teams and they develop styles of play that are robust to external disruptions (such as rule changes and tactical advances). In this respect, sports teams are no different from other biological organisms in the struggle for the survival of the fittest.

Affordance Use

Interactions with features of the environment provide opportunities to perceive and use new affordances because adaptations of developing skills lead to increased biological functionality (Kauffman, 1995). In sport, the use of relevant affordances (i.e., related to task goal) is a major feature of each individual's capacity to coadapt to task and environmental constraints through competitions that coaches facilitate. Recall that affordances are relational properties of an individual–environment system and capture the action-specific relations that exist between the capacities (effectivities) of an individual performer and the action-relevant properties of the substances, surfaces, objects, others, and events of a performance environment (Gibson, 1979). Using this conceptualization in sport, the term *fitness* has a different meaning than we normally associate with it. In this sense, fitness is based on the functionality of an athlete's performance behaviors and the relations between the ever-changing demands of a competitive performance environment.

To use affordances of team games, individual athletes need to be able to use different capacities to enhance their performance functionality. Some may invest in physical resources (e.g., velocity, strength, flexibility), whereas others emphasize their perceptual abilities (e.g., increasing their awareness of covered space or the quality of their visual attention to informational sources to anticipate movements of opposition and teammate movements). Some individuals enhance their functionality by seeking an advantage through performing risky behaviors (e.g., being innovative and playing with flair), whereas others may seek to perform with caution, moving conservatively and avoiding risky decisions (see figure 9.3). Collectively, these behaviors will shape the overall functionality and competitiveness of a sport team. In this way, coadaptation can enhance innovation and creativity as individuals exploit system degeneracy to arrive at varied performance solutions for achieving the same performance goal (see chapter 8).

Coadaptation in Small-Sided and Conditioned Games

Competing in team sports is predicated on the coadaptive interactions of individual athletes who are continually affected by information available in key task constraints. Coadaptation between teammates can be developed by implementing small-sided and conditioned games (SSCGs) (Davids, Araújo, Correia, and Vilar, 2013). Practice design in SSCGs differ from many traditional drills and rehearsed movements (such as shadow play) in the richness of information and uncertainty present in them and the adaptive variability required of players. Learners can address contextual challenges in different SSCGs by using perception and action continuously to solve problems and make decisions for using affordances in the environment. During performance, the rules of competition frame the copositioning of players, relative to each other, and to boundaries, markings, and scoring targets in the playing area. In SSCGs, these coadaptive moves emerge during continuous interactions between teammates and opponents, providing the greatest sources of information and affordances to be perceived and used for team sports performers.

The nonlinearity of a sport team as a complex adaptive system signifies that its emergent properties (in the form of decisions, intentions, and actions of competing and cooperating players) need to be anticipated by participants during performance. Just as it is impossible to completely predict how changes in the environment will affect a biological system during team sport performance, it is challenging to completely predict in advance how other players will coadapt to pressures exerted by actions of teammates and opponents in

FIGURE 9.3 Athletes successfully exploit system degeneracy to achieve the same task goal. In basketball, players can score points by shooting close to the basket or from further away using a variety of shooting techniques.

the timescale of milliseconds and seconds. For example, in this timescale for perception and action, attackers continuously change their positions on field to escape the attentions of defenders marking them closely, often using deception to cause misperceptions. In this way, they are providing affordances for other players, inviting specific actions of teammates and opponents through their own actions (Vilar et al., 2014). Research on these continuous coadaptations has emphasized the importance of information from the environment for affordances (e.g., reachable space, distance to another defender, the trajectory of the ball in the playing area, and subtle sources such as angles to goal target and distance to sidelines) for decision making and organization of actions of competing and cooperating team games players (see table 9.1).

As James Gibson noted "Behavior affords behavior . . . all [types of behaviors] depend on the perceiving of what another person or other persons afford, or sometimes on the misperceiving of it" (1979, p. 135). This quote from Gibson was not written with team sports in mind, but it is amazingly relevant for understanding performance behaviors in that context. It suggests that practice task designs should seek to faithfully simulate aspects of these environmental and task constraints that invite players to interact and to explore specific paths of an affordance landscape. What are the key features of research into skill acquisition in team sports that can help sport practitioners design fruitful learning experiences?

SPORTS ORGANIZATIONS SHOULD ENSURE THAT THEIR WORK IS COHERENT, UNIFIED, AND BASED ON EVIDENCE.

In high-performance sport, many types of specialists analyze athletic performance as closely as possible to identify advantages that might lead to success. Indeed, it has rapidly become the norm for Olympic and international-level sports teams to employ support staff that includes coaches, teachers, sport scientists, trainers, performance analysts, and psychologists, to name a few. To ensure that all practitioners work together as a team to implement learning design principles in a coordinated fashion, elite sports organizations should develop a substantial theoretical framework to support the work of a department of methodology. It won't surprise you that we believe ecological dynamics can and should provide this underpinning.

It has become clear that learning designs need to help team sport players find information to organize and manage their coordinated interactions in competitive performance contexts. Interactions in training and practice can help athletes form specific, temporary, intended synergies in different performance subphases. A department of methodology can implement a performance model approach to appropriately constrain the self-organizing tendencies of players by engaging them with principles of play and specific game models. A game model could be implemented as a unifying background (global) to capture the specific self-organizing interactions of teammates (local) in order to achieve performance goals (compete successfully). A game model needs to be flexible and dynamic and very much aligned with the view that sports teams are complex adaptive systems. Such a notion of a game model is constrained but not restricted to preferred playing styles of coaches, competitive goals of the sport organization, and the characteristics of the individuals on the team. To reach this level of adaptive flexibility, sports teams need an instantaneous high level of communication between members of the department of methodology and also between them and the players. A sport team needs intelligent team performers (see Key Concept) on the field and a shared understanding that instant and continuous adaptations to changing competitive constraints is a fundamental part of competing together.

MANIPULATION OF CONSTRAINTS IN TEAM SPORTS SHOULD NOT CREATE BARRIERS TO LEARNING AND DEVELOPMENT.

The first edition of this book stated that a significant challenge for sports practitioners was to manipulate key task constraints in order to enhance learning opportunities and the quality of learning experiences for individual athletes (Davids, Button, and Bennett, 2008). This idea was distinguished from the obvious statement that many hours of intensive, specialized training and dedicated practice are needed to enhance expertise, acquire skill, and develop talent (Davids, Araújo, Vilar, Pinder, and Renshaw, 2016). An important feature of practice task design is *constraints manipulations*, defined as subtle variations and modifications of information from a performance context such as space, time available, location on field, angle to scoring target, and positioning relative to playing-area markings. A considerable body of evidence demonstrates that these constraints interact to influence player organization in team sports (summarized in table 9.1).

Table 9.1 Empirical Evidence of Influential Task Constraints on the Organization of Players in Various Team Sports

Task constraints	Sport	Research study
Lateral and longitudinal displacements of the ball and competing teams	Futsal	Travassos, Araújo, Duarte, and McGarry (2012)
Numbers of players involved	Futsal	Vilar, Araújo, Davids, Correia, and Esteves (2013)
Practice designs with different directions and orientations of passing	Soccer	Travassos, Duarte, Vilar, Davids, and Araújo (2012)
Time to contact between a shooter and goalkeeper	Soccer	Shafizadeh, Davids, Correia, Wheat, and Hizan (2015)
Number of players and field dimensions	Rugby union	Silva and colleagues (2015)
Starting distance between defenders	Rugby union	Correia and colleagus (2012)
Space occupation (number of players, interpersonal distances between players and to the basket)	Basketball	Esteves and colleagues (2015)
Service action modes	Volleyball	Paulo, Araújo, and Davids (2018)
Players' relative positioning on court	Tennis	Carvalho and colleagues (2013)
Players' distances to the centerline of the court and to the center of the net	Tennis	Carvalho and colleagues (2014)

(continued)

Case Study *(continued)*

However, practitioners must be cautious not to modify constraints simply because they can be modified. Barriers to learning and development can emerge if coaches and teachers *overconstrain* (narrowing the field of affordances) or *underconstrain* (asking a novice to search an affordance landscape rather than a specific field within it) in a practice program. Learning is still likely to occur when over- or underconstraining, but the steepness of the learning curve will limit effective progress and may cause an inefficient use of time. To manipulate constraints effectively and efficiently, skilled coaches need to identify the relevant constraints on performance, manipulate them in an appropriate way, and ensure that they are targeted at the skill level of the learners. This type of skill and precision in constraints manipulation is predicated on the deep experiential knowledge of the sports practitioners designing the learning environment.

COORDINATED TACTICAL PATTERNS OF PLAY DO NOT MERELY EMERGE FROM SPONTANEOUS SELF-ORGANIZED INTERACTIONS BETWEEN TEAM PLAYERS.

Research data and theory have shown how intrinsic self-organization processes are spontaneous (e.g., Kelso, 1995). This idea is powerful and yet needs clarification if it's not to be misconstrued as an assumption that tactical behaviors in sports teams can *spontaneously* emerge from the system. In fact, it's important to note that tendencies for self-organization are spontaneous and emergent but continuously influenced by surrounding constraints (both internal and external to a sports team as a complex adaptive system) (e.g., Vilar, Araújo, Davids, and Bar-Yam, 2013; Passos et al., 2009). Spontaneity of self-organization here does not mean that players should always be left to their own devices and that team sports players will immediately gel and produce highly effective performances in competition.

Tendencies for self-organization need to be continuously shaped in practice by constraints of a competitive environment as players work together. For example, success would not be guaranteed if a hypothetical very rich professional basketball team were simply to buy all the best players in the league for each position. The assembled players would need to train and practice together and develop astute tactical awareness through the local-to-global interactions that have been described earlier in this chapter. Even then, the individual players may not gel as a team if the players do not display the game intelligence to coadapt and coordinate their actions effectively. Coaches play a valuable role in helping to develop functional interactions between players and thereby improving the collective tactical abilities of the team.

USE SHARED AFFORDANCES IN PRACTICE SETTINGS TO ACHIEVE PERFORMANCE GOALS.

Shared affordances in team sports are opportunities for collective actions that exist in a performance environment, and the aim of training and practice is to facilitate their use for achieving performance goals (Araújo and Davids, 2016a). In team sports practices, practitioners can design games and tasks around the key *principles of play* as pathways to guide players toward the key affordances. Principles of play in team sports are universal (e.g., advance forward in a playing area to attack the opposition territory by using width and depth). Passos and colleagues (2013) proposed that constraints manipulation could be used by sport practitioners to guide players toward specific fields of affordances. For example, a field of affordances for teammates counterattacking a zone defense in basketball could be explored in practice by varying (1) the number of attackers versus defenders (exploring opportunities for action in overloads and underloads), (2) the starting distances between attackers and defenders, (3) the initial space between defenders, and (4) the time allowed for the completion of a shot at the basket before the ball is turned over. It is important to note that learners need to be confronted with information for actions in practice tasks that help them perceive and use the affordances available in a performance environment. The information can be *augmented* with instructions from a coach, teacher, or sport scientist, but there must be a clear rationale in ecological dynamics for *how* these supplementary verbal instructions and visual images should be used, which we address next.

USE AUGMENTED VERBAL COMMENTS AND FEEDBACK AS SUPPLEMENTARY INSTRUCTIONAL CONSTRAINTS IN PRACTICE.

In sport, a performer's *intentions* frame the use of perception and action to achieve their task goals. In team games, these intentions could include context-related information underpinning perception and action related to time constraints of competition (e.g., chasing a losing scoreline with 5 minutes of the match remaining, defending a lead). Regardless of the specifics of a competitive context, principles of play provide support for athletes in achieving their performance goals. Practice games and tasks can focus on these principles, and coaches can briefly highlight them for learners, communicating through visual and acoustic media (e.g., video analysis, verbal comments that nudge players). The aim is to avoid *verbal monologues* in this part of the coaching process, but instead to use verbal information sparingly to *guide* learners toward relevant affordance fields for further exploration in

(continued)

Case Study *(continued)*

the practice contexts. The intention is most definitely not to impart knowledge and information to learners by using full verbal descriptions of actions in the form of if-then statements that address every contingency. A major challenge in practice design is to build on agreed-on intentions and principles through continuous development of implicit communication of teammates within learning environments.

HOW DONOR SPORTS CAN BE USEFUL IN ATHLETE DEVELOPMENT.

Facilitating coadaptive moves in team sports training allows learners to enhance their dexterity (Bernstein, 1967) through constant interactions with the other players in the performance environment. Dexterity helps players become more flexible in synergy formation, reorganizing system degrees of freedom, and exploring different information sources to satisfy changing task constraints (Chow, 2013). In this section, we propose that a variety of sporting experiences can help learners to develop dexterity. At an early age, children should experience fun and enjoyment in *playing* during a variety of physical activities and sports that may not seem to have specific relations with a target team sport (Wormhoudt, Savelsbergh, Teunissen, and Davids, 2018). The main idea is to develop more skillful individuals through exposure to a variety of specific and nonspecific practice while supporting more functional learning capacities for later specialization (Güllich, 2018).

Are Parkour and Futsal Donor Sports for Other Team Sports?

Relevant, functional athletic qualities, including coordination, balance, turning ability, body awareness, strength, and reaction speed can be augmented through an affordance landscape shared between a donor sport activity that supports exploratory learning and an athlete's main target sport (Wormhoudt et al., 2018). Ideally, donor sport activities should use many of the same basic movement skills required in the target sport, but they can also be useful when a particular skill, relevant in the target sport, is underdeveloped in an athlete (Wormhoudt et al., 2018). For example, Strafford, Van Der Steen, Davids, and Stone (2018) proposed that the sport of parkour could provide a representative and adaptive platform for developing athletic skills such as coordination, timing, balance, agility, spatial awareness, and muscular strength.

The potential overlap of performance-enhancing affordances in the donor sport landscape presents opportunities for development of key athletic skills that may be instrumental for specialization in an individual's target sport (e.g., the specific postural control and balance capabilities required for movement on and off the ball). Additionally, participating in donor sports offers potential psychological benefits such as enhanced perception, cognition, and emotional self-regulation. For instance, athletes may learn to regulate stress and anxiety during competitive training scenarios that are transferable to their main target sport in which they are expected to perform calmly under pressure. In team sports, transfer can be enhanced by choosing donor sports that have perception–action demands similar to those in the target sport. These ideas suggest that compared with playing multiple sports in the early diversification phase of development, donor sports offer a greater level of congruence and correspondence with target sports by capturing the specifying information available to regulate actions, representative tasks, and action modes that are functional (related to goal attainment). For example, archery is unlikely to be a donor sport for a team game like soccer because of its inherent static nature. On the other hand, futsal may be considered a donor sport for soccer because of its dynamic tendencies for enhancing ball manipulation skill and perceptual awareness. This relationship can be harnessed during later specialized training while avoiding the documented risks associated with too much early specialization. Next, we discuss two potential donor sports in more detail.

Parkour Parkour is an acrobatic sport in which practitioners explore their movement capabilities (e.g., running, climbing, jumping, landing on one and two legs, vaulting, balancing, stepping, hurdling, quadrupedal movement, and rolling) to negotiate environmental features and properties (e.g., gaps, obstacles, surfaces, and inclines) in the most innovative and efficient manner. Abilities deemed critical to athlete specialization for performing in team sports can be donated by parkour, such as fluidity of movement, safe landing and falling strategies, creativity in negotiating gaps and obstacles, and related decision making. Integrating parkour-style activities into practice landscapes could develop athleticism and skill transfer in young athletes who play team sports because of the overlap of performance-enhancing affordances and adaptive functional movement capabilities. Practicing parkour-like activities also requires learners to judge distances, gap sizes, and surface properties and to focus attention, solve problems, make decisions, and innovatively negotiate environmental features. A network of shared affordances in the environment can invite specific actions that provide opportunities for athletic skill development as athletes become more adaptive at sampling a variety of environmental properties intrinsic to parkour and the team sport being targeted. It's worth pointing out again that we are referring to parkour-style training that involves interacting with indoor and outdoor installations in different ways. We are definitely *not* referring to extreme manifestations of parkour such as freerunning or BASE jumping, where the aim is to interact with the naked environment in an adventurous and skillful manner. These are altogether different activities.

One appeal of parkour-style training is that it may transfer to several team sports. For example, many team ball sports require fluid and dynamic movement patterns in which athletes are required to quickly reposition their body relative to an opponent's movements with respect to the ball position, direction, and speed (Esteves et al., 2015). Parkour practitioners similarly emphasize the importance of fluidity and dynamism in movement exploration within a performance environment. An example is the precise foot placement required to negotiate constraints such as the location and orientation of objects in a performance environment. This type of activity could be implemented into the training and warm-up phase of contact team sports to develop foot placement and orientation with respect to a target (e.g., an obstacle or an opposing player). Parkour can also help develop an athlete's ability to effectively use stopping, starting, turning, and cutting movements suggested as critical skills in team sports such as basketball and dodgeball. Safe-landing strategies as a means of recovering balance, initiating a change of direction, and postural control following physical challenges are critical for preventing injuries (Taylor, Wright, Dischiavi, Townsend, and Marmon, 2017). Parkour could help develop landing skills after jumping and enhance awareness of proprioceptive and haptic information from the soles of the feet and from the lower limbs. This is important because, like in team sports, parkour requires the ability to regain balance and postural control following physical challenges. Resourcefulness in movement exploration afforded through parkour helps athletes recover from forced landings in sports such as gridiron football, rugby league, and rugby union in which players tackle one another to regain possession of the ball (Passos et al., 2016).

Parkour emphasizes enjoyment and fosters creativity in movement exploration rather than focusing on developing movement skills in a specific sport as advocated in traditional drill-based approaches to skill learning. Emphasizing enjoyment and creativity reduces boredom and enhances movement coordination and control because every obstacle an athlete meets during parkour needs to be negotiated in a distinct way. Interactions with a surface or an obstacle may not have an obvious solution, so athletes must use their creativity to interact with them in meaningful ways. Sport practitioners in youth team development programs can exploit the exploratory and creative nature of parkour to enable physical conditioning while at the same time developing self-regulation capacities and enhancing movement skills in an enjoyable way. These ideas suggest that designs of playscapes may require fundamental shifts in playgrounds to include features, limitations, or boundaries that constrain the reorganization of motor system degrees of freedom at different levels (Bernstein, 1967; Sparrow and Newell, 1998). Where financial constraints are not an issue, sporting academies should construct or regularly visit a parkour training environment (Wormhoudt et al., 2018). Parkour-style training can act as a vehicle for athletic development and skill transfer by exploiting guided-discovery learning in a diversified sport experience environment. This approach would counteract the negative effects of early specialization, which can be too repetitive and drill based, lacking essential exploratory activity.

Futsal as a Donor Sport for Soccer   Whereas parkour may be a suitable donor sport for many team sports, futsal is the obvious donor for one sport: soccer. Futsal is a small-sided game (5v5) played on a court smaller than its bigger cousin. It is played with a ball smaller and heavier than a soccer ball and that has less bounce (Araújo, Davids, Bennett, and Button, 2004). Consequently, a significant emphasis for futsal players is on ball control and manipulation: taking different types of touches on the ball in tight spaces (e.g., using soft feet to shield the ball from opponents); using different parts of the feet (e.g., the sole, side, back, and toe); and adjusting the timing for passing, shooting, and dribbling the ball. Contrast this with soccer, in which the emphasis is more on performance of gross movements because of the increased space and game durations that require more strength and aerobic endurance. Associated with the need to move the ball quickly and with precision or to maintain defensive equilibrium to recover ball possession, futsal promotes general individual agility in terms of coordination, perception-action coupling, reaction, rhythm, and balance.

Despite some of these differences, futsal shares many commonalities with soccer, making it a good candidate to be a donor sport (Travassos, Araújo, and Davids, 2018). Most obviously, in both sports, the ball is typically manipulated with the feet to move it around the field, and the common objective is to score more goals than the opponent. From a collective system perspective, both sports require equilibrium in defensive and offensive moves, with precise adjustments according to variations in the space–time interrelations between teammates and opponents. These demands promote the development of players' spatial orientation and the ability to functionally manage space and time during performance. The constant changes in players' copositioning increases variability in space covered and in relationships established with teammates and opponents, providing a broader perception of game relations. Because there are fewer players on a futsal team than on a soccer team, futsal contributes to the development of a wider range of technical and tactical abilities. Futsal also provides more frequent opportunities to perform skills and engage with the ball than during an 11-per-side soccer game (see Davids, Araújo, Correia, and Vilar, 2013; Fenoglio, 2003). Futsal encourages up to three times as many opportunities to use (affordances for) visual exploration activity (scanning behaviors) during play, compared to soccer (Oppici, Panchuk, Serpiello, and Farrow, 2017). Furthermore, every player needs to use both feet to perform the skills needed during competition and to engage in collective tactical behaviors with and without the ball.

Finally, futsal promotes transfer effects in practice because of the different perceptual-motor adaptations of actions caused by the type of ball used, the characteristics of futsal court surfaces, and even the type of futsal shoes worn. Also, by taking up futsal at an early stage, developing soccer players have the opportunity to explore different offensive and defensive tactical behaviors that will enrich their developing perceptual-motor landscape. This landscape can provide a resource of developing movement patterns and behaviors that players can exploit when seeking to enhance transfer between donor and target sports. The complementary nature of the two sports can be exploited for skill acquisition in early diversification through emphasizing selected performance-based affordances, behavioral correspondence between sports, and self-evident advances toward task goals. We will revisit these ideas in chapter 12.

Summary

In this chapter, we have discussed how multiple sports performers cooperating, competing, and coadapting together in the same playing area can be likened to a complex, dynamic system. The organization of players or athletes in team sports is influenced by external factors (global-to-local interactions) such as coaches and tactical instructions as well as by continuous, internal self-organizing tendencies among players (local-to-global interactions). Rich patterns of coordinated movement (synergies) emerge in team sports as a function of the constraints that envelop them. Teams of athletes on the field are often supported by teams of practitioners off the field (e.g., coaches, analysts, physical therapists, and fans), and as we discussed, a department of methodology approach can embrace the ecological dynamics framework to provide a coherent and functional scaffold for successful performance. Practitioners should look for strategies to develop intelligent team performers who can identify crucial moments in a game and instigate collective behaviors to exploit them. Finally, we discussed the emerging idea of donor sports as a way to develop team sport players. Donor sports are activities like parkour that have movement and perceptual skills in common with the target sport. Practicing donor sports can help to emphasize and improve certain performance attributes and thereby reduce the risk of engaging in high volumes of repetitive, specialized practice early in an athlete's career.

Self-Test Questions

1. Imagine that the players on a basketball team spontaneously change their organization and formation during a game to exploit an opponent's weakest player. Does this adaptation represent a global-to-local process or a local-to-global process? Justify your answer.

2. Suggest to a team sport coach practical strategies she might use to improve the coordination and communication of the players on her team.

3. How can you design practices and games to encourage learners to become more intelligent team performers? Illustrate your answer with one example from three team sports.

4. In this chapter, it was suggested that futsal may act as a donor sport for soccer. Can you think of candidate donors for other sports or physical activities?

5. Explain why these donor sports might help learners become better at a specific target sport.

Laboratory Activity

Coadaptation in Teams

Using a laboratory activity, you can better highlight how coadaptation and shared affordances can be present in the completion of a collective task.

Experimental Problems

- Identify a task that can be achieved in a competitive way (e.g., reaching a target as fast as possible by dribbling against an opponent) but can be achieved with a higher outcome (faster or more accurately) in a collective way (e.g., reaching the target by passing instead of dribbling).

- Thereafter, rules (or constraints) can be progressively included to exclude individual action (e.g., dribbling) and to promote (force) collective action in order to share affordances and coadaptation (e.g., all players must touch the ball once or twice to traverse the pitch and reach the target, but each player can only take steps). The number of players, the number of steps, the size of the pitch, the number and size of the target, the number of opponents, and the roles of the opponent can be changed to design a rich landscape of shared affordances.

- You must still attempt to complete the task goal of reaching the target and use different interpersonal coordination organizations to achieve the same task goal.

Equipment and Resources

- Selection of different equipment (balls, targets), players, and field for a collective task

- Open laboratory space or gymnasium

- Video camera or GPS

Use the video camera and GPS to capture the different interpersonal coordination organizations to attempt to achieve the task goal and to identify how affordances are shared. Describe how players coadapt when the constraints are changed.

CHAPTER 10

Modified Perceptual Training for Athletes

CHAPTER OBJECTIVES

After completing this chapter, you will be able to do the following:

- Identify a range of perceptual-motor training methods and explain why they might be beneficial for learning
- Discuss the advantages and disadvantages of different ways to assess perceptual-motor training
- Provide a practitioner with recommendations for manipulating vision and maintaining representative learning design
- Explain the factors that influence the effectiveness of demonstrations

---

Throughout this book we have acknowledged that search and discovery are important learning processes. In practical terms, however, it is often unwise to pursue a totally discovery-based pedagogical approach. A completely unstructured practice environment would be inefficient in terms of the time it may take to learn a skill (Daly, Bass, and Finch, 2001), and it also might be physically and mentally harmful to the learner. This is why we and many others have proposed the strategy of directing learners' search for functional coordination solutions (e.g., Correia, Carvalho, Araújo, Pereira, and Davids, 2019).

Since the first edition of this book in 2008, digital technologies have advanced considerably, creating intriguing new opportunities to measure and develop the perceptual skills of athletes. In this chapter, we examine how perceptual training techniques can be used to direct and constrain the learner's search activities during practice. In particular, we discuss one of the most popular coaching strategies in the form of demonstrations as a type of perceptual training. It will become clear that several factors influence whether the learner can attune to key information sources. We also review evidence for manipulating availability of visual information (e.g., occluding vision) for learning. Regardless of how information is presented to the learner, the aim is not to prescribe a specific course of action, but instead to use modified perceptual training to promote perceptual-motor degeneracy on the pathway to skillful behavior (Seifert, Button, and Davids, 2013).

What Is Modified Perceptual Training and Why Do It?

As we discussed in chapter 3, a variety of sources of perceptual information are used to regulate actions. Information in various forms, such as light, sound, pressure, temperature, and inertia, is continuously detected and used by athletes to adapt their movement patterns. The process by which humans learn to attune to relevant (related to goal achievement) information sources can be influenced and potentially enhanced through modified perceptual training (MPT). MPT includes strategies that coaches or learners themselves can employ to improve perceptual skill. MPT strategies that have been popular include sport-specific video review and reaction-time training, whereas emerging approaches such as virtual reality, brain training, and wearable monitoring devices are gaining traction.

A review of MPT tools was undertaken by Stephen Hadlow and colleagues at the Australian Institute of Sport (Hadlow, Panchuk, Mann, Portus, and Abernethy, 2018). These authors proposed a new framework for MPTs that can help practitioners to evaluate the effectiveness of the different tools that are now available. It was also noted that three assumptions underlie the presumed usefulness of MPT tools: (1) The targeted perceptual skill should discriminate between athletes of different skill levels, (2) improvements in the skill of interest should be possible through training, and (3) any improvement in that skill should transfer to performance environments (i.e., to enhance competitive performance). While a large body of empirical work has addressed the first two assumptions, investigations of transfer following MPT are rare, but let us first consider why MPT can be an effective strategy.

It is well established that modifying information can destabilize perception–action couplings in several ways (e.g., anchoring, perturbing, scaling) and it therefore has the power to assist the learner if manipulated appropriately (Chow, Davids, Button, and Renshaw, 2016). Important for practitioners, information can provide a shortcut for the learner to begin exploring specific (rather than global) areas of the perceptual-motor landscape available during practice. On the other hand, information also has the potential to distract and weaken perception–action links, so one must use it wisely. For example, providing additional instructions on how to perform motor skills is often not helpful when feedback related to the task goal is already naturally available to constrain the learner's search activities (Hodges and Franks, 2001). Furthermore, providing learners with both detailed instructions and feedback related to concurrent movements can often prove to be too much, particularly in complex tasks in which spatiotemporal demands are high.

Current technology provides the capacity for sport scientists and performance analysts to gather masses of information on athlete behaviors on and off the training area. However, there is an obvious danger of providing too much augmented information in an attempt to facilitate motor learning. Generally speaking, information supplied during motor skill practice enhances performance, but when it is subsequently withdrawn it can lead to performance deficits in retention tests. Practitioners must consider carefully how to manipulate information (e.g., to add, reduce, or highlight existing sources) in order to avoid oversaturation and creating a dependence on the use of outside information. Also, certain individuals have more to gain than others from receiving augmented information to help them learn (Magill, 1994). For example, early learners struggling to understand a task goal clearly benefit from receiving instruction or demonstration. Furthermore, individuals experiencing injury or illness that reduces their typical motor or sensory capacity may well require additional information to compensate for their altered level of function.

MPT can also help to motivate learners and to promote self-assessment during practice. In a study of children learning gymnastics (Potdevin et al., 2018), an intervention group that received video feedback was contrasted with a control group that received the same training but without feedback. The video feedback group improved its techniques in key activities. Furthermore, the intervention group improved in terms of self-assessment scores and motivation when surveyed after practice. Interestingly, providing video that highlighted key movement changes was particularly effective in helping the learners to identify and modify the joint angles necessary to execute the required movements more effectively.

Assessment Techniques

There are many potential means by which perceptual skill can be assessed. While the following is by no means an exhaustive list, these examples demonstrate how emerging digital technologies are opening up exciting new possibilities to monitor and further develop perceptual-motor behavior (Appelbaum and Erickson, 2018). Note that assessment techniques often neglect or downplay the role of movement in generating information. As we now appreciate from earlier chapters in this book, skill is neither just perceptual nor just motor, but instead perceptual-motor!

Digital Assessments of Visual Function

Numerous software programs and apps have emerged in recent years that use computers or devices to expose learners to diverse stimuli to which they must respond. Indeed, a number of "vision and brain training" tools are enthusiastically promoted on-line, and purportedly help to develop visual function in sport and other performance domains. However, a lack of concrete evidence regarding the effectiveness of such tools has arguably hampered their acceptance as worthwhile learning aids (Appelbaum and Erickson, 2018). As 3-D presentation options are becoming more accessible, it is likely that more of these tools will continue to enter this potentially lucrative market. Indeed, given the huge success of recreational video games in recent decades, it seems inevitable that considerable interest and growth in these assessment platforms will continue.

Visual–Motor Reaction Time

Reacting quickly to visual stimuli is a key attribute that many skilled athletes exhibit. Consequently, several instruments have been created to evaluate and train visual-motor reaction time. For example, the Batak reaction-time trainer requires athletes to press randomly lit buttons in a fixed configuration as rapidly as possible. Numerous similar commercial products are available, including Dynavision and the Wayne Saccadic Fixator. It is not surprising that these tools are promoted to detect concussions in sports in combination with other motor and neuropsychological measures (Wilkerson, Nabhan, Prusmack, and Moreau, 2018). However, while apparently appealing to coaches of many high-performance sports, more evidence that directly links visual-motor reaction time training to on-field performance is required (Appelbaum and Erickson, 2018).

Foveal Vision: Eye–Movement Registration Systems

Eye movements indicate how athletes visually scan their environment. Means to measure eye movements include placing electromyographical sensors on the ocular muscles responsible for controlling eye movement. However, a lack of portable equipment has limited gaze behavior studies and constrained researchers to studies that restrict participant movement. As Dicks, Button, and Davids (2010) remind us, constraining athletes to respond in unrealistic ways alters how they scan their environment (see Spotlight on Research: What Do Soccer Goalkeepers Look At?).

A video-based technique to measure eye movements is preferred by many researchers for its portability and convenience of preparation. The equipment is typically composed of a pair of modified glasses with miniaturized cameras mounted around the frame and a recording device to store video footage. These systems usually detect the location of **foveal vision** within a scene through integration of two eye features: the pupil and the reflection from the cornea. The fovea is the small region on the retina that provides the highest level of visual acuity. Portable eye-movement systems compare the vector between the pupil and the cornea, from which the system's software computes point of gaze. An additional camera records the viewpoint of the participant and this perspective is interlaced with the eye motion video. A positional cursor highlighting the point of visual gaze is then digitized and superimposed onto the scene camera by custom-written software.

Unlike early manifestations of eye-tracking technology, mobile eye trackers are relatively portable, allowing the examination of gaze in athletes such as climbers (Button, Orth, Davids, and Seifert, 2018) or cricketers (Croft, Button, and Dicks, 2010) in naturalistic environments (see figure 10.1). It should be noted that various limitations associated with using portable systems that register eye movement remain (van Maarseveen, Savelsbergh, and Oudejans, 2018); not least is how the point-of-view data are obtained and analyzed. While we should not rely on eye-tracking data alone to assess perceptual skill, it remains a fascinating topic worthy of future research.

Courtesy of James Croft.

FIGURE 10.1   The climber in this image is wearing a mobile eye tracker that can record the location of fixations as the wearer navigates his environment.

Spotlight on Research

What Do Soccer Goalkeepers Look At?

Using a portable eye-movement registration system, Matt Dicks and colleagues (2010) wanted to find out what information soccer goalkeepers attend to when facing penalty kicks. To see how task constraints influenced their eye-movement strategies, the goalkeepers watched the same penalty taker in a series of presentation conditions and response modes: (1) video simulation with verbal response (VSV), (2) video simulation with movement (VSM), (3) in situ with verbal response (ISV), (4) in situ with movement (ISM), and (5) in situ with interception (ISI). In effect, the five conditions represented a continuum of representative design for the goalkeepers, with the ISI condition being the most realistic (or lifelike). The eye-tracking data is summarized in figure 10.2. The circles represent fixations, and the larger the circle, the greater the frequency of fixations at that location. For clarity, the circles are accompanied by a letter. "A" denotes the highest fixation frequency location, with descending frequency represented by subsequent letters.

The results showed that goalkeepers spent more time fixating on information from the penalty taker's movements than to ball location for all perceptual judgment conditions involving limited movement (e.g., verbal responses, joystick movement, and simplified body movement). In contrast, an equivalent amount of time was spent fixating on the penalty taker's relative motions and the ball location for the ISI condition that required goalkeepers to attempt to make penalty saves (figure 10.2). These results suggest that gaze and movement behaviors function differently depending on the experimental task constraints selected for empirical investigations. This study highlighted the need for research on perceptual-motor behaviors to be conducted in representative experimental conditions to allow appropriate generalization of conclusions to performance environments.

FIGURE 10.2 Eye-movement strategies differ depending on the presentation mode of information and how the viewer responds. The images summarize the most common fixation locations for skilled goalkeepers when watching a penalty taker at different time points during their approach.

Reprinted by permission from M. Dicks, C. Button, and K. Davids, "Examination of Gaze Behaviors Under in Situ and Video Simulation Task Constraints Reveals Differences in Information Pickup for Perception and Action," *Attention, Perception and Psychophysics* 72, no. 3 (2010): 706-720.

Application

Consider the implications of this study for the strategy of conducting perceptual skills training without including a realistic movement response. The results suggest that eye-movement strategies are quite specific to the task constraints imposed on the learner. Therefore, consider how you might design a perceptual-motor training session for a soccer goalkeeper to practice saving penalties in a representative fashion.

Manipulating Vision

Modified perceptual training can take many forms, including highlighting key information (e.g., through demonstration or improving visual contrast), occluding or masking it (e.g., practicing with eyes shut), and changing information (e.g., manipulating the size of or distance to a target). In this section, we consider common strategies for manipulating visual information in training.

Occlusion Techniques

Sports place considerable demands on the athlete's visual system, and it is well known that **occlusion** of visual information results in reduced motor performance and accuracy (Davids, Williams, and Williams, 2005). Indeed, the strategy of training in conditions of reduced or diminished vision has considerable research support. Although using blindfolds or visual occlusion goggles during volleyball, soccer, and basketball practice may seem unusual, several recent studies have supported the idea of occluding various information sources during learning to direct players to alternative perceptual information sources. Occlusion devices such as blindfolds, protruding bibs worn around the waist, and LCD stroboscopic glasses (that intermittently flash between opaque and clear) have been used in various sports to develop eye–hand coordination. For example, they have been used in volleyball to direct a blocker's search for acoustic information from a setter's hand–ball contact, in basketball to prevent players from watching their hands as they bounce a ball, in soccer to direct players to raise their heads and search for visual information in the environment as they dribble the ball, and in golf to focus the player's attention on the proprioceptive feel of the golf swing. The key point is that practitioners can remove information to help learners augment underdeveloped information–movement couplings.

Demonstrations: Directing Visual Attention

The nature of the constraints placed on learners limits their search for more functional movement patterns. The more constraints that learners need to satisfy, the less opportunity there is for experimentation and exploration through self-directed or discovery learning. In this respect, a visual demonstration of a skill should be conceptualized as an instructional constraint (part of the subset of task constraints) that guides learners' exploratory activity. For example,

Spotlight on Research

How Removing Vision Can Benefit Catching Performance

In this one-handed catching experiment by Bennett, Button, Kingsbury, and Davids (1999), three groups of children were selected using a pretest of catching ability. Only participants who caught less than 10% of trials were investigated. One group of children practiced the task with restricted vision (RV group) while wearing a helmet with an opaque screen attached to it (see figure 10.3a). The helmet was designed to remove visual information from the catching limb. The researchers predicted that in the absence of visual information, the children would be forced to search for alternative information sources such as proprioceptive information from the catching arm. The RV group transferred to a normal vision condition after 120 practice trials. A second group had vision available (VA group) during the practice trials but then transferred to the RV condition for 20 transfer trials. Finally, a control group trained for the same period of trials with normal vision throughout.

As shown in figure 10.3b, each group improved catching performance from pre- to posttest. Of particular interest was the significantly greater improvement of the RV group compared with the VA group. During transfer tests, the RV group showed no detrimental effects of catching in normal vision. However, the VA group

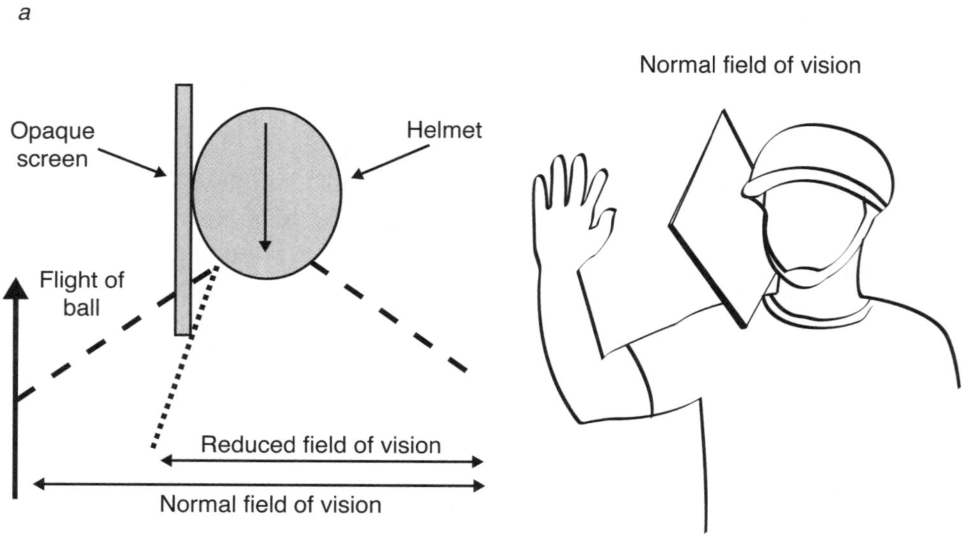

FIGURE 10.3a Manipulating access to information of the catching arm can benefit catching-skill acquisition by directing the learner's search for relevant information for catching a ball to underutilized sources.

Reprinted by permission from S. Bennett, C. Button, D. Kingsbury, and K. Davids, "Manipulating Visual Informational Constraints During Practice Enhances the Acquisition of Catching Skill in Children," *Research Quarterly for Exercise and Sport* 70, no. 3 (1999): 220-232.

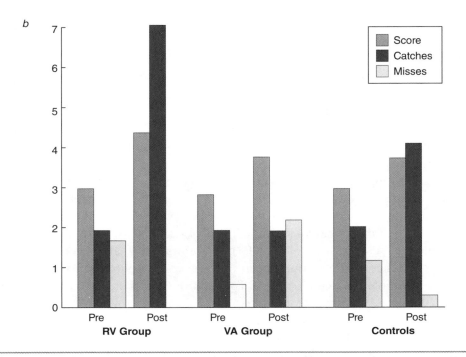

FIGURE 10.3b Catching performance in terms of score (0-5 scale) and number of catches or misses before and after the practice phase of the study.

Reprinted by permission from S. Bennett, C. Button, D. Kingsbury, and K. Davids, "Manipulating Visual Informational Constraints During Practice Enhances the Acquisition of Catching Skill in Children," *Research Quarterly for Exercise and Sport* 70, no. 3 (1999): 220-232.

performed poorly when vision of the catching arm was occluded. The sensitivity of the VA group to removal of visual information suggests that catchers in this group had relied heavily on vision and were somewhat less adaptable when this information was restricted. Another suggestion was that the RV group benefited from being directed toward information sources provided by vision of the ball early in flight, proprioception from the catching arm, and acoustic information from the ball machine.

Application

In summary, the data supported the use of equipment aids as a teaching strategy to direct novices toward appropriate information sources. Whether more experienced learners would show similar benefits in long-term performance in response to these types of manipulations during practice is an interesting question for future work. In what other types of movement activities could learners benefit from practice with restricted vision? From the context of rehabilitation after injury, provide a similar example of how a practitioner might direct a patient toward critical information sources (e.g., acoustic, haptic, visual) that support movements such as postural control, balance, or locomotion toward a target.

taekwondo students who practice a kick previously demonstrated by a teacher can be constrained by the model's action. However, if the learners are not given a demonstration but are simply asked to defend themselves against an opponent, this type of exploratory practice would represent a lower level of constraint because the learners' search activities have not been directed by the model's demonstration.

Imitating a model such as a parent, skilled performer, or coach demonstrating a motor pattern is a common activity in daily life and is intended to facilitate motor skill acquisition (De Maeght and Prinz, 2004). Also known as observational modeling, **observational learning** is the process whereby a person adopts or replicates the behavioral patterns and actions of others as a direct consequence of observing those behaviors (Ashford, Bennett, and Davids, 2006). Observational learning initially became a focus of study in social psychological research on imitation (e.g., Bandura, 1969) and has experienced a recent resurgence in popularity in areas such as neurosciences, robotics, and artificial intelligence (Jeon and Lee, 2018). Observers can include spectators, learners, students, teammates, and opposing athletes. The observed individuals could include demonstrators, performers, or models. Furthermore, some dance instructors use mirrors as an alternate way to augment or highlight visual feedback to the learners about their actions. The fact that many practitioners commonly use observational learning methods suggests that its role is recognized and well understood.

While a variety of theoretical explanations have been proposed over the years for interpreting observational learning effects, the visual perception perspective advocated by Scully and Newell (Scully, 1986; Scully and Newell, 1985) provides a theoretically based account of the visual processes underlying this learning phenomenon. Specifically, it emphasizes the nature of the perceptual information that observers pick up to constrain movement production. According to this view, changes in motor behavior following observational learning depend on the perception of relative motion information from a model, which observers use to assemble stable coordination patterns during a particular movement activity. The term **relative motion** refers to the specific spatiotemporal relationships among and within limbs, as well as the organization of the performer's limbs relative to the surrounding environment. The literature on biological motion (Johansson, 1973) demonstrates that relative motion is the principal source of visual information that observers use to identify and classify different types of human movement activities such as walking, cycling, and gymnastic moves.

Once a learner perceives relative motion (i.e., the movements of body segments relative to one another), it acts as an informational constraint on the emergence of a coordination pattern that is essential to a task being learned. Recall from chapter 3 that informational constraints guide the learner's search for effective task solutions within the perceptual-motor landscape (Warren,

1990). Some evidence exists for the idea that observation of relative motion information is enough to guide the search for appropriate coordination solutions during motor learning. For example, Ward, Williams, and Bennett (2002) examined the relationships among visual-search strategy, anticipation, and biological motion perception in tennis. Tennis players were required to perform motor responses to forehand and backhand drive shots presented in video film format and as point-light images. The point-light images were created by attaching reflective markers to the players' major anatomical sites before recording the players performing various shots against a black background. In this scenario, the point-light display presentations contained the same relative motion pattern as conveyed in the video but with the background and structural information removed. When viewing point-light sequences, participants employed fewer fixations (5.8 versus 7.2) of longer duration (597 versus 457 milliseconds) to a smaller number of fixation locations (3.8 versus 4.6) compared with the normal video display. Despite these differences in fixation usage, participants under the point-light constraints were able to perceive as much relevant relative motion information to support movement approximation as when viewing videos.

Although it has been argued that some motor learning can occur without movement (McCullagh and Weiss, 2001), when observational modeling is used as an instructional protocol to facilitate acquisition of new movement behaviors, it is rarely used in isolation. Instead, it is typically used in conjunction with other learning strategies, including verbal instructions, visual imagery, and physical practice, to establish information–movement couplings. An important aim in future research is to understand how these modes of transmitting information to learners interact to constrain search activities.

Effect of Relative Motion Information on Intrinsic Dynamics

Horn, Williams, and Scott (2002) also reported changes in search behavior when female soccer players viewed demonstrations of a chipped soccer pass presented in point-light compared with video format. Compared with controls, no learning differences were reported for the point-light display and video-presentation groups. Interestingly, the point-light display group showed a more selective visual-search strategy than the video-presentation group. The differences in search strategy resulted from the removal of key environmental information related to the mainly irrelevant background structure within the display. These variations in search strategy illustrate how performers might acquire information to guide skill acquisition.

The presentation of key informational constraints in relative motion of models can direct learners' search for coordination solutions and constrain visual-search activities (Horn et al., 2002; Ward et al., 2002). It follows that coaches and teachers need to identify the nature of information that learners acquire so that the content and presentation of information during a visual demonstration can be enhanced to promote skill acquisition. Linking these findings to Newell's (1985) model of motor learning, it seems that visual demonstrations should facilitate the early stage of skill learning by conveying relative motion information essential for the assembly of a novel coordination pattern (Scully and Newell, 1985). Later in learning, when the goal of the task demands the refinement of an already established coordination pattern, observational modeling should help the perception of dynamic features for optimal scaling of a movement pattern (e.g., producing a pattern that varies in force, timing, or duration).

An interesting application of these ideas has emerged recently through which some sports clothing and equipment designers are astutely capitalizing. Garments and equipment can be designed to highlight or disguise motion characteristics to the advantage of the user. For example, the recent trend of brightly colored soccer and rugby shoes (as opposed to the more traditional plain, black designs) may help to direct an opponent's attention to a player's feet when perhaps it would be better directed to their torso. Indeed, Smeeton, Varga, Causer, and Williams (2018) showed that sports players (netballers and handball players) wearing clothing that disguised the relative motion characteristics of their throwing action were able to disrupt the anticipatory responses of their opponents. Perhaps there is more to the recent fashion trends in sports than meets the eye!

Characteristics of the Model

If modeling constrains a learner's search activities, then we would expect the characteristics of a model to have an important bearing on learners' practice activity. Hence, model characteristics have to be carefully selected to facilitate search. For example, children learning to ski may benefit from watching a child rather than an adult because of the closer fit between the psychophysical constraints of the learner and model. Differences in limb lengths, strength, and center of mass between an adult model and child learner might result in demonstrated movement solutions that are less useful to the learner.

Existing evidence has shown that using peer-group models is beneficial in motor learning, particularly when there is a skill differential between learners and models. d'Arripe-Longueville, Gernigon, Huet, Cadopi, and Winnykamen (2002) found that in a swimming task for children, peer models who were more skilled elicited more effective learning, primarily by constraining the children's desire to emulate the models through hard work in practice. Novice models did not influence the self-efficacy of learners as much as the skilled peer-group models. In another study, d'Arripe-Longueville, Gernigon, Huet, Winnykamen, and Cadopi (2002) found that gender differences in peer-group modeling led to a greater amount of modeling in asymmetrical (different-gender) dyads, particularly affecting the number of practice trials undertaken by male children.

Another explanation of these findings is that when watching a model possessing similar attributes to themselves, learners are more actively involved in problem solving and goal attainment than when observing a skilled model, for example (Hodges and Franks, 2002). In addition, learners benefit from receiving variable information during practice and discovering what works and what does not work. These factors may also contribute to the apparent benefits of learners observing models and not simply copying an idealized technique.

Clearly, further work is needed on the psychophysical constraints of models on learners, particularly concerning child–adult variations and gender differences between model and learner. Another interesting issue is whether models for athletes with disabilities need to have the same physical characteristics as the learners. For example, would a model with a disability or a model without best facilitate the practice of learners with an injury or a disability? If modeling directs learners' search, then it follows that congruence between model and learner constraints should be relatively high to optimally constrain exploratory activities. It appears that model characteristics need to be calibrated with those of the learners to enhance the benefit to be gained from visual demonstrations.

Feedback and Learner–Regulated Scheduling

The proliferation of digital technologies in the early 21st century (e.g., smartphones, wearable sensors) means that movement feedback has become a convenient and simple practical tool for the general public. For example, the fact that most mobile phones contain high-quality video cameras provides a ready means to collect and record movement. However, just because it is easier to take video footage during practice doesn't mean we should. Janelle, Barba, Frehlich, Tennant, and Cauraugh (1997) considered two questions of particular interest. First, is video feedback better than other types of feedback? Second, to what extent do learners benefit from choosing when and how much feedback they receive? Janelle and colleagues used a precision ball-throwing task with the nondominant limb to address these questions. To ascertain whether movement-related feedback (KP) was of greater benefit than knowledge of results (KR), three groups of learners received KP via video feedback while another group received KR. Another concern was whether learners should receive KP in summary format. For this reason, one of the KP groups received video feedback after every five trials (summary format). The researchers suggested that learners would benefit most from choosing the schedule of KP provision (Janelle et al., 1997). Therefore, the final two groups consisted of a group that decided when KP was provided (self) and a group that had no choice but did have a feedback schedule matching that of the self-group (yoked). All participants were recorded performing the acquisition trials and had access to KR as they observed where the ball landed on the target.

The form scores from Janelle and colleagues' (1997) study clearly supported the use of video feedback (see figure 10.4). The KR group consistently showed poorer throwing form than the KP groups. Accuracy scores were also lowest in the KR group. During acquisition trials, the summary and self groups performed equally well. However, in no-feedback retention trials, the better movement form came from the self group. Finally, the yoked group appeared to have suffered from not being able to choose when KP was administered. Despite receiving the same amount of KP at the same time as the self group (on 11% of trials), the retention of the yoked group was not as high.

The findings of Janelle and colleagues (1997) raise several questions for practitioners and performers alike. First, the similarity in movement form and outcome scores indicates that when learners focus on achieving good form, they tend to successfully achieve outcomes as a by-product. Second, it seems important to allow the learner some control in determining when move-

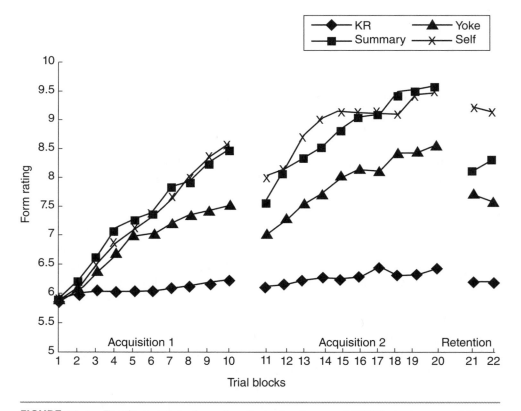

FIGURE 10.4 The form scores from Janelle and colleagues' (1997) study support the benefits of self-choice in when learners should receive video feedback. The self group chose when they received video footage of their movement form while throwing at a target.

Adapted by permission from C.M. Janelle et al., "Maximizing Performance Feedback Effectiveness Through Videotape Replay and a Self-Controlled Learning Environment," *Research Quarterly for Exercise and Sport* 68, no. 4 (1997): 269-279.

ment-related feedback is supplied. It is likely that self-regulation of feedback enhances motivation and also leads to more effective learning strategies. Also, this research has clearly demonstrated that in tasks with multiple degrees of freedom, KR alone is insufficient to optimize learning. The learner benefits most from a modest provision of movement-related feedback in order to develop the most salient aspects of the skill. Finally, as Newell (1996) pointed out, demonstrations only provide the learner with kinematic information about motion. Tasks like precision throwing that are primarily regulated by kinetic feedback may also benefit from other forms of feedback delivery.

Augmented Perceptual Training

The current era in human history is often referred to as the digital information age, signifying the transition from traditional industries to an economy based on digital information transmission. Numerous technological developments in recent decades have allowed humans to record and share information in ways that were simply not possible in previous generations. Information-transmitting devices for learning that are in vogue at the time of writing include location and activity trackers (e.g., GPS), active video games with motion analysis (e.g., Microsoft Kinect or Nintendo Wii), 3-D screens, motion sensors in devices (e.g., smartphones, rackets, clothes), and practice simulators to name but a few. Similarly, the Internet and social media in particular make sharing information among large groups of people a relatively simple task in contrast to just a decade ago. Indeed, it is already difficult to remember an era in which sharing videos, photos, and other media on the Internet was not possible, yet today these activities occupy a significant portion of many people's lives. Clearly, our much enhanced capacity to record, analyze, and share movement patterns has the potential to significantly affect the motor-learning process, but is there evidence of this impact in the research literature?

Farrow (2013) wrote a review on the effectiveness of practice-enhancing technologies for motor learning. He points out that use of new technologies to facilitate practice in the high-performance setting has increased, yet at the same time, a comparatively modest volume of research has reported on the efficacy of such approaches. The key issue for many training aids is the extent to which they can mimic realistic information–movement couplings (i.e., action fidelity or behavioral realism).

This gap in the motor-learning literature is understandable given the challenges of undertaking effective analyses of motor-learning interventions over extended timescales. Nevertheless, abundant evidence confirms the effect that practice-enhancing technology has on the development of perception–action couplings that emerge during performance. The evidence from performance studies suggests that these interventions can support the formation and stabilization of perception–action couplings in athletes. For example, Stone, Maynard, North, Panchuk, and Davids (2015) showed that ball-projection technology (traditionally used for practicing interceptive actions such as hitting or catching a ball) could be enhanced by integrating video images to provide advanced visual information of an event or action preceding ball flight. These types of analyses are not common because advanced visual information from a thrower's actions is typically removed when athletes practice interceptive actions with the aid of a ball-projection machine (Pinder, Renshaw, Davids, and Kerhervé, 2011). Previous work has indicated that manipulating access to this type of information can alter hand movements (movement of the catching arm and grasping actions) and eye movements that emerge during one-handed catching performance (Panchuk, Davids, Sakadjian, MacMahon, and Parrington, 2013).

In their study, Stone and colleagues (2015) manipulated participant access to advanced information of a thrower's actions provided in a video as well as information from ball-flight projection (slowing or increasing speed relative to the video image of a thrower's actions) while recording whole-body kinematic and kinetic data. Participants attempted to perform or simulate (with a micromovement) one-handed catches in three experimental contexts: (1) a condition that included integrated video images of advanced visual information and ball-flight projection, (1) video images of a thrower's actions only, and (3) ball-flight projection information only. The results of the study revealed that when video images of a thrower's actions and ball-projection information were integrated, lower-limb adjustments were used primarily to regulate posture and attempt interceptions. However, movement was initiated earlier when advanced visual information was available before ball flight, resulting in more stabilized perception–action coupling and superior catching performance in the integrated condition. When only advanced visual information of a thrower's action was presented without ball-flight information, Stone and colleagues (2015) observed the catcher didn't adjust his position and lower his center of gravity by bending his legs as much as when integrated video and ball-flight information and ball-flight-only information were available.

The findings of Stone and colleagues (2015) are significant because they illustrate how technology (e.g., ball-projection machine with video) can be integrated to highlight relevant information sources. Note, however, that it is important to ensure that practice technologies be predicated on principles of ecological dynamics, specifically the integration of information from actions before ball flight with ball-trajectory information to provide representative task constraints to stabilize perception–action couplings (see also chapter 7).

Summary

Practice can be described as a search process in which learners find appropriate coordination solutions for movement problems under varying task constraints. Modified perceptual training, or MPT, is a collective term that describes strategies for manipulating perceptual information to educate the learner's attention (Hadlow et al., 2018). The assumed benefit of MPT methods is to channel learners' search activities so that they are directed to key information sources more efficiently. Investigators now are more likely to use a wide range of methodologies to explore MPT, including various neuropsychological brain-scanning techniques (e.g., Jeon and Lee, 2018), visual eye-tracking procedures (e.g., Dicks et al., 2010), and qualitative or quantitative movement analysis (e.g., typically approximated to the modeled action) allied with traditional performance outcome measures. There remains an ongoing need for the extensive use of statistical techniques such as meta-analysis to verify specific trends and establish theoretically grounded models on which new and emerging tools can be judged (Hadlow et al., 2018). This important research provides an evidence-backed approach to ensure reliable generalization of the principal effects associated with demonstrations.

Videotaped demonstrations or watching someone else perform a skill is one example of a popular form of MPT. Demonstrations can help learners find suitable coordination solutions more quickly and safely, although the aim should not be to imitate the model's behavior. Rather, the model demonstrates a possible coordination solution that may guide learners' physical practice activities. The role of the demonstration is to get learners in the ballpark, so to speak, so they can find relevant coordination solutions. To this extent, learners may benefit from choosing how and when they view demonstrations or augmented feedback, therefore taking greater responsibility for their own learning (Janelle et al., 1997). Emerging technologies in recent decades, such as simulators, optical illusion garments, and virtual reality games, are of increasing interest in both research and practical perspectives in MPT (Appelbaum and Erickson, 2018). Thanks to the digital information age, the future of practice may be quite different from what we have been accustomed to.

Self-Test Questions

1. List the advantages and disadvantages of a learner engaging in discovery learning without intervention from a practitioner.

2. Choose a motor skill from a sport you are familiar with and identify relative motion characteristics. Plan a demonstration that will guide an observer's practice of the motor skill.

3. What factors should a practitioner consider when planning a practice session that includes demonstrations?

4. How can learner-regulated feedback be an effective strategy for practitioners?

CHAPTER 11

Practitioners as Designers

CHAPTER OBJECTIVES

After completing this chapter, you will be able to do the following:

- Understand the important relationship between experiential knowledge and empirical findings in supporting effective skill acquisition
- Describe the role of coaches and teachers as designers of practice
- Acknowledge how the constraints-led approach can be applied in a range of sports
- Gain new insights from the case studies presented to enhance your own practice

---

Interactions among constraints are dynamic in nature and are instrumental in shaping the emergence of movement behavior. As we have already seen from earlier chapters, it is practically impossible for a learner to repeat the same exact movement solution over time and trials. The role of the practitioner is to facilitate exploratory behaviors among learners rather than to prescribe explicit movement forms to accomplish a movement task goal. From this perspective, practitioners can be conceived as designers of practice environments, providing the ingredients for adaptable and robust skill learning that can account for learner–environment interactions. Practitioners have to design rich landscapes of affordances that contain an abundance of relevant information to guide action (Rietveld and Kiverstein, 2014).

Practitioners face a significant challenge when they attempt to integrate their practical experience with new knowledge and theories provided by emerging research. This is especially challenging when new insights provided by scientific evidence conflict with what they have been practicing. It is important to understand that the interaction between theory and practice is a two-way process and that theory can also be shaped by existing practices. Indeed, if the goals of practitioners and scientists were better aligned, it could allow both parties to realize the benefit of combining practice and theory. An example is when practitioners use new insights gained from theory and empirical findings to enhance their own practices. Additionally, researchers have been prompted to consider emotion as a fundamental principle in representative learning design because of practitioner dissatisfaction about its relative absence from motor learning theory (Headrick et al., 2015). This chapter presents case studies contributed by practitioners to show how ideas from ecological dynamics can be enacted in different sports and learning contexts in diverse performance environments.

Case Studies

The following case studies have been contributed by a variety of practitioners (e.g., elite to subelite coaches, coach educators, and physical education teachers) from different types of sport (e.g., individual, team, indoor, outdoor). The common element that links the case studies is the application of an ecological dynamics theoretical approach (often via constraints-led strategies) in designing effective practice environments.

ICE-SKATING

Garrett Lucash

I am a United States figure skating champion, world team member, cofounder of Athlete Centered Learning, and cofounder of Athlete Centered Skating (ACS). Contrasting training experiences ignited my powerful curiosity to explore athlete development and motor skill acquisition research. ACS programming integrates those experiences and research into an evolving curriculum.

Figure skating is an extremely demanding early-specialization sport. Figure skaters must perform extremely complex skills with equal parts pertaining to technical and artistic mastery. The majority of practice involves motor skill acquisition: Skaters are introduced to new skills; they practice, improve, and eventually perform those skills again in competition. Figure skating pedagogy is heavily rooted in traditional notions that expertise culminates from repetition, linearity, and idealistic movement patterns. ACS, in contrast, is firmly grounded in ecological dynamics principles, which stipulate that expert performance is manifested through exploration, nonlinearity, and adaptability.

Our goal was to establish a training environment that nurtures confident, capable, and resilient learners positioned to achieve success in figure skating and life after sport, which enriches the value of participation. We challenged tradition—even seemingly timeless hand-me-down practices that many seem to take for granted. Reformation involved several key objectives. First, transform each practice into unique information-rich experiences that maximize learning. Second, transform skaters into active agents of their own learning (i.e., self-directed and exploratory learning).

Adding variability and novelty to the general practice structure and training of individual skills can help us achieve the first objective (i.e., ensuring an information-rich experience). ACS skaters now practice warm-up exercises, jumps, and spins in different orders and combinations and through variable speeds, amplitudes, and patterns on the ice. Some sequences are simple and preplanned and others are completely random. Gone is the antiquated notion that skills must be practiced in the same way and order every practice. Our skaters no longer strive to be perfect—an impossible and psychologically damaging goal. Instead they strive to be adaptable—an achievable and psychologically empowering goal.

To transform ACS skaters into active agents of their own learning, the second objective, we discarded the traditional notion of feedback, which reflects a one-way transmission of information from coach to skater, and adopted a transactional approach that identifies feedback as a dialogue between coach and skater. To achieve this, we had to delay, even withhold, our commentary and allow skaters to struggle through the task and perhaps to fail at times. Most importantly, we started asking the following questions to skaters: What did that feel like? What adjustment did you try to make? What would you like to work on next? What will you do to improve the skill? Now, our skaters tend to think more deeply about their training; they are more aware, more responsible for their work, and importantly, more self-directed in their learning.

From the two-way dialogue, we can move away from being prescriptive to more conceptual in the skill acquisition process and no longer view technique as a specific motor pattern blueprint that all skaters must duplicate. Over time, technique morphed into a collection of core concepts for skaters to integrate in their own unique and context-specific ways (performer constraints) to solve the task at hand (task constraint). Each core concept is now explained externally through movement outcomes (rather than the movement form themselves). The benefits of this intervention are significant and immediately observable. According to ACS skaters, technique is easier to understand, remember, implement, and transfer to other contexts. The coach–skater dialogue is simplified. Multiple corrections, which used to be addressed as isolated prescriptions, can now be integrated through a single core concept (perhaps an analogy). And perhaps most important, the behaviors that are underpinned by the core concepts are easy to observe.

To further increase training variability, ACS adopted creative tasks and games to engage the feedback exchange. We vary how, when, and who (coach or skater) will initiate the dialogue, the number of trials to include, and the emphasis of the task or game. Sometimes multiple skaters work together in groups while we observe to nurture their evaluative judgment and make training more of a social interaction. This intervention diminished both the monotony of practice and the skaters' reliance on coaches to tell them what to do after every trial. Skaters can also now remain focused and be engaged in practice longer.

We firmly believe that the role of coaches should not be limited to demonstrating their own wisdom but rather to facilitate the athlete's acquisition of wisdom. The greatest challenge of the ACS program has been that it sits almost diametrically opposed to traditional coaching practices. As a result, it has been challenging at times to go against the grain, but there is value in what we do, and we strive to work harder. Undoubtedly, we must communicate, educate, experiment, philosophize, promote, and network. We do not walk a pathway long since cleared, but one that is stunted, ironically, by tradition. Instead, we ascend our own trails, clearing obstacles, and challenging existing dogmas as we go, and this is exactly how to elevate sports performance to levels not seen before.

ROCK AND ICE CLIMBING

Ludovic Seifert

I am a professor in motor control and learning at the University of Rouen, in France, and I am a mountain guide certified by the International Federation of Mountain Guide Associations. I coach a regional team of junior mountaineers from the French Alpine Club Federation. As a practitioner, I have always been intrigued by how climbing on rock and artificial climbing walls can help to prepare someone involved in mountaineering, mixed-route climbing (i.e., combination of rock and ice, see figure 11.1), and ice climbing. Does skill transfer between indoor and outdoor occur and how does it? Separately, what is the skill transfer between rock and ice climbing? Indeed, as there are no mountains, no snow, and no ice in the Normandy region where I live (near the northern coast of France), climbers mainly train on rock and artificial climbing walls.

The implication is for climbers to be able to adapt to using ice tools when climbing on rock, notably by hooking the blade in a jug or by jamming the blade in a crack, because swinging the ice axes into the rock to anchor the blade is challenging or even counterproductive. Based on the resources that I have to work with in Normandy, I heavily leverage the constraints-led approach (CLA) by focusing on manipulating task constraints (e.g., using various types of ice axes), environmental constraints (e.g., using various supports and textures, such as mixed route, alternating icy and rocky sections), and performer constraints (e.g., wearing gloves or climbing with bare hands). By skillfully manipulating and taking into account the relevant constraints, climbers can learn to adapt and expand their repertoire of actions to enhance their adaptability.

Infusing variety in environmental constraints in practices is critical in encouraging climbers to explore different motor solutions. For example, I always try to select ice waterfalls with complex shapes that allow a climber to explore a variety of actions, postures, and paths. When the icefall is dense, climbers must swing their ice tools to anchor them, and when the icefall has many holes and indents, they learn to hook the blade in the holes to conserve energy. However, during this process, climbers sometimes cross their left and right hands because the presence of holes on the rocks invite them to follow a zigzag path instead of following a vertical pathway. The learner–environmental mutuality cannot be overlooked. Attunement to environmental information is crucial in supporting adaptive behavior. A nonrepresentative practice environment (in the absence of relevant informational constraints), such as trying to learn rock and ice climbing with a ladder under symmetric support and following a vertical and linear displacement, does

© Ludovic Seifert

FIGURE 11.1 A climbing route composed of a mixture of rock and ice (mixed-route climbing).

not develop attunement to ice properties (e.g., temperature, thickness, density, color, sounds, shape, inclination).

Nevertheless, it is still possible to use CLA to train climbing on artificial climbing walls by helping the climbers to focus on functional properties (i.e., opportunities for climbing offered by the environment according to the climber's ability) rather than on structural properties (e.g., size, shape, and distance between holds) because once the climbers go outdoors, there will be an absence of those structural features. Therefore, I prefer to get the climbers to focus their attention on whether the rock is climbable. In practice, this means an emphasis on relying on the texture of the surface and the friction it affords and to rely on the orientation of holds to make possible a swinging action of the body so it oscillates like a pendulum.

In climbing, it is important to help climbers develop perceptual attunement to functional information (i.e., information that invites actions and is critical for effective decision making). Variable practice should not be done just for the sake of incorporating variability. Variability can be targeted to help exaggerate relevant perceptual information and to avoid routines that are irrelevant. This is especially important in outdoor climbing and mountaineering where climbers must continuously adapt to changing climbing conditions, weather, fatigue, and potential falls. Skills transfer between environment (indoor to outdoor, rock to ice) is a key feature of expertise that reflects adaptability in climbing. Thus, route setters have a huge responsibility to design routes that can provide a rich landscape of affordances (i.e., various ways to succeed that could be transferred to other contexts).

HAMMER AND JAVELIN THROWING

Jean-François Gregoire

I am now a lecturer in sports sciences, having previously been a physical education teacher and a hammer thrower in athletics. I competed in the hammer throw until 1995 and have been coaching the sport since then. As a coach and athlete, I have always been intrigued by the challenge to find ways to simplify the throwing skill to make it easy for learners to acquire the required movement to find success in the sport. The difficulty is in avoiding a situation of decomposition of the movement so much that it becomes almost impossible to perform in its entirety (as a single multiarticular movement). Here, I will use two throwing events to illustrate how I have adopted the constraints-led approach (CLA) to enhance skill acquisition: hammer throw and javelin throw.

The hammer throw is a spectacular movement that highlights the athlete–environment mutuality (i.e., the athlete–hammer system). The objective is to maximize the speed of hammer release after a series of rotations by the athlete within a confined space. Traditionally, the skill acquisition processes have emphasized the need to attempt a throw after one loop and then move on to two loops and so on and so forth. The use of an analogy to perform the heel-plant movement has also been quite common. However, these approaches have been futile and the athlete quickly realizes that adding loops over time does not take into account the required movement dynamics and that it is not reasonable to assume that one can learn to turn by using the specific heel-plant movement without the hammer. Task simplification works more effectively and could include requiring the athlete at the first session to perform multiple loops and throw the hammer toward the target area (without an emphasis on the movement form itself). One simple single task constraint is to look at the hammer while keeping the arms extended, and the task goal is to rotate as quickly as possible.

With practice, the athletes learn to balance themselves during the rotating motion by adjusting the forces needed to resist the centrifugal force generated by the hammer. Self-organization of movement can emerge during this process. For example, athletes can make adjustments to their head position, trunk, or lower limbs at the individual level to enhance stability. Exploration of what works for individual athletes can occur because the coach can manipulate task constraints to affect the rotation of the athlete–hammer system. For example, the coach may ask an athlete to get from point A to point B in a certain number of rotations without worrying about rotating by using the heel-plant movement. This approach (manipulating informational constraints) allows athletes to feel comfortable with the rotations and experience the effects of this movement: head spinning, loss of benchmarks, muscle tension. Awareness of these sensations may be absent using a more analytical approach that focuses on a specific movement form.

Similar to hammer throwers, javelin throwers must generate the highest flight speed to the javelin to perform effectively, but they must also ensure an appropriate javelin trajectory so that the aerodynamic properties of the javelin are fully exploited. At the final phase of the throw, skilled athletes will typically have a javelin that is parallel to an imaginary line between the two arms and the shoulders (the javelin tip is at the level of the eye). Conversely, less skilled athletes tend to exhibit a nonparallel alignment.

Using CLA, I typically ask the athlete to throw a volleyball instead of the javelin to attempt to induce a better alignment of the javelin with the imaginary line between both arms. Because it is not possible to hold the ball in the hand, athletes are forced to carry it with the palm of their hands facing the sky and with their hand above the level of the shoulder to keep from dropping the ball. In conclusion, CLA allows for better adaptability so athletes can effectively face variable changes to the performance environment. Changes caused by maturation, training effects, or injuries require athletes to adapt to these changing constraints quickly, and CLA affords the necessary adaptability.

YOUTH SOCCER

Mark O'Sullivan

I am involved in coach education and player development at AIK Stockholm Football Club, Sweden. Soccer is a dynamic team sport characterized by players having to switch between attack and defense. To inform our session design and analysis, we conceptualize this dynamic ebb and flow between attack and defense as (1) in possession: search, discover, and exploit space and gaps using soccer interactions and (2) recovering the ball: close space and gaps, minimize possibilities for opponent's soccer interactions, and win the ball.

The vernacular of soccer interactions helps us to elucidate the ideas of CLA. Soccer interactions (dribble, pass, shoot, move without the ball) refer to how players coordinate their behavior with the dynamics of performance environments, which operate at different timescales. That is, not only how they behave in relation to immediate physical and informational (i.e., situational) demands but also in interaction with historical and sociocultural constraints (Uehara, Button, Falcous, and Davids, 2018).

A challenging concept has been the notion of designing environments around ideas of adaptive efficiency. By this, we mean fostering evolution in the coaching practice that works effectively through time beyond the reproduction and rehearsal of predetermined techniques that often give the impression of working at a moment in time (i.e., looking organized and giving the illusion that the coach is in control of the learning). This is a major obstacle for us because these reductionist methods have until recently been an integral part of the formal coach education courses in Sweden and contribute to an ideological inertia that has required us to conduct regular interactions with coaches, players, and parents in the form of educational seminars and meetings. Examples of these traditional assumptions appeared in the yearly organizational and planning document of various teams for 2018.

> "We will use coordination ladders, rings, and cones to train on different moments and movements. Of course, we will also play soccer. There will be a focus on dribbling technique, receiving, and turning." —2018 boys under-9 team

The acquisition of skill by a young learner involves what Gibson (1966, 1979) referred to as *educating their attention*. Moving from theme-based sessions toward sessions defined by principles of play (interactions) has proven helpful. This involves designing tasks that simulate aspects of the performance environment, observation of emergent behaviors, and selectively introducing the young player to the correct aspects of the environment and their affordances. Therefore, we also need to look at educating the coaches' attention, helping coaches learn how to observe interactions as opposed to just actions. How are the players exploring the wide range of affordances in the environment?

> "I was very skeptical when AIK introduced this way of working. Now I love it and I see how it motivates the kids." —Field note from a parent coach, 2018 under-8 boys team

In the quote above, I share a practical example from working with the AIK under-8 boys team. When working with young players (who often have tendencies to move toward the ball), we do not need to explicitly tell them to create width and depth. Instead, we can give value to the idea of moving away from the ball through task design and manipulation of task constraints (e.g., number of players, field size, rules, start position of ball feed and players) and challenge players to investigate whether it is harder to defend a large space or a small space and what this means for the team in possession. The kids then decide that when in possession, they need to try to create a large space (how large, of course, depends on the situation) to play in that makes it hard for their opponents to recover the ball. Thus, in this example, we are giving value to the idea of moving away from the ball. When the team in possession behaves like this, learning how to optimize space, they are creating opportunities and opening up possibilities to exploit gaps and space using soccer interactions.

Further recommendations and thoughts on implementing CLA include the need to develop a common language that coaches and players can understand without the technical jargon present in the theory underpinning such approaches. There is also the need to reduce coach intervention and feedback. The first feedback a player receives should come directly from the task design. The coach can help nudge self-organization by guiding and shaping player interactions to enable them to adapt toward possible solutions.

SWIMMING

Philippe Hellard

I have a PhD in sport sciences, and I was also a coach at the national swimming center, as well as for the French team. In addition, I headed the research department of the French Swimming Federation for 20 years and was part of the staff for the French swimming team, which won three European championships from 2009 to 2012.

I do not subscribe to a single theoretical framework to support my practice. However, I have found conceptual ideas from cognitive sciences, social interaction, and ecological dynamics to be relevant to how it has informed me about practice. My collaborations with top-level coaches have also provided me with insights; many of them have constructed their own technical model of swimming and used methods of learning based on a mixture of the previously mentioned theoretical frameworks. Those technical models and methods of learning are based on the complexity and the constraints during swimming in comparison to land-based sports. To note, swimming is performed in water, where reducing drag is a key challenge to moving fast. Indeed, when moving in water, drag on the human body is about 780 times larger than the drag involved when moving through air. On the other hand, contrary to the terrestrial locomotion, hands and feet sweep through the water because there is no fixed support in swimming. Moreover, vision is not oriented in the direction of the displacement, and the breathing is constrained. These environmental and task constraints require specific perceptual-motor and physiological adaptation of humans to the aquatic environment. Moreover, my experience with top-level coaches also taught me that we must take into account the performer constraints (e.g., morphological type and physical, physiological, and psychomotor abilities) of the swimmers, and we must adapt our training methods to ensure that we can meet the needs of individual swimmers. From CLA, this is a critical consideration because we must be cognizant of the various interactions among environmental, task, and performer constraints. Internal constraints include the swimmer's strength, buoyancy, fatigue, and anthropometric characteristics, and external constraints include swimming stroke, swimming speed and stroke rate, active drag, and instructions from the coach.

For example, we can consider how fatigue constrains performance at the end of a 100-meter front crawl: the muscular strength of the swimmer decreases by 20% to 40%. The swimmers slow their hand speed during the underwater phase and spend more time in the aerial phase of the cycle without applying high force and generating high power. The relative duration of the arm recovery increases and therefore the interarm coordination is modified. Depending on the level of fatigue and swimming speed, various adaptations of the coordination can emerge, some of which can affect effectiveness or economy of movement effort. In my view, coaches should identify any dysfunctional behavior that may emerge and aim to find functional coordination solutions. Swimmers should learn to adapt their behavior and intentions accordingly. The coach should find ways to invite swimmers to continuously adapt to changing performance contexts (e.g., fatigue, injuries). The key is in manipulating constraints (e.g., training load, swimming speed, time and intensity to reach the task goal) to design suitable training situations and then introduce pacing and instructions to explore new solutions and adapt intention.

In practice, I organize training and performance analysis based on the following:

- I consider fundamental technical principles and not movement form itself.
- I focus on the individual swimmer and do not prescribe a single expected movement form for the swimmer.
- I am attuned to the intentions of the swimmer and what needs to be done to achieve a set target.
- I am mindful of the global performance of the task even though I may be trying to improve one technical aspect of the movement.
- I understand that changing one aspect of the movement can have implications for other parts of the overall movement solution.

SNOWBOARDING

Tom Willmott

I am the head coach of Snow Sports NZ's park and pipe program. Our team includes athletes competing in the freeskiing and snowboarding disciplines of halfpipe, slopestyle, and big air, which are all now part of the Winter Olympics. I have been coaching our national team since 2005 through four Winter Olympic cycles. Our athletes have achieved multiple medals at major events, including World Cups, X-Games and, most recently, two bronze medals at the 2018 Winter Olympics. I consider myself a "pracademic," having completed a Professional Doctorate in Elite Performance from the University of Central Lancashire in England, a master's degree in physical education from the University of Otago in New Zealand, and a bachelor's degree with honors in sports coaching from the University of Wales. I enjoy applying skill acquisition theories to make performance gains in our sport, which is subjectively judged, has a high level of athlete autonomy, and is inherently fun.

In our high-performance program, we usually train individually or in groups of two to four athletes. Our sport is ripe for using ideas from CLA, and the best coaches will constantly manipulate the training environment, the task, and individual factors to maximize learning. One training approach that we often use is derived from a well-known skateboarding game: SKATE, which is based on the basketball game of HORSE. Athletes are pitted against each other, and the first athlete chooses and attempts a certain trick. Once she lands it, the other athletes in the group attempt the same trick. Any of the athletes unable to complete the trick get an S. The next athlete attempts a trick of his choice and the others follow. The game continues with athletes collecting the letters S-K-A-T-E as they fail at trick attempts. Once an athlete has collected all five letters by failing five tricks, she is out. The winner is the last athlete remaining.

This game is a great way to expand an athlete's comfort zone; athletes are bound to learn new tricks or ways of doing things by mirroring their peers and attempting to outperform each other. The coach can set this up and take a backseat, just watching the progression. Or the coach can intervene to specify the environment, challenge athletes further, serve as the judge to decide whether the tricks have been performed exactly as the first performer did, throw in "curve balls" for the athletes to achieve, or simply join in. With a group of highly skilled athletes that possess a large trick repertoire, this game can take some time, but they will be challenged to come up with new and innovative tricks to outdo their peers. This is indeed a great way to challenge the athletes to explore new ways to perform tricks.

While a coach should have a range of games or tools in her tool box, one of the most exciting elements of coaching is devising new games and approaches to challenge specific performance elements and make individual or group gains. We have experimented using long fishing rods to dangle targets in the halfpipe. Athletes work on their amplitude by projecting up into the air at takeoff to try to touch the target with their hand. We have manipulated other task constraints such as using a 3 × 3 grid on jump landings. Athletes play tic-tac-toe to challenge speed judgment and directional control. We use massive airbags to provide a safe and errorless training environment among various other approaches. Sometimes the simplest games or training manipulations are the best.

RUGBY

Richard Shuttleworth

I completed my PhD and studied the role of affordances in elite rugby players from an ecological dynamics perspective. In the past I have worked as a professional coach development manager for England rugby and as a skills acquisition specialist at the Australian Institute of Sport. I also provided support for England's international performance coaches, including England U20's coach, Rory Teague, who won a World Cup.

Analysis of World Cup performances has shown that scoring tries win tournaments. Therefore, in preparation for the 2016 U20 Rugby World Cup, coaches and players worked on an adaptation of Pierre Villepreux's playing model (Deleplace, Bouthier, and Villepreux, 2018) based on principles of play, including go forward, support ball, and support space to pressure the opposition into conceding points. Playing an adaptive game model limits emphasis on preplanning player movements and instead focuses on player's skills and coadaptive behaviors with teammates and opponents (Passos et al., 2008). This approach encourages players to skillfully engage and interact with multiple opportunities for action in a field of relevant affordances (Withagen, Araújo, and de Poel, 2017). There was a deliberate change from a coach-directed environment present in the previous Six Nations tournament to a guided discovery, coach-supportive environment that would introduce players to a relevant part of the affordance field representing the Junior World Cup (JWC) performance niche. Coaches preferred players to solve performance problems themselves and to transfer these skills into solving problems in the JWC, rather than being provided with solutions.

Intelligent performers were key in codesigning new performance-based affordances into training by setting appropriate match-related scenarios to solve in practice or by designing solutions beforehand to problems identified through opposition analysis

(Rietveld and Kiverstein, 2014). Coaches implemented 12v12 scaled (reduced numbers) conditioned games so that decisions had to be made to address positioning in support and committing to the ruck (breakdown in play) due to lack of numbers and opposition threats. Time constraints were imposed on game practices. Intensive game scenarios were created by physically stressing players by inducing intensity peaks representative of, and frequently exceeding, game intensity during critical periods. Coaches manipulated game rules to induce variety in attack and transition. It was key to start skill games with general movement by tactically rolling the ball into spaces giving a tactical advantage, disadvantage, or balance while using game situations to develop principles of play in attack and defense and action-based problems for players to solve. Players had restricted time to practice self-selected preplanned plays (to disorganize defense) while they were physically and mentally stressed, thereby intertwining the training of perception, cognition, and action (Davids, Button, Araújo, Renshaw, and Hristovski, 2006). Regular breakouts into mixed small-sided games (SSGs) encouraged alternative player combinations to explore affordances in central and wider spaces, creating the potential for opponents to invite go-forward opportunities.

The adaptive game model provided the flexibility to solve problems arising from varying playing styles across opposition teams and find solutions to going forward, and this required that the team interact with opponents to solve complex, dynamic problems. Playing with an intent to collectively go forward and perceptually attend to specifying information provided the team with multiple shared affordances in attack (width and depth). Coadaptive behavior during local (subunit) and global (tactical) interactions were identified as key performance skills for adjusting to changes relative to opponents' actions and styles across all five international performances.

TENNIS

Anna Fitzpatrick

I am a doctoral researcher and associate lecturer at Sheffield Hallam University in England. I am also a former professional tennis player and British national champion. My goal is to help bridge the gap between academia and applied practice within my area of sport science and performance analysis in tennis. The work I would like to share is based on my experience of coaching children's tennis.

I first came across Newell's (1986) constraints-led approach while working on my undergraduate degree. Coincidentally, I had just started coaching mini tennis, a scaled version of tennis, with modified court dimensions, ball characteristics, and scoring format. Newell's theory instantly drew me in, allowing me to objectively reflect on both my training as a professional player and my current coaching practice.

Mini tennis was designed to facilitate children's functional movement behaviors and reduce the speed of the game so that their behaviors closely reflect those needed in the adult version of the sport. After a little research I learned that, although versions of mini tennis had been implemented around the world, there was little empirical evidence to suggest that it achieved its intended purpose.

I investigated this concept further (Fitzpatrick, Davids, and Stone, 2018) and identified a fundamental flaw: Mini tennis players performed considerably more forehands than backhands (a ratio of up to 6:1 in favor of the forehand), whereas a ratio of close to 1:1 is typical in adult tennis. I understood that such a disparity was likely to lead to a skill imbalance over time, potentially to the detriment of children's development and progression in the sport. I applied my theoretical understanding of constraints and experiential knowledge of tennis to design three simple manipulations to attempt to ameliorate the asymmetry in players' emergent behaviors through this training intervention (Fitzpatrick et al., 2018):

1. Internal court dimensions
   - During coaching sessions, children are often asked to attempt to perform a forehand when the incoming ball lands to the right of the center line and a backhand when the ball lands to the left of the centerline for right-handed players. It is opposite for left-handed players. I repositioned the centerline slightly to the right of the standard centerline (all players were right-handed) in order to increase the amount of space to the backhand side of the line (see figure 11.2).

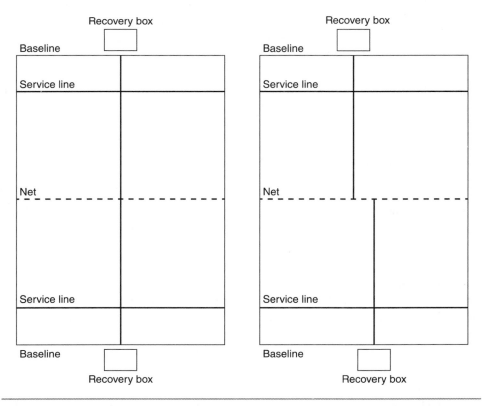

FIGURE 11.2 Recovery box and centerline locations for the control group (left) and experimental group (right).
Provided by Anna Fitzpatrick

2. Recovery box location

- Recovery boxes are often placed behind the center of the baseline to encourage appropriate court positioning. I moved each player's recovery box slightly to the right, directly behind their repositioned centerline, thus increasing the distance between the recovery box and the sideline on the player's backhand side (see figure 11.2). As usual, players were asked to recover to the box after each stroke.

3. Scoring format

- During points-based activities, bonus points were awarded when a player hit a winner or forced her opponent out of position (i.e., created a perturbation) using her backhand.

After 8 weeks (1-hour coaching per week), players were performing 17% more backhands (and 17% fewer forehands), and the forehand-to-backhand ratio corresponded to that of adult tennis (i.e., close to 1:1). The original mini tennis constraints had afforded the children sufficient time to move around the ball and perform a forehand, when a backhand could otherwise be played. Repositioning their centerlines and recovery boxes slightly to the forehand side of the court meant that players were constrained to move a greater distance if they wanted to move around the ball and perform a forehand. Thus, this behavior became less likely to emerge because players were required to adapt and explore different solutions (i.e., active exploration of the backhand stroke).

As well as successfully ameliorating the forehand–backhand asymmetry, the constraint manipulations elicited further favorable emergent behaviors. The children's ability to maintain a rally (i.e., mean rally length) increased to a greater extent than the control group, who were not exposed to the constraint manipulations. They committed fewer backhand errors and were able to create perturbations more often than the control group, using their backhands. Finally, the children's backhand and forehand technical proficiency improved more than those of the control group.

I had expected the manipulations to redress the forehand–backhand asymmetry, reduce the number of backhand errors, and improve players' backhand technique, but I was initially surprised that improvements were also evident in their forehand technique; after all, they were performing 17% fewer forehands. On reflection, however, it became clear. If a player moves around an incoming ball to perform a forehand, particularly when a backhand would be more appropriate, the forehand technique elicited is unlikely to be functional. However, if the constraint manipulations applied here reduced the temptation to move around the ball, the player may be more likely to perform and acquire a more functional action response by electing to pay a backhand instead. So, in facilitating active backhand exploration, the manipulations also reduced the number of technically poor forehands that were performed at times when a backhand would have been more appropriate. Essentially, the players were electing to perform forehands only when the incoming ball was appropriate for that stroke, and they were therefore exhibiting more functional forehand technique.

Overall, my experiences of applying CLA to tennis coaching have been incredibly positive; the model has become embedded within my role as a coach and educator. Designing environments that encourage learners to explore different solutions to problems and observing the effects of carefully considered manipulations can be very rewarding. However, I have also learned that manipulating the learning environment can lead to secondary, potentially contraindicated behaviors. As such, it is vital to plan constraint manipulations thoroughly and holistically and to constantly assess performers' emergent behaviors and prepare to adapt if undesired, dysfunctional behaviors begin to emerge.

Summary

These case studies nicely demonstrate how practices can be designed based on CLA and, more broadly, on the theoretical ideas of ecological dynamics. No emphasis is placed on a prescribed movement solution; instead, the focus is on recognizing that individualized movement solutions are the norm rather than the exception. It is important to recognize that designing effective practices is both an art as well as a science. Several of the case studies allude to the important role that emotion-laden practice has in skill acquisition, and a common emergent theme seems to be the challenge and fun learners experience through CLA. The relevance of both experiential practical knowledge from practitioners coupled with what the theory can offer from CLA is critical. It is apparent that the practice designers played a facilitative role rather than an overly prescriptive role in determining how learning should occur for the students and athletes. Teaching, coaching, and learning are always context and learner dependent. Accounting for learner–environment mutuality is key to understanding why some constraints can be manipulated effectively at some instances but could fail dramatically in others.

Self-Test Questions

1. Choose one of the practice activities described in this chapter and adapt it for the sport or activity of your choice.
2. How might you as a coach design the practice to manipulate task difficulty?
3. How can coaches identify which constraints to manipulate and which to leave alone?
4. From the practitioners profiled in this chapter, which has impressed you the most in terms of his or her application of theoretical ideas and why?

CHAPTER 12

Expertise and Talent Development in Sport

CHAPTER OBJECTIVES

After completing this chapter, you will be able to do the following:

- Explain how learning designs in practice can exploit general and specific transfer to help develop talent
- Associate specific training with near transfer of motor learning and general training with far transfer
- Describe different talent development pathways that include either early specialization in one sport or diversification in multiple sports
- Consider how the interaction of specificity of practice in a given sport with earlier variable nonspecific practice experiences benefits the potential for long-term talent development
- Describe future directions for motor development and skill acquisition research

---

Throughout this book, our challenge has been to clarify theoretical concepts that provide principles for designing effective practice tasks and learning activities to prepare for the numerous demands of competitive performance (Chow, Davids, Button, and Renshaw, 2016). Termed the microstructure of practice (Davids, Renshaw, Pinder, Greenwood, and Barris, 2016; Davids, Güllich, Shuttleworth, and Araújo, 2017), these activities refer to the work of coaches and sports practitioners on an hourly, daily, weekly, and monthly basis to enhance skill and athletic performance. To help athletes achieve their potential, a major task for sports practitioners is to facilitate the learners' ability to perceive and use *affordances* (opportunities for actions) from a rich available landscape (Rietveld and Kiverstein, 2014) matched to their specific capacities, skills, and experience (Davids, Araújo, Seifert, and Orth, 2015).

In this final chapter, we discuss implications of these ideas for transfer of training in relation to talent development. This is undoubtedly a big issue, and it remains a hotly debated topic around the world (e.g., Epstein, 2019; Rea and Lavallee, 2017). To consider this complex issue systematically, we address two primary questions. First, how can an ecological dynamics rationale guide the design of an affordance landscape during practice to facilitate transfer to competitive performance environments in sport? Second, what are the different outcomes of specific and general transfer of training and how might that understanding benefit athletes across the macroscopic timescale of talent development?

Transfer in Learning: Where Does Generality and Specificity of Transfer Originate?

The concept of transfer is central to a discussion of learning design in sport programs focused on athlete development and performance (chapter 7). High-quality practice sessions are high-quality *simulations* of how the learner wants to perform in competition. Put another way, effective learning designs require an understanding of how to transfer learning from a practice environment to a competitive performance environment. At the onset of the previous century, Woodworth and Thorndike (1901) proposed the identical elements theory of transfer. They argued that in successful transfer of learning, elements of a practice task must be tightly coupled to relevant properties (information, tasks, and responses) in a performance task. As we discussed in chapter 7, tasks with *near* transfer are those tasks that share common properties and are likely to incur effective transfer. On the other hand, *far* transfer involves tasks and performance with limited properties that are shared between training and performance environments.

A significant number of empirical studies have looked at the specificity of practice effects. Performance of a practiced task or nearly identical tasks can be improved through designs that emphasize near transfer. Generic, noncontextual training interventions (emphasizing far transfer) have been perceived to have limited benefits, but only if a practitioner is interested in accelerated learning on a specific task. However, the proliferation of learning designs that overemphasize specificity of transfer have raised valid concerns about the effects of early specialization in sports (see Chow, Davids, Shuttleworth, and Araújo, in press). In terms of athlete development over the macroscale of talent development (long term), ecological dynamics has implicated the important role of the more generalized training associated with (far) transfer practice effects (Davids et al., 2017). In this chapter, we discuss the benefits of far transfer effects that lie in athlete enrichment programs to prepare learners for sport specialization later in athletic development (Stone, Stafford, North, Toner, and Davids, 2019; Renshaw et al., 2019).

How Should We Interpret Specificity of Learning in Sport?

In chapter 1, we explained that specifying information variables should be present in practice task designs that seek to faithfully simulate performance conditions. More faithful simulations of a competitive environment during practice have enhanced specificity because of the very specific nature of the information designed into practice tasks, leading to more specific transfer from practice to performance (Chow et al., 2016). Specificity of transfer will enhance the coupling of perception and action, which is fundamental to the accelerated acquisition of skill and expertise in sport (Davids, Button, and Bennett, 2008). Specifying perceptual variables is a term from ecological psychology that is equivalent to the gold standard of information needed to regulate specific actions in sport, such as vision of the takeoff board to regulate run-ups for long jumpers or the position of the umpire at the stumps for cricket bowlers approaching the bowling crease (Greenwood, Davids, and Renshaw, 2016) (see figure 12.1). In traditional approaches to learning design, too much emphasis has been placed on practice tasks structured for the repetitive reproduction of specific *actions*. While specificity of practice is undoubtedly relevant *at the right time* in athlete development, problems related to an overemphasis on specificity of training and practice over extended periods from an early age have been well documented. These concern the physical, psychological, and emotional issues that can emerge in individuals

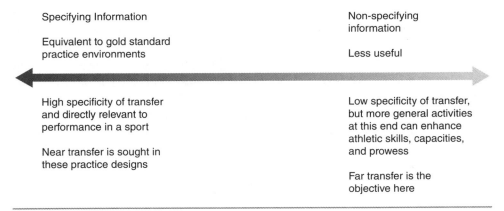

FIGURE 12.1   Methodologies in the microscale of practice and physical activity for enhancing skill acquisition. Traditional practice design has a default mode situated at the highly structured end of the affordance landscape, focusing on direct teaching, coaching, and verbal instructions. Coaches need to focus on learning design and move among different regions of the affordance landscape based on the individual needs of each athlete.

(Davids et al., 2017). Furthermore, it has been proposed that competitive performance in many sports is composed of an athlete self-regulating during interactions with a performance environment (see the Case Study later in this chapter; Renshaw et al., 2019).

The Distinction Between Practicing Actions and Interactions in Sport

In team sports, with active defenders and teammates present, small-sided and conditioned games (SSCGs) provide a more representative context for *interactions* with field markings, spaces, target areas (goal, basket, try line), gaps, and defenders positioned to prevent attackers from gaining an advantage. When practicing a skill in isolation (i.e., when other performers are not present), an athlete tends to focus on rehearsing *actions*. For team sports such as netball, soccer, or basketball, unopposed practice in the absence of a defender, dribbling around cones, passing in static pairs, shooting at a scoring target in isolation, or running in straight lines are all practice activities that reduce the levels of specifying information sources needed to regulate a learner's interactions with a performance environment. The distinction between interactions and actions can be summarized by the presence of relevant others (teammates and opponents) in a practice task design and relevant informational constraints such as line markings, surfaces, target areas, gaps, and specific locations to regulate performance in a performance area.

Prolonged practice of actions under simplified practice task constraints (exemplified by drills in isolation) will lead to slower learning and the formation of less stable and reliable perception–action couplings because athletes learn to rely on nonspecifying information sources such as cones and grid markings. There is also a risk of boredom and lack of enjoyment if practice task design is based for extensive periods on nonspecifying information sources. Some argue there are limited occasions when practice tasks with nonspecifying information sources are warranted. These include very early in learning for a limited amount of time, when an athlete is recovering movement stability after severe injury or illness, and when a coach and athlete want to initiate practice of an innovative performance behavior in an isolated practice context.

Interactive practice task designs contain specifying perceptual variables (chapter 1) for athletes to pick up and use to regulate performance. These information-rich variables could be designed into practice tasks with high specificity of transfer exemplified by the following:

- Opportunities to practice performance behaviors in a simulated competition setting (e.g., diving from a springboard into a pool rather than into a foam pit, climbing on a low rocky outdoor surface rather than on an indoor wall, jumping into a sand pit after a long run-up rather than running through the pit)

- Learning to manipulate sports equipment (such as a ball or stick) with the hands or feet while active defenders are present rather than in isolation

- Boxing against a moving opponent rather than hitting a static heavy bag

- Practicing tactical patterns of play against active defenders in team games rather than using shadow play rehearsal without defenders present; practicing with field or court markings rather than gridlines; and playing against active, moving defenders to denote changing availability of space, passing, or dribbling lines and gaps to exploit or close

- Learning to swim in an outdoor aquatic environment in which currents, flows, eddies, waves, wind, and changes in ambient temperature affect performance rather than in a calm indoor swimming pool with a constant ambient temperature and no effects of currents and water flows

These examples reference the key information sources that need to be available during practice for skill acquisition in different sports and activities. In all these practice environments, sport practitioners need to understand *how* affordances (invitations for interactions) can be designed in the microstructure of practice to make transfer more *specific* (leading to more accelerated athlete development) rather than *general* (leading to slower rates of development). To avoid overemphasizing specificity of training and its potentially negative effects, important questions for practitioners concern (1) when and how in the development of talent may general transfer contribute to enhancing athlete development and performance, and (2) what the potential value of unstructured play and practice experiences in athlete development is.

Finding the Right Balance: Specific and General Transfer in Talent Development

Effective learning designs can enhance talent development processes (in programs that last months and years) by promoting relevant experiences for sport specialization and diversification in developing athletes (Davids et al., 2017). This mix of specific sports training and more generalized experiences of physical activity and sports prevents the problems with early specialization identified in the sport science literature and underpins an athlete's capacity to self-regulate while interacting with constraints of a performance environment. Under highly varying performance contexts, functional behaviors in sport need to vary over the macrotimescale of years and decades as sports evolve, constrained by changes in tactical trends, innovations in equipment and technology, surfaces, rules, and regulations.

These changes to sports are captured in a mix of environmental and task constraints that require athletes to functionally adapt behaviors to achieve intended performance goals. For example, the performance constraints of batting and bowling in cricket test matches, which can last 5 days, differ from the constraints of limited overs cricket matches, e.g., the 20-20 format (lasting a few hours). An athlete's capacity to self-regulate while interacting with task and environmental constraints in different competitive performance constraints is predicated on *dexterity* (adaptive expertise). Bernstein (1967, p. 228; italics in the original) conceptualized dexterity as

> *the ability to find a motor solution for any external situation, that is, to adequately solve any emerging motor problem correctly* (i.e., adequately and accurately), *quickly* (with respect to both decision making and achieving a correct result), *rationally* (i.e., expediently and economically), *and resourcefully* (i.e., quick-wittedly and initiatively).

Exploratory activity is an integral part of human development available to exploit. Babies, for example, spend a lot of time in infancy exploring their environment to learn about affordances of objects and surfaces and other people (Gibson, 1988). Continuous exploratory interactions with the environment, termed "experiments on the world" by E.J. Gibson (1988, p. 7) are typical in human development and lead to *general* skills that can be harnessed in later athletic development when people start to specialize in competitive sport.

Ecological dynamics emphasizes that expertise in sport can be developed by enhancing an athlete's dexterity (through interactions) and not by the optimization of a specific movement pattern through repetition and rehearsal (see Glazier and Davids, 2009). Interactive practice designs could enhance an athlete's expertise in specific sports by helping her to become more adaptive, innovative, and flexible in coping with variations in task and environmental constraints (Chow et al., 2016; Davids et al., 2008; Davids et al., 2017). For example, in the sport of rugby union, a challenging decision is when to kick the ball upfield to create attacking opportunities and when to run at a defense with ball in hand. Designing an affordance field in practice encourages athletes to coadapt their decisions and actions to what an opposition's defensive pattern *invites* at any moment. This example indicates how the microstructure of practice should abound with problem-solving scenarios (promoting athlete interactions) as implied by Bernstein's (1967) ideas on developing dexterity.

CASE STUDY: EMERGENCE OF EXPERT PERFORMANCE FROM INTERACTIONS

Bob Beamon's Incredible Leap

In the 1968 Olympics, held at Mexico City, Bob Beamon set the world record in the long jump with a mark of 29 feet, 2.25 inches (8.90 m), breaking the existing record by 21.6 inches (55 cm). This created an abrupt transition in the incremental progress that had served as the hallmark for track and field world records (see figure 12.2). Beamon's record lasted an astonishing 23 years, until Mike Powell of the United States jumped 29 feet, 4.25 inches (8.95 m) in 1991. After Powell, the best jumps of the year ranged from 27 feet, 4.75 inches (8.35 m) (the same mark as the 1965 world record that Beamon broke in 1968) and 28 feet, 8 inches (8.74 m). Analysis of background information provides important insights on the cognitions, emotions, and actions of this elite performer while he was self-regulating during an Olympic final. It also describes the state of the environment in explaining the emergence of this special performance outcome (see Araújo and Davids, 2018).

Bob Beamon was 22 years old and before the Olympics had a personal best jump of 27 feet, 4.75 inches (8.33 m) after just 5 years of traditional training in long jump. Before he started to participate in track and field, he played basketball. In the final of the Olympic Games of 1968, he jumped alongside Ralph Boston of the United States, who was a coholder of the world record at the time of 27 feet, 4.75" (8.35 m) and was 29 years old; Lynn Davies of England, who was a former Olympic champion and 26 years old; and Igor Ter-Ovanesyan of the Soviet Union, who was the other world record coholder and 30 years old. The competition was intense. Beamon later recorded his last thought (main intention) before hitting the board as "Don't foul." He also noted that "my mind was blank during the jump. I was as surprised as anybody at the distance" (Araújo and Davids, 2018, p.146). After Beamon, Klaus Beer of East Germany (26 years old) was second in 26 feet, 10.5 inches (8.19 m), Ralph Boston was third in 26 feet, 9.25 inches (8.16 m), Ter-Ovanesyan was fourth in 26 feet, 7.75 inches (8.12 m), and Lynn Davies was ninth in 26 feet, 0.5 inches (7.94 m). Mexico City is 7,382 feet (2,250 m) above sea level. At this altitude, the thinner air provides less air resistance. Mexico City is also farther from the center of the Earth than most athletics venues, so gravitational

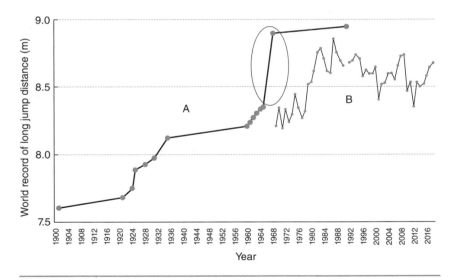

FIGURE 12.2 *(a)* Official world records in the long jump over time. *(b)* Best marks of the year from 1968 to 1991 and after the 1991 world record. The ellipsis signals the abrupt transition from previous world records to Beamon's 29 feet, 2.25 inches (8.90 m) jump in 1968 (black marker).

Reprinted by permission from D. Araújo and K. Davids. "The (Sport) Performer-Environment System as the Base Unit in Explanations of Expert Performance," *Journal of Expertise* 1, no. 3 (2018): 144-154.

forces are smaller. According to Allain (2012) these conditions can provide an advantage to long jumpers of up to 2.75 inches (7 cm), compared to a corresponding jump under more typical ambient temperatures and pressure at sea level.

The night before the final, Beamon had been concerned with personal problems. He had lost his scholarship at the University of Texas at El Paso shortly before his departure for Mexico City for participating, with other African American students, in a boycott of a track and field meet against Brigham Young University, a Mormon institution whose racial policies bothered them. He also was not getting along with his young wife. "Everything was wrong," he said. "So I went into town and had a shot of tequila. Man, did I feel loose" (Araújo and Davids, 2018, p.146).

Implications for Talent Development in Sport

Beamon's experience at the 1968 Olympics suggests that no single variable, located solely in the performer or environment, can explain the emergence of expert performance. Expert performance cannot be acquired or possessed by individuals (or be located in an environment), but instead it emerges from the specific interactions of system components. To performance analysts in track and field, Beamon was a slim, long-legged athlete, who used an inconsistent technique. This means that on some occasions his technique facilitated good performances and in others it did not. The influence of altitude, weather conditions, his weight-to-strength ratio, his psychological state because of the agitation of the previous night, the intense competition with the other high-level athletes, the fast runway of Estadio Olímpico, and his past variable sport practice experiences may have coalesced to support his performance at that single moment. All these constraints may have influenced his actions to self-organize in a performance that cannot be explained by referring to any single component of performance. Self-organization tendencies can result in an emergent system solution that is richer and more functional than the sum of the parts. When a system establishes a state (e.g., Beamon performing the long jump task in the Estadio Olímpico in Mexico City), as a result of the dynamical interactions among several interacting system components, self-organization tendencies causally facilitate such a state.

Application

In track and field events like long jumping, small performance variations include properties of the track, air resistance (altitude), and weather conditions such as ambient temperature and wind velocity and direction (McCosker, Renshaw, Greenwood, Davids, and Gosden, 2019). When running to place the foot on a target, an athlete's kinematics and kinetics of locomotion vary during each attempt, and indeed from stride to stride (captured in variables like speed, stride lengths, lower-limb joint angles, and dynamics). Moreover, optical information from objects located near the takeoff board as well as light reflected from the takeoff board itself can help skilled jumpers regulate their gait during the approach phase. These variables reflect information sources that can be designed into practice tasks to provide opportunities for athletes to self-regulate during interactions. Key constraints that can be manipulated include competition scenarios (reflecting intentions, psychological and emotional states, peer competition), different training locations (varying altitude, weather conditions, fast or slow runways, wind directions and variations).

Specialization and Diversification Pathways to Talent Development

In ecological dynamics, the development of talented athletes is, in part, the result of their responsiveness to the design, types and modes of activities experienced during practice, and play (Davids et al., 2017; Coutinho, Mesquita, and Fonseca, 2016). Research has revealed three main talent development pathways from junior (childhood) to senior (elite) athletic performance: **early specialization**, **early diversification**, and **early engagement** (Côté, Baker, and Abernethy, 2007). These typical pathways are characterized by the amount of time spent in the microstructure of practice and competitive play *in a single sport* (typically characterized by rehearsal and repetition of dedicated movement patterns) or *more than one sport* (characterized by opportunities to explore many different actions in varied performance contexts). The early specialization pathway involves a large amount of intense practice (often deliberate) in a specific sport domain, a low amount of play activity in one sport, and experience of relatively few, or no other sports, in the early years (table 12.1). Research on the early-specialization pathway has identified numerous negative consequences of undertaking many hours in

Table 12.1 Three Potential Talent Development Pathways

	Early specialization	Early diversification	Early engagement
Range of sports and activities practiced	Low (largely focused on one sport)	High initially, decreasing after puberty	High
Amount of deliberate play	Low	High initially, decreasing after puberty	High
Potential for skill transfer	Low	High	High
Likely outcomes	• High level of sports performance • Increased potential of burnout or injury • Reduced enjoyment of sport	• High level of sports performance • Enhanced fitness and health • High enjoyment of sport	• Recreational level of participation • Enhanced fitness and health • High enjoyment of sport

specific practice dominated by one sport during early development. These consequences include burnout, dropout, overuse injuries, and lower levels of enjoyment and attainment (e.g., Baker, Cobley, and Fraser-Thomas, 2009). The early diversification pathway involves the sampling of a diverse range of activities until approximately puberty after which the learner begins to specialize in his preferred sport. Côté and colleagues (2007) suggest that this pathway favors the long-term health of the junior athlete in contrast to early specialization. Finally, early engagement also involves diverse sampling of activities early in childhood followed by engagement at a recreational level in activities that are more focused on fitness and health, as opposed to sport performance.

Güllich and colleagues have shown that early specialization in sport may result in performance success at the *junior* level (e.g., Güllich, Kovar, Zart, and Reimann, 2016). They also have shown that an early-diversification approach, which avoids many documented problems of early specialization, is associated with success at the *senior* level (supported by data from Coutinho et al., 2016). An early-diversification pathway involves exposure to different affordances designed into the microstructure of practice in varied sports, often including large amounts of unstructured play and practice in the early years. Research on this developmental experience has shown that children who follow this pathway may engage in at least six sports in addition to their main sport. The early-diversification pathway is thought to lead to enhanced sport expertise because high levels of intrinsic motivation arise from increased levels of fun and enjoyment and deeper engagement. It has been suggested that the physical competencies and physiological conditioning developed through diversified sport experiences in childhood may be transferable, although the exact nature of these transfer processes are still being conceptualized in ecological dynamics (Ng and Button, 2018).

Key Concept

What Is Talent?

Talent has been conceptualized in ecological dynamics as an enhanced functional relationship between an individual and a performance environment (Araújo et al., 2010). Talent can be enhanced through practice designs that emphasize *discovery* and *exploitation* of functional action solutions in a varied field of affordances to improve an individual's performance effectiveness. In talent development programs, coaches could work with skill acquisition specialists to design dedicated practice environments replete with specific affordances that can be perceived and used depending on the needs of an individual athlete. Learning designs that enhance the functionality of an athlete in a sport performance environment will develop the talent of an athlete.

Including *specifying information* in practice designs for developing athletes is vital to their ability to learn how to regulate their actions in particular performance environments. For example, Seifert, Wattebled, Herault, and colleagues (2014) showed that experts explored combinations of subtle kinesthetic, haptic, acoustic, and visual information from tool use (i.e., ice axes, crampons, ropes and screws, etc.) to regulate their actions while climbing, whereas beginners relied predominantly on one source of information. Hence by using a variety of specifying and nonspecifying information sources, skilled performers can exploit general transfer processes to determine more appropriate actions for a wider range of situations.

It should be noted that using combinations of specifying and nonspecifying information can lead to slower skill acquisition because most learning situations do not mimic the target skill closely enough. For example, practicing on an indoor climbing wall can provide opportunities to improve strength, agility, and flexibility; to scan a surface for affordances of holds; to support and transfer weight on holds of different shapes and sizes; and to grasp a hold with the fingers or hands. These underlying capacities can enrich the skills of a climber so that he can transfer some of these general processes to meet the challenge of ascending a vertical surface on a mountain.

This climbing example suggests that the microstructure of practice could be designed to contain both specifying and nonspecifying information for regulating an athlete's functional performance behaviors (see figure 12.1). Generalized skill transfer occurs when more-fundamental processes and activities (which can enhance perception, action, and cognitions) are experienced in learning. These include processes involved in information detection; fundamental movement behaviors like agility, balance, and general athleticism; and mental attributes like resilience, self-regulation, and decision making under pressure. Transfer of specificity and generality can be induced through continuous interactions between athletes and the equipment, space, other individuals, and events during sport training and practice (Davids et al., 2017).

How can specific and general transfer be used in learning designs to enhance fundamental actions like throwing and catching? More generally, practicing ball skills such as throwing and catching may be transferable to performing specific movement skills in different team games. For example, elements of throwing actions exist in the volleyball overhead serve, badminton overhead clear, and pitching in baseball. Later in skill development, throwing and catching can be embedded in small-sided conditioned games (e.g., 3v3 net-barrier game of throwing and catching within a badminton court) to facilitate use of a wider range of affordances in the microstructure of practice. These more general task constraints can facilitate the interactions of players in other invasion games (such as soccer, field and ice hockey, and rugby union). The affordances used in these dynamic game environments may be transferable to other types of invasion games that have the same underlying tactical requirements.

To summarize, practice task designs that contain specifying information lead to effective, efficient, and rapid (specific) transfer of training, whereas nonspecifying information may enhance athletic development and lead to more general transfer of training (Chow et al., 2016). The use of moderately informative information sources is likely to lead to more *general* transfer in learning when a coach uses nonspecifying information as part of sport practice. Greater specificity in transfer occurs when highly informative variables are included in later practice designs. Designing practice tasks that offer more general transfer early in learning may prevent the problems caused when children specialize too early (through too much exposure to intense performance contexts in practice). Additionally, more general transfer may help develop core perceptual and cognitive skills and movement competencies, which can be harnessed later during more specialized training and performance.

Structured and Unstructured Play and Practice in the Transfer of Training in Sport

This information about the rich mixture of generality and specificity of transfer highlights the value of **unstructured play** in practice experiences, and this concept has figured strongly in the development of many elite athletes (Coutinho et al., 2016; Forsman et al., 2016). Structured practice can be described as deliberately organized sport-specific activities involving typical elements such as supervision, coaches, officials, specialized equipment, and time limits. Because structured practice is designed to enhance performance in a particular targeted sport or activity, the assumed transfer to other activities is not particularly high, although that depends on the principles discussed in the previous section. In contrast, unstructured experiences have been defined as activities that are not led by a coach or adult, but emerge from interactions between learners who organize their own activities and games (Davids et al., 2017). Unstructured learning experiences expose athletes to diverse affordances that support athletic development such as opportunities for enjoyment and fun, affiliation with peers, expression of leadership, resilience, and autonomy. They also afford possibilities to explore creative and innovative action performance solutions away from the critical evaluations by adults, teachers, coaches, and parents (Davids et al., 2017).

Although structured and unstructured play and practice activities are not completely divergent, more research is needed to understand how benefits of unstructured practice and play can be exploited for use in formal athlete development programs (Uehara, Button, Falcous, and Davids, 2018). Powerful motor learning principles underpin the design of these important developmental activities. This conceptualization can help sport practitioners to support developing athletes in designing their own fields of affordances in play environments (ensuring rich variations in use of space, equipment, textures, surfaces, objects, and markings while promoting fun and enjoyment). Our improving understanding of how unstructured play augments motor development can support practitioners' appreciation of the crucial value of these activities in the development of children's athleticism, physical literacy, and movement competencies (Roberts, Newcombe, and Davids, 2019).

Important questions that need to be resolved in future research concern how much time developing athletes should spend in specialized training and in more generalized, unstructured athletic experiences (Forsman et al., 2016). When specialization and more fundamental generalized athletic experiences should occur is also a relevant issue in ecological dynamics. Arne Güllich and colleagues (2016) have shown that diversified engagement in different sports occurred very early for many world-class performers and typically lasted until late adolescence (mean ages in different studies was 16 to 20 years).

Data from research by Güllich and colleagues (2016) suggest that variable learning experiences (diversified engagement) early in athletic development can boost learning effectiveness during later specialized training and specific practice programs. This approach requires a subtle balance of learning experiences in which specialized training occurs at a later stage in athlete development after being supported by generalized experiences as part of an athlete enrichment program.

Physical Literacy as the Foundation to a Healthy Life Span

As we approach the conclusion of this book, it seems appropriate to speculate briefly on the future and comment on some of the significant issues facing skill acquisition. In chapters 6 through 10, we discussed how the digital age, in which 21st century society has taken its first steps, presents both opportunities and challenges for humans in terms of motor skill acquisition. Indeed, technological advances such as the Internet, social media, remote sensing devices, and virtual reality simultaneously enhance the capacity for learners to explore their environment and search for movement solutions while at the same time provide distractions and potential barriers to physical activity. The emerging influence of these important macrolevel environmental factors can be linked to the numerous talent development pathways discussed earlier in this chapter. More so than ever before, learners have the freedom and ability to explore their movement capacity with or without guidance, yet we remain uncertain about how or whether to deviate from traditional practice strategies. This uncertainty reinforces our conviction echoed throughout these pages that robust, empirically informed theory should underpin skill acquisition practice.

Physical inactivity has been described as perhaps the greatest threat to global health in the 21st century (Blair, 2009). Physical literacy is a multidimensional concept that includes movement competence and psychological, social, and emotional constructs that underpin a person's ability to engage in physical activity throughout her life span (Whitehead, 2010). A physically literate individual has the competency to transfer perceptual-motor skills across different activities and has the desire and confidence to express himself through movement. Cairney, Dudley, Kwan, Bulten, and Kriellaars (2019) place physical literacy at the center of a conceptual model that links physical activity and life span health (figure 12.3). However, considerable work is still needed to increase our understanding of physical literacy and its implications for practitioners. Indeed, the measurement of physical literacy is by no means a simple matter, let alone knowing how to develop it in the future (see Giblin, Collins, and Button, 2014).

Throughout this book we have outlined the theoretical ideas of ecological dynamics, and we conclude that they are well aligned with emerging models of motor development such as physical literacy and the athletic skills model (ASM). The ASM advocates that early play and practice experiences of children should involve participation in "multisports," which involve a variety of movement experiences and activities (Wormhoudt, Savelsbergh, Teunissen, and Davids, 2018). In the multisport stage, children need to be exposed to a

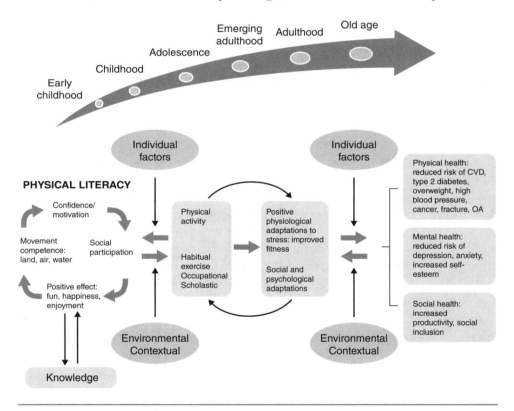

FIGURE 12.3 Conceptual model linking physical literacy, physical activity, and health (CVD: cardiovascular disease, OA: osteoarthritis).

Reprinted by permission from J. Cairney et al., "Physical Literacy, Physical Activity and Health: Toward an Evidence-Informed Conceptual Model," *Sports Medicine* 49, no 3 (2019): 371-383. doi:10.1007/s40279-019-01063-3

variety of learning contexts that will support their athletic development while they explore functional movement behaviors that enhance psychological, physical, and physiological capacities (i.e., physical literacy). These ideas are consistent with those expounded in a nonlinear pedagogy that advocate a nuanced balance between specificity of practice and enrichment of each learner's capacities for perception, action, and using cognition (see Chow, Davids, Shuttleworth, and Araújo, in press).

In talent development programs, enriched athlete capacities provide **effectivities** that can support the perception and use of affordances in a performance landscape. The holistic development of individual athletes, when interacting with different fields of the performance landscape, supports their functional coadaptation with environmental and task constraints (see Araújo et al., 2010). It's important not to underestimate the value of the pleasure and fun associated with the constant exploration of movement competencies while experiencing new individual action possibilities. During play in different performance contexts, engagement in multiple sports and physical activities has the potential to increase the long-term motivation for practice, essential in elite specialized-sports programs (Wormhoudt et al., 2018). The ASM suggests that through multisport experiences, effectivities (movement competencies) can be transferred into five major components of performance: stability, flexibility, agility, power, and endurance. At an early age, children should experience fun and enjoyment in *playing* a variety of physical activities and sports that may not seem to specifically relate to a target team sport (Wormhoudt et al., 2018). These suggestions lie in stark contrast to the philosophies espoused by many high-performance sport academies in which early identification of talented athletes and punishing specialized practice regimens seem to be an acceptable cost of success.

As the human population continues to grow and medical treatments of life-threatening conditions improve, the consequences of an aging population will inevitably come under the spotlight. As the model depicted in figure 12.3 suggests, successful aging requires renewed attention to the role and types of physical activity that humans engage in as they get older (see also Chodzko-Zajko, Schingel, and Park, 2008). From a skill acquisition perspective, it will be interesting to see more work done with older-adult learners in an attempt to disprove the notion that "you can't teach an old dog new tricks." A consistent message throughout this book has been that although it can be difficult to get people to try new ways of doing things (particularly if they have been doing something in a particular way for a long time), it is well worth the effort.

Summary

This chapter discussed an ecological dynamics rationale for how learning designs in practice can exploit general and specific transfer in the development of athlete expertise and talent in sport. Research suggests that interaction of specificity of practice in a given sport with earlier variable nonspecific practice experiences (for athlete enrichment) benefits the potential for long-term development of excellence. We highlighted and identified how affordance landscapes could be exploited in learning designs using examples from elite and subelite sports practice. We explained the roles that specifying and nonspecifying information incorporated into learning environments play, and we discussed implications of enhancing athlete dexterity in skill acquisition. We outlined important issues for skill acquisition research to address both now and in the future. And finally, we discussed the intriguing concept of physical literacy and how it might be linked to physical activity and long-term health.

Self-Test Questions

1. Explain how a learning rock climber might benefit from the inclusion of specifying and nonspecifying information in the microstructure of practice activities.

2. Which is better for the development of a young athlete and why: early specialization in a sport or diversification in a range of sports?

3. How does the physical literacy of a child influence her likely physical activity in adulthood and ultimately her long-term health as she ages?

4. Considering the likely directions of skill acquisition research, list the three most interesting questions about learning that you would like to see addressed.

GLOSSARY

action readiness—During learning, an individual develops a tight coupling with opportunities for action available in an affordance landscape. The strength of this coupling leads to action readiness in which an individual is primed to act on affordances that are detected and used during performance. Action readiness can be enhanced in well-designed practice programs.

action fidelity—The extent to which the movement demands of a real-world task are simulated or re-created in a practice situation. Reduced action fidelity means that movement responses are downplayed, or not accurately reproduced, in the simulated activity.

adaptability—The capacity of the movement system to adapt to constraints to consistently satisfy a task goal.

affective learning—When motor learning acknowledges and simulates the emotional response that is typically associated with performance of an activity.

affordance—James Gibson (1979) coined the term affordance to describe the properties of the environment that provide opportunities or possibilities for action for each individual with appropriate capacities for these interactions. More recently, Rob Withagen and colleagues have proposed that affordances may be described as invitations for action to capture how individuals may detect and select between affordances. The relationship with an affordance depends on the strength of the coupling developed between an athlete and an affordance.

Archimedes force—The buoyancy or lift force that is created when a solid object is immersed or partially immersed in a fluid. Archimedes principle suggests that this force is equal to the weight of the fluid that the object displaces.

athlete intelligence—An intelligent performer in work, education, sport, and military contexts is a highly adaptive individual who has developed the capacity to make decisions and solve problems in complex and dynamic situations.

attractors—Stable and functional patterns of organization exhibited by open systems.

attunement—The process through which performers learn to identify and use information that is relevant to guiding their actions.

autonomy—An individual's sense of control and freedom of choice. One of the three key constructs of self-determination theory.

behavioral information—Information that helps to specify how an action should be performed. For example, handles on implements and doors help to specify how the implement or door should be grasped and moved.

bifurcation—A split in the movement system's phase space where at least two qualitatively different patterns are available.

calibration—The mapping of an individual's personal capabilities with the demands presented by a task.

coadaptation—In evolutionary biology, the term coadaptation refers to how one species adapts its structure and function to changes in another species or the environment. At the shorter timescale of learning, development, and performance, individual athletes can use the process of coadaptation to modify their behaviors with respect to a practice environment designed by a coach or the tactical activities of a competitor.

coadaptive moves—How performers move to ensure a successful fit between environment and task demands. Such actions are made in response to perceived changes in the performance situation.

cognition—The active maintenance of a robust performer–environment system, achieved by coordinated perception and action.

competence—An individual's sense that she can accomplish a given outcome to a required standard. One of the three key constructs of self-determination theory.

complex adaptive systems—Complexity refers to systems that technically have two or more interacting parts (often in the scale of hundreds, thousands, etc.). It is the potential for interaction between the components that can lead to the emergence of rich behaviors as these systems adapt to changes in a performance environment. Sensitivity to surrounding information and the potential to form synergies between system components (coordinative structures that can help these systems achieve performance goals) are two defining features of a complex adaptive system.

consolidation—Describes the process by which a movement pattern's stability is enhanced in the absence of physical practice (e.g., during postpractice or sleep). Referred to in cognitive psychology as off-line learning.

coordinative structure—Bernstein's description of the initial solutions employed by the human movement system early in the learning process.

creativity—The discovery and creation, through exploratory behaviors, of unconventional affordances.

decision making—Transitions in the course of action.

degeneracy—The ability of elements that are structurally different to perform the same function or yield the same output.

degrees of freedom (dfs)—Independent components of a system that can fit together in many different ways.

department of methodology—The integration of the work of a group of practitioners in sport who cooperate under a unified theoretical framework to support athlete learning and preparation for high-performance sport. This group of practitioners could include, for example, coaches, strength and conditioning trainers, psychologists, health and well-being specialists, performance analysts, clinical and rehabilitation specialists, administrators. and managers.

dynamical systems—Systems that change over time, transiting through different states of organization, such as stability, instability, and metastability, are considered dynamical in nature. The behaviors of such systems can be mathematically modeled to describe their states of organization as well as their transitory trajectories.

early diversification—One of numerous talent development pathways. In early diversification, during childhood, the learner is exposed to a variety of diverse sports and physical activities until approximately puberty. At this time, the learner begins to specialize in his preferred sport.

early engagement—Involves a diverse sampling of activities early in childhood followed by engagement in recreational-level activities that are more focused on fitness and health than on sport performance.

early specialization—Typically involves a large amount of intense practice (often deliberate) in a specific sport, a low amount of play activity in one sport, and experience of relatively few or no other sports in the early years.

ecological dynamics—A theoretical framework that combines key ideas from ecological psychology and dynamical systems theory.

effectivities—Movement capabilities such as strength, power, and agility that enable an individual to move competently.

embodied cognitions—Cognitive processing that implicitly accounts for an individual's action capabilities.

emergence—The spontaneous occurrence of behavior from interacting constraints that was not predetermined or planned.

environmental constraints—Sociocultural aspects and physical variables such as ambient light, temperature, altitude, gravity, or Archimedes force.

exosystem (e.g., demography)—The exosystem comprises the settings in which the developing person participates. It is one of four nested sublevels in the bioecological model of development.

foveal vision—The small portion of the visual field in which discrimination of detailed features is possible. The fovea is the small region on the retina that provides the highest level of visual acuity.

general transfer—When intrinsic and task dynamics do not cooperate closely, and the individual athlete has the potential to further develop only general capacities that exist as part of her current intrinsic dynamics.

habituation—Refamiliarization with an activity or environment that facilitates subsequent performance. Habituation effects lead to more variable performance than when habituation is no longer necessary.

informational constraints—The various forms of energy flowing through the system.

intentionality—Directedness or purposiveness toward objects, events, or people.

invariants—Features of the informational array that remain static, or fixed, despite changes of the perceiver's perspective or of the perceived feature relative to the individual.

knowledge about—Perception mediated by language, pictures, and other symbols, which may constrain future action.

knowledge of—Perception based on information to control action, which constrains actual action.

macrosystem (e.g., national historical context)—The broadest level of the bioecological model of development, it contains the links between all the other sublevels.

mesosystem (e.g., training facility)—Entails interrelations emerging between two or more settings containing the developing person. When people move between microsystems, they create a mesosystem. It is one of four nested sublevels in the bioecological model of development.

metastability—The capacity of a system to adopt multiple stable states with equal probability. Metastability provides the movement system with inherent flexibility to adapt to different situations, scenarios, and challenges.

microsystem (e.g., family support)—The innermost level of the bioecological model in which the developing person is directly involved in relationships with the immediate physical, social, and symbolic features of his environment.

moment of inertia—The resistance of an object to movement. It is calculated as a product of the mass of an implement and the radius of rotation.

nonlinear pedagogy—A pedagogical approach with specific design principles that emphasizes exploratory learning based on the understanding of how goal-directed behaviors emerge from the interaction of constraints.

nonlinearity and nonproportionality—Relates to cause–effect proportionality. In a linear system, a large change in a system's behavior needs to be preceded by a large change in its cause or causes, while in nonlinear systems, a large change in causes may produce both minor or large qualitative changes in the system's behavior, but also multistability.

nonspecifying information—Information that doesn't directly specify or isn't coupled to a movement response. While potentially unreliable, such information can be used to anticipate how best to move or how to adapt in a given situation.

observational learning—The process whereby a learner adopts or replicates the behavioral patterns and actions of others as a direct consequence of observing those behaviors.

occlusion—To block, mask, or restrict vision in some form.

optic array—The informational field that is detectable by an organism with sensory features that are attuned to optics (e.g., humans with healthy visual system).

organismic constraints—A person's characteristics. They could be structural, such as genotypes and anthropometric parameters, or functional, such as motivations and emotions.

pelada—An informal, pickup style of soccer practiced (among other places) in Brazil. Literally translated from Portuguese as *naked soccer*.

perceptual-motor landscape—A manifold of all the possible movement possibilities that are available to an individual.

perturbation—A disruption to the human movement system.

phase space—All the hypothetical states of organization into which a dynamical system can evolve.

physical constraints—Structural or functional characteristics of the human movement system.

pluripotentiality—The potential involvement or removal of biomechanical degrees of freedom to increase stability or flexibility of the system. Describes how one synergetic structure can be mapped to many functions.

prospective control—How actors adapt behavior in advance to the physical and informational constraints in the environment.

relatedness—An individual's sense of social fit, of belonging to a group or network. One of the three key constructs of self-determination theory.

relative motion—The specific spatiotemporal relationships among and within limbs, as well as the organization of the performer's limbs relative to the surrounding environment.

representative design—An important concept introduced by ecological psychologist Egon Brunswick (1956), it refers to the degree to which a sampled environment is representative of the original that it simulates.

scanning procedure—An experimental technique through which the learner's intrinsic dynamics can be revealed.

self-organization—The capacity for a complex system to organize itself into regular, ordered patterns when placed under constraint. No central organizer or stored plan is necessary for self-organization to occur.

shared affordances—Invitations for actions perceived by all members of a team. Being able to perceive and use shared affordances as they emerge in performance supports coordination of actions in team synergies formed in a local-to-global direction.

shift—A subtle alteration in pattern dynamics that can accompany learning. In contrast to a global and marked change (bifurcation), shifts are typically gradual and smaller in magnitude.

similarity—A multidimensional term relating to the degree of similarity between tasks. Could be expressed in terms of movement similarity, task complexity, or proximity of the tasks in the perceptual-motor workspace.

specific transfer—Can emerge under practice task constraints in which existing intrinsic dynamics of an individual *cooperate* with the dynamics of a new task to be learned, facilitating emergence of successful performance behaviors.

specifying information—Information that can be used to directly regulate an action.

stable—Robustness to external or internal perturbations.

synergies—The formation of functional relationships between components of a complex adaptive system. In team sports, synergies underpin the coordination of functional group actions by players to achieve task goals, as captured by principles of play (e.g., to advance toward the opposition scoring area or to defend space in a collective way).

task constraints—Task goals, specific rules associated with an activity, implements or tools, surfaces, ground areas, and boundary markings such as pavements, barriers, line markings, and posts.

task simplification—Systematically modifying the task constraints to provide a challenging task without sacrificing representative learning design (i.e., preserving important information–movement couplings).

tau—The symbol denoted to an optical invariant that may contribute to the control and coordination of interceptive actions. Tau represents the optical information specified by the relative rate of expansion of the visual solid angle enclosed by these contours of a perceived object or surface.

transitions—Changes from one state of coordination to the other that are not intentional but that result from the self-organizing properties of the motor system.

unstructured play—Practice activities that are not supervised or guided by a coach, teacher, or referee (official).

REFERENCES

Abbott, A., Button, C., Pepping, G. J., and Collins, D. (2005). Unnatural selection: Talent identification and development in sport. *Nonlinear Dynamics, Psychology, and Life Sciences, 9*(1), 61-88. Retrieved from http://www.ncbi.nlm.nih.gov/pubmed/15629068

Ackerman, P. L. (2014). Nonsense, common sense, and science of expert performance: Talent and individual differences. *Intelligence, 45*, 6-17.

Adé, D., Seifert, L., Gal-Petitfaux, N., and Poizat, G. (2017). Artefacts and expertise in sport: An empirical study of ice climbing. *International Journal of Sport Psychology, 48*(1), 82-94.

Allain, R. (2012, August 4). Olympic physics: Air density and Bob Beamon's crazy-awesome long jump. *Wired*. Retrieved from https://www.wired.com/2012/08/long-jump-air-density.

Anderson, J. R. (2014). *Rules of the Mind*. New York: Psychology Press.

Andersson, J., and Maivorsdotter, N. (2017). The 'body pedagogics' of an elite footballer's career path–analysing Zlatan Ibrahimovic's biography. *Physical Education and Sport Pedagogy, 22*(5), 502-517.

Andy, C. Y., Wong, T. W. L., and Masters, R. S. W. (2017). Examining motor learning in older adults using analogy instruction. *Psychology of Sport and Exercise, 28*, 78-84.

Appelbaum, L. G., and Erickson, G. (2018). Sports vision training: A review of the state-of-the-art in digital training techniques. *International Review of Sport and Exercise Psychology, 11*(1), 160-189.

Araújo, D., and Davids, K. (2009). Ecological approaches to cognition and action in sport and exercise: Ask not only what you do, but where you do it. *International Journal of Sport Psychology, 40*(1), 5-37.

Araújo, D., and Davids, K. (2011). What exactly is acquired during skill acquisition? *Journal of Consciousness Studies, 18*(3-4), 7-23.

Araújo, D., and Davids, K. (2015). Towards a theoretically-driven model of correspondence between behaviours in one context to another: Implications for studying sport performance. *International Journal of Sport Psychology, 46,* 268-280.

Araújo, D., and Davids, K. (2016a). Team synergies in sport: Theory and measures. *Frontiers in Psychology, 7*, 1449. doi:10.3389/fpsyg.2016.01449

Araújo, D., and Davids, K. (2016b). Towards a theoretically-driven model of correspondence between behaviours in one context to another: Implications for studying sport performance. *International Journal of Sport Psychology, 47*(1), 745-757.

Araújo, D., and Davids, K. (2018). The (sport) performer-environment system as the base unit in explanations of expert performance. *Journal of Expertise, 1*(3), 144-154.

Araújo, D., Diniz, A., Passos, P., and Davids, K. (2014). Decision making in social neurobiological systems modeled as transitions in dynamic pattern formation. *Adaptive Behavior, 22*(1), 21-30.

Araújo, D., Davids, K., Bennett, S., Button, C., and Chapman, G. (2004). Emergence of sport skills under constraints. In A. M. Williams and N. J. Hodges (Eds.), *Skill acquisition in sport: research, theory and practice* (pp. pp. 409-433). London: Routledge, Taylor and Francis.

Araújo, D., Davids, K., Cordovil, R., Ribeiro, J., and Fernandes, O. (2009). How does knowledge constrain sport performance? An ecological perspective. In D. Araujo, H. Ripoll, and M. Raab (Eds.), *Perspectives on cognition and action in sport* (pp. 119-131). Hauppauge, NY: Nova Science Publishers.

Araújo, D., Davids, K., and Hristovski, R. (2006). The ecological dynamics of decision making in sport. *Psychology of Sport and Exercise, 7*, 653-676.

Araújo, D., Davids, K., and Passos, P. (2007). Ecological validity, representative design, and correspondence between experimental task constraints and behavioral setting: Comment on Rogers, Kadar, and Costall (2005). *Ecological Psychology, 19*(1), 69-78.

Araújo, D., Fonseca, C., Davids, K. W., Garganta, J., Volossovitch, A., Brandão, R., and Krebs, R. (2010). The role of ecological constraints on expertise development. *Talent Development and Excellence, 2*(2), 165-179.

Araújo, D., Hristovski, R., Seifert, L., Carvalho, J., and Davids, K. (2017). Ecological cognition: Expert decision-making behaviour in sport. *International Review of Sport and Exercise Psychology*, 1-25. doi:10.1080/1750984X.2017.1349826

Araújo, D., and Kirlik, A. (2008). Towards an ecological approach to visual anticipation for expert performace in sport. *International Journal of Sport Psychology, 39*, 157-165.

Ashford, D., Bennett, S. J., and Davids, K. (2006). Observational modeling effects for movement dynamics and movement outcome measures across differing task constraints: A meta-analysis. *Journal of Motor Behavior, 38*(3), 185-205.

Baker, J., Côté, J., and Abernethy, B. (2003). Learning from the experts: Practice activities of expert decision makers in sport. *Research Quarterly for Exercise and Sport, 74*(3), 342-347.

Baker, J., Cobley, S., and Fraser-Thomas, J. (2009). What do we know about early sport specialization? Not much! *High Ability Studies, 20*(1), 77-89.

Baldwin, T. T., and Ford, J. K. (1988). Transfer of training: A review and directions for future research. *Personnel Psychology, 41*(1), 63-105.

Bandura, A. (1969). *Principles of Behaviour Modification*. New York: Rinehart-Winston.

Barab, S. A., and Roth, W. M. (2006). Curriculum-based ecosystems: Supporting knowing from an ecological perspective. *Educational Researcher, 35*(5), 3-13.

Barnett, S. M., and Ceci, S. J. (2002). When and where do we apply what we learn?: A taxonomy for far transfer. *Psychological Bulletin, 128*(4), 612-637.

Barris, S., Farrow, D., and Davids, K. (2014). Increasing functional variability in the preparatory phase of the takeoff improves elite springboard diving performance. *Research Quarterly for Exercise and Sport, 85*(1), 97-106.

Beak, S., Davids, K., and Bennett, S. J. (2002). Child's play: Children's sensitivity to haptic information in perceiving affordances of rackets for striking a ball. In J. E. Clark and J. Humphreys (Eds.), *Motor development: Research and reviews,* Vol. 2 (pp. 120-141). Reston, VA: NASPE.

Beamon, R. and Beamon, M. W. (1999). *The man who could fly: The Bob Beamon story*. Columbus, MS: Genesis Press.

Beilock, S. L., Carr, T. H., MacMahon, C., and Starkes, J. L. (2002). When paying attention becomes counterproductive: Impact of divided skill-focused attention on novice and experienced performance of sensorimotor skills. *Journal of Experimental Psychology: Applied, 8*(1), 6-16.

Bennett, S. J., Button, C., Kingsbury, D., and Davids, K. (1999). Manipulating visual information constraints during practices enhances the acquisition of catching skill in children. *Research Quarterly for Exercise and Sport, 70*(3), 220-232.

Berkinblit, M. B., Feldman, A. G., and Fukson, O. I. (1986). In search of the theoretical basis of motor control. *Behavioral and Brain Sciences, 9*(4), 626-638.

Bernstein, N. A. (1967). *The coordination and regulation of movements*. London, UK: Pergamon Press.

Bernstein, N. A. (1996). On dexterity and its development. In M.L. Latash and M.T. Turvey (Eds.), *Dexterity and its development* (pp. 1-244). Mahwah, NJ: Lawrence Erlbaum Associates.

Berthouze, L., and Lungarella, M. (2004). Motor skill acquisition under environmental perturbations: On the necessity of alternate freezing and freeing of degrees of freedom. *Adaptive Behavior, 12*(1), 47-64.

Bingham, G. P. (1988). Task-specific devices and the perceptual bottleneck. *Human Movement Science, 7*(2-4), 225-264.

Bizzi, E., and Ajemian, R. (2015). A hard scientific quest: Understanding voluntary movements. *Daedalus, 144*(1), 83-95.

Blair, S. N. (2009). Physical inactivity: The biggest public health problem of the 21st century. *British Journal of Sports Medicine, 43*(1), 1-2.

Bootsma, R. J. (1998). *Ecological movement principles and how much information matters.* Paper presented at the Second Symposium of the Institute for Fundamental and Clinical Human Movement Sciences, Amsterdam.

Bootsma, R. J., Bakker, F. C., van Snippenberg, F. J., and Tdlohreg, C. W. (1992). The effects of anxiety on perceiving the reachability of passing objects. *Ecological Psychology, 4,* 1-16.

Bootsma, R. J., and van Wieringen, P. C. W. (1990). Timing an attacking forehand drive in table tennis. *Journal of Experimental Psychology: Human Perception and Performance, 16,* 21-29.

Boschker, M. S., Bakker, F. C., and Michaels, C. F. (2002). Memory for the functional characteristics of climbing walls: Perceiving affordances. *Journal of Motor Behavior, 34*(1), 25-36. doi:10.1080/00222890209601928

Bradshaw, E. J., and Sparrow, W. A. (2002). The effects of target length on the visual control of step length for hard and soft impacts. *Journal of Applied Biomechanics, 18*(1), 57-73. doi:10.1123/jab.18.1.57

Broderick, M. P., and Newell, K. M. (1999). Coordination patterns in ball bouncing as a function of skill. *Journal of Motor Behavior, 31,* 165-188.

Bronfenbrenner, U. (1979). *The ecology of human development.* Cambridge, MA: Harvard University Press.

Bronfenbrenner, U. (1995). Developmental ecology through space and time: A future perspective. In P. Moen, G. H. Elder Jr., and K Luscher (Eds.), *Examining lives in context: Perspectives on the ecology of human development* (pp. 619-647). Washington DC: American Psychological Association.

Bronfenbrenner, U. (2005). *Making human beings human: Bioecological perspectives on human development.* Thousand Oaks, California: Sage.

Bronfenbrenner, U., and Morris, P. A. (1998). The ecology of developmental processes. In W. D. R. M. Lerner (Ed.), *Handbook of child psychology: Theoretical models of human development* (pp. 993-1028). Hoboken, NJ: John Wiley and Sons.

Bronfenbrenner, U., and Morris, P. A. (2006). The bioecological model of human development. In *Handbook of child psychology: Theoretical models of human development,* Vol. 1, 6th ed. (pp. 793-828). Hoboken, NJ: John Wiley and Sons.

Brunswik, E. (1956). *Perception and the representative design of psychological experiments* (2nd ed.). Berkeley, CA: University of California Press.

Buszard, T., Farrow, D., Reid, M., and Masters, R. S. (2014). Modifying equipment in early skill development: A tennis perspective. *Research Quarterly for Exercise and Sport, 85*(2), 218-225.

Button, C. (2016). Aquatic locomotion: Forgotten fundamental movement skills? *New Zealand Physical Educator, 49*(1), 8-10.

Button, C., Bennett, S. J., and Davids, K. (2001). Grasping a better understanding of the intrinsic dynamics of rhythmical and discrete prehension. *Journal of Motor Behavior, 33*(1), 27-36.

Button, C. and Davids, K. (2004). Acoustic information for timing. In: H. Hecht and G.J.P. Savelsbergh (Eds.). *Time-to-Contact. Advances in Psychology series.* (pp.355-370) Amsterdam, Holland: Elsevier.

Button, C., Lee, M. C. Y., Mazumder, A. D., Tan, C. W. K., and Chow, J. Y. (2012). Empirical investigations of nonlinear motor learning. *The Open Sports Sciences Journal, 5*(1), 49-56.

Button, C., MacMahon, C., and Masters, R. S. W. (2011). Keeping it together: Motor control under pressure. In D. Collins, A. Abbott, and H. Richards (Eds), *Performance psychology: A practitioners' Guide* (pp. 177-190) . London: Elsevier.

Button, C., Orth, D., Davids, K., and Seifert, L. (2018). The influence of hold regularity on perceptual-motor behaviour in indoor climbing. *European Journal of Sport Science, 18*(8), 1090-1099.

Button, C., and Pepping, G. J. (2002). Enhancing skill acquisition in golf: Some key principles. Retrieved from www.coachesinfo.com/category/golf

Cairney, J., Dudley, D., Kwan, M., Bulten, R., and Kriellaars, D. (2019). Physical literacy, physical activity and health: Toward an evidence-informed conceptual model. *Sports Medicine, 49*(3), 371-383.

Camponogara, I., Rodger, M., Craig, C., and Cesari, P. (2017). Expert players accurately detect an opponent's movement intentions through sound alone. *Journal of Experimental Psychology Humam Perception and Performance, 43*(2), 348-359. doi:10.1037/xhp0000316

Carello, C., Thuot, S., and Turvey, M. T. (2000). Aging and the perception of a racket's sweet spot. *Human Movement Science, 19*, 1-20.

Carlson, R. (1988). The socialization of elite tennis players in Sweden: An analysis of the players' backgrounds and development. *Sociology of Sport Journal, 5*(3), 241-256.

Carvalho, J., Araújo, D., Travassos, B., Esteves, P., Pessanha, L., Pereira, F., and Davids, K. (2013). Dynamics of players' relative positioning during baseline rallies in tennis. *Journal of Sports Sciences, 31*(14), 1596-1605.

Carvalho, J., Araújo, D., Travassos, B., Fernandes, O., Pereira, F., and Davids, K. (2014). Interpersonal dynamics in baseline rallies in tennis. *International Journal of Sports Science and Coaching, 9*(5), 1043-1056. doi:10.1260/1747-9541.9.5.1043

Chemero, A. (2009). *Radical embodied cognition.* In Cambridge, MA: MIT Press.

Chiviacowsky, S. (2014). Self-controlled practice: Autonomy protects perceptions of competence and enhances motor learning. *Psychology of Sport and Exercise, 15*(5), 505-510.

Chodzko-Zajko, W., Schwingel, A., and Chae Hee Park, H. P. (2009). Successful Aging: The Role of Physical Activity. *American Journal of Lifestyle Medicine, 3*(1), 20-28. https://doi.org/10.1177/1559827608325456.

Chollet, D., Chalies, S., and Chatard, J. C. (2000). A new index of coordination for the crawl: Description and usefulness. *International Journal of Sports Medicine, 21*(01), 54-59.

Chollet, D., and Seifert, L. (2011). Inter-limb coordination in the four competitive strokes. In L. Seifert, D. Chollet, and I. Mujika (Eds.), *The world book of swimming: From science to performance* (pp.153-172). Hauppauge, New York: Nova Science Publishers.

Chow, H. M., Kaup, B., Raabe, M., and Greenlee, M. W. (2008). Evidence of fronto-temporal interactions for strategic inference processes during language comprehension. *NeuroImage, 40*(2), 940-954. doi:10.1016/j.neuroimage.2007.11.044

Chow, J. Y. (2010). Insights from an emerging theoretical perspective in motor learning for physical education. In Chia, M. and Chiang, J. (Eds.) *Sport Science in the East: Reflections, Issues and Emergent Solutions*, (pp. 59–78). Taiwan: World Scientific. InEds.

Chow, J. Y. (2013). Nonlinear learning underpinning pedagogy: Evidence, challenges, and implications. *Quest, 65*(4), 469-484.

Chow, J. Y., and Atencio, M. (2014). Complex and nonlinear pedagogy and the implications for physical education. *Sport, Education and Society, 19*(8), 1034-1054.

Chow, J. Y., Button, C., Davids, K., and Koh, M. (2007). Variation in coordination of a discrete multiarticular action as a function of skill level. *Journal of Motor Behavior, 39*(6), 463-479.

Chow, J. Y., Davids, K., Button, C., and Koh, M. (2006). Organization of motor system degrees of freedom during the soccer chip: An analysis of skilled performance. *International Journal of Sport Psychology, 2-3*, 207-229.

Chow, J. Y., Davids, K., Button, C., and Koh, M. (2008). Coordination changes in a discrete multi-articular action as a function of practice. *Acta Psychologica, 127*(1), 163-176.

Chow, J. Y., Davids, K., Button, C., and Rein, R. (2008). Dynamics of movement patterning in learning a discrete multiarticular action. *Motor Control, 12*, 219-240

Chow, J. Y., Davids, K., Button, C., and Renshaw, I. (2016). *Nonlinear Pedagogy in Skill Acquisition: An introduction.* Oxon, UK: Routledge: Taylor and Francis.

Chow, J. Y., Davids, K. W., Button, C., Renshaw, I., Shuttleworth, R., and Uehara, L. A. (2009). Nonlinear pedagogy: Implications for teaching games for understanding (TGfU). In T. Hopper, A. J. Butler, and B. Storey (Eds.), *TGfU: Simply good pedagogy: Understanding a complex challenge* (pp. 131-143). Vancouver, British Columbia, Canada: Physical and Health Education (PHE) Canada.

Chow, J. Y., Davids, K., Button, C., Shuttleworth, R., Renshaw, I., and Araujo, D. (2006). Nonlinear pedagogy: A constraints-led framework for understanding emergence of game play and movement skills. *Nonlinear Dynamics, Psychology, and Life Sciences, 10*(1), 71-103.

Chow, J. Y., Davids, K., Button, C., Shuttleworth, R., Renshaw, I., and Araújo, D. (2007). The role of nonlinear pedagogy in physical education. *Review of Educational Research, 77*(3), 251-278.

Chow, J. Y., Davids, K., Hristovski, R., Araújo, D., and Passos, P. (2011). Nonlinear pedagogy: Learning design for self-organizing neurobiological systems. *New Ideas in Psychology, 29*(2), 189-200.

Chow, J. Y., Davids, K. W., Renshaw, I., and Button, C. (2013). The acquisition of movement skill in children through nonlinear pedagogy. In J. Cote and E. Lidor (Eds), *Conditions of children's talent development in sport* (pp. 41-59). Morgantown, WV: Fitness Information Technology.

Chow, J. Y., Davids, K., Shuttleworth, R., and Araújo, D. (In Press). Ecological Dynamics and transfer from practice to performance in sport. In N. Hodges and M. Williams (Eds.), *Skill Acquisition in Sport, Third Edition* (pp. 1-20). London: Routledge.

Chow, J. Y., Koh, M., Davids, K., Button, C., and Rein, R. (2013). Effects of different instructional constraints on task performance and emergence of coordination in children. *European Journal of Sport Science* (ahead-of-print), 1-9.

Chow, J. Y., I. Renshaw, Button, C., Davids, K., and Tan, C. W. K. (2013). Effective learning design for the individual: A nonlinear pedagogical approach in physical education. In: A. Ovens, T. Hopper and J. Butler. (Eds.) *Complexity Thinking In Physical Education: Reframing Curriculum, Pedagogy and Research.* (pp. 121-134) London, Routledge.

Clark, J. E. (1995). On becoming skillful: Patterns and constraints. *Research Quarterly for Exercise and Sport, 66,* 173-183.

Clarke, D., and Crossland, J. (1985). *Action systems: An introduction to the analysis of complex behaviour.* London: Methuen.

Cordier, P., Dietrich, G., and Pailhous, J. (1996). Harmonic analysis of a complex motor behavior. *Human Movement Science, 15*(6), 789-807.

Cordovil, R., Araújo, D., Pepping, G.-J., and Barreiros, J. (2015). An ecological stance on risk and safe behaviors in children: The role of affordances and emergent behaviors. *New Ideas in Psychology, 36,* 50-59. doi:https://doi.org/10.1016/j.newideapsych.2014.10.007

Correia, V., Araújo, D., Duarte, R., Travassos, B., Passos, P., and Davids, K. (2012). Changes in practice task constraints shape decision-making behaviours of team games players. *Journal of Science and Medicine in Sport, 15*(3), 244-249.

Correia, V., Carvalho, J., Araújo, D., Pereira, E., and Davids, K. (2019). Principles of nonlinear pedagogy in sport practice. *Physical Education and Sport Pedagogy, 24*(2), 117-132. doi:10.1080/1 7408989.2018.1552673

Côté, J., Baker, J., and Abernethy, B. (2007). Practice and play in the development of sport expertise. *Handbook of Sport Psychology, 3,* 184-202.

Côté, J., Macdonald, D. J., Baker, J., and Abernethy, B. (2006). When "where" is more important than "when": Birthplace and birthdate effects on the achievement of sporting expertise. *Journal of Sports Sciences, 24*(10), 1065-1073.

Court, M. L., Bennett, S. J., Williams, A. M., and Davids, K. (2002). Local stability in coordinated rhythmic movements: Fluctuations and relaxation times. *Human Movement Science, 21*(1), 39-60.

Court, M. L. J., Bennett, S. J., Williams, A. M., and Davids, K. (2005). Effects of attentional strategies and anxiety constraints on perceptual-motor organisation of rhythmical arm movements. *Neuroscience Letters, 384*(1-2), 17-22.

Coutinho, P., Mesquita, I., and Fonseca, A. M. (2016). Talent development in sport: A critical review of pathways to expert performance. *International Journal of Sports Science and Coaching, 11*(2), 279-293.

Craig, C. (2013). Understanding perception and action in sport: how can virtual reality technology help? *Sports Technology, 6*(4), 161-169.

Croft, J., Button, C., and Dicks, M. (2010). Visual strategies of sub-elite cricket batsmen in response to different ball velocities. *Human Movement Science, 29*(5), 751-763.

d'Arripe-Longueville, F., Gernigon, C., Huet, M.-L., Cadopi, M., and Winnykamen, F. (2002). Peer tutoring in a physical education setting: Influence of tutor skill level on novice learners' motivation and performance. *Journal of Teaching in Physical Education, 22*(1), 105-123.

d'Arripe-Longueville, F., Gernigon, C., Huet, M.-L., Winnykamen, F., and Cadopi, M. (2002). Peer-assisted learning in the physical activity domain: Dyad type and gender differences. *Journal of Sport and Exercise Psychology, 24*(3), 219-238.

Daly, R. M., Bass, S. L., and Finch, C. F. (2001). Balancing the risk of injury to gymnasts: How effective are the counter measures? *British Journal of Sports Medicine, 35*(1), 8-18.

Davids, K. (2000). Skill acquisition and the theory of deliberate practice: It ain't what you do it's the way that you do it! Commentary on Starkes, J. "The road to expertise: Is practice the only determinant?" *International Journal of Sport Psychology, 31*, 461-465.

Davids, K., and Araújo, D. (2010). The concept of 'Organismic Asymmetry' in sport science. *Journal of Science and Medicine in Sport, 13*(6), 633-640. doi:10.1016/j.jsams.2010.05.002

Davids, K., Araújo, D., Correia, V., and Vilar, L. (2013). How small-sided and conditioned games enhance acquisition of movement and decision-making skills. *Exercise and Sport Sciences Reviews, 41*(3), 154-161. doi:10.1097/JES.0b013e318292f3ec

Davids, K., Araújo, D., Hristovski, R., Passos, P., and Chow, J. Y. (2012). Ecological dynamics and motor learning design in sport. In M. Williams and N. Hodges (Eds.), *Skill acquisition in sport: Research, theory and practice* (2nd ed.) (pp. 112-130). London, Routledge.

Davids, K., Araújo, D., Hristovski, R., Serre, N. B., Button, C., and Passos, P. (2013). *Complex systems in sport: Routledge research in sport and exercise science* (Book 7). New York, NY: Routledge.

Davids, K., Araújo, D., Seifert, L., and Orth, D. (2015). Expert performance in sport: An ecological dynamics perspective. In J. Baker and D. Farrow (Eds.), *Routledge handbook of sport expertise* (pp. 130-144). New York, NY: Routledge/Taylor and Francis Group.

Davids, K., and Baker, J. (2007). Genes, environment and sport performance - why the nature-nurture dualism is no longer relevant. *Sports Medicine, 37*(11), 961-980.

Davids, K., Button, C., Araújo, D., Renshaw, I., and Hristovski, R. (2006). Movement models from sports provide representative task constraints for studying adaptive behavior in human movement systems. *Adaptive Behavior, 14*(1), 73-95.

Davids, K., Button, C., and Bennett, S. J. (2008). *Dynamics of skill acquisition: A constraints-led approach*. Champaign, IL: Human Kinetics.

Davids, K., Gullich, A., Shuttleworth, R., and Araújo, D. (2017). *Understanding environmental and task constraints on talent development: Analysis of micro-structure of practice and macro-structure of development histories*. In J. Baker, S. Cobley, J. Schorer, and N Wattie (Eds.), *Routledge handbook of talent identification and development in sport*. Routledge International Handbooks (pp. 192-206). Abingdon, UK: Routledge.

Davids, K., Kingsbury, D., Bennett, S. J., and Handford, C. (2001). Information-movement coupling: Implications for the organisation of research and practice during acquisition of self-paced extrinsic timing skills. *Journal of Sports Sciences, 19*, 117-127.

Davids, K., Renshaw, I., Pinder, R., Greenwood, D., and Barris, S. (2016). The role of psychology in enhancing skill acquisition and expertise in high performance programmes. In S. T. Cotterill, G. Breslin, and N. Weston (Eds.), *Applied sport and exercise psychology: Practitioner case studies*. (pp.241-260). London: Routledge.

Davids, K., Savelsbergh, G. J. P., Bennett, S. J., and van der Kamp, J. (2002). *Interceptive actions in sport: Information and movement*. London: Routledge, Taylor and Francis.

Davids, K., Williams, J. G., and Williams, A. M. (2005). *Visual perception and action in sport*. New York, NY: Routledge.

Davis, B., and Sumara, D. (2006). Complexity and Education: Inquiries into Learning. *Teaching, and Research*. Mahwah, New Jersey, London: Lawrence Erlbaum Associates.

de Bruin, L. R. (2018). Evolving regulatory processes used by students and experts in the acquiring of improvisational skills: A qualitative study. *Journal of Research in Music Education, 65*(4), 483-507.

De Maeght, S., and Prinz, W. (2004). Action induction through action observation. *Psychological Research, 68*(2-3), 97-114.

de Wit, M. M., de Vries, S., van der Kamp, J., and Withagen, R. (2017). Affordances and neuroscience: Steps towards a successful marriage. *Neuroscience and Biobehavioral Reviews, 80*, 622-629. doi:https://doi.org/10.1016/j.neubiorev.2017.07.008

Deci, E. L., and Ryan, R. M. (2000). The "what" and "why" of goal pursuits: Human needs and the self-determination of behavior. *Psychological Inquiry, 11*(4), 227-268.

Deleplace, M., Bouthier, D., and Villepreux, P. (Eds.). (2018). *René Deleplace. Du Rugby de Mouvement à un Projet Global Pour l'EPS et les STAPS*. Villeneuve d'Ascq. Presses universitaires du Septentrion.

Dewey, J. (1896). The reflex arc concept in psychology. *Psychological Review, 3*(4), 357-370. doi:10.1037/h0070405

Dicks, M., Button, C., and Davids, K. (2010). Examination of gaze behaviors under in situ and video simulation task constraints reveals differences in information pickup for perception and action. *Attention Perception and Psychophysics, 72*(3), 706-720. doi:10.3758/app.72.3.706

Diedrichsen, J., White, O., Newman, D., and Lally, N. (2010). Use-dependent and error-based learning of motor behaviors. *Journal of Neuroscience, 30*(15), 5159-5166.

Duarte, R., Araújo, D., Folgado, H., Esteves, P., Marques, P., and Davids, K. (2013). Capturing complex, non-linear team behaviours during competitive football performance. *Journal of Systems Science and Complexity, 26*(1), 62-72.

Dunwoody, P. T. (2009). Theories of truth as assessment criteria in judgment and decision making. *Judgment and Decision Making, 4*(2), 116-125.

Edelman, G. M., and Gally, J. A. (2001). Degeneracy and complexity in biological systems. *Proceedings of the National Academy of Sciences of the United States of America, 98*(24), 13763-13768.

Ehrlich, P. R. (2000). *Human natures: Genes, cultures, and the human prospect*. Washington, D.C.: Island Press.

Epstein, D. (2013). *The Sports Gene: Inside the Science of Extraordinary Athletic Performance*. Yellow Jersey Press: London.

Epstein, D. (2019). *Range: Why Generalists Triumph in a Specialized World*. Riverhead Books: New York.

Esteves, P., Silva, P., Vilar, L., Travassos, B., Duarte, R., Arede, J., and Sampaio, J. (20156). Space occupation near the basket shapes collective behaviours in youth basketball. *Journal of Sports Sciences, 34*(16), 1557-1563.

Fajen, B. R., Riley, M. A., and Turvey, M. (2009). Information, affordances, and the control of action in sport. *International Journal of Sport Psychology, 40*(1), 79-107.

Farrow, D. (2013). Practice-enhancing technology: A review of perceptual training applications in sport. *Sports Technology, 6*(4), 170-176.

Fenoglio, R. (2003). The Manchester United 4 v 4 pilot scheme for U-9's part II: The analysis. *Insight: FA Coaches Association Journal*, 21-24.

Fink, P. W., Foo, P. S., and Warren, W. H. (2009). Catching fly balls in virtual reality: A critical test of the outfielder problem. *Journal of Vision, 9*(13), 14-14. doi:10.1167/9.13.14

Fitch, H. L., Tuller, B., and Turvey, M. T. (1982). The Bernstein perspective: III. Tuning of coordinative structures with respect to perception. In J. A. S. Kelso (Ed.), *Human motor behavior: An introduction* (pp. 271-282). Hillsdale NY: LEA.

Fitzpatrick, A., Davids, K., and Stone, J. A. (2018). Effects of scaling task constraints on emergent behaviours in children's racquet sports performance. *Human Movement Science, 58*, 80-87.

Forsman, H., Gråstén, A., Blomqvist, M., Davids, K., Liukkonen, J., and Konttinen, N. (2016). Development of perceived competence, tactical skills, motivation, technical skills, and speed and agility in young soccer players. *Journal of Sports Sciences, 34*(14), 1311-1318.

Fox, P. W., Hershberger, S. L., and Bouchard, T. J. (1996). Genetic and environmental contributions to the acquisition of a motor skill. *Nature, 384*, 356-358.

Gandevia, S., Allen, G. M., Butler, J. E., and Taylor, J. L. (1996). Supraspinal factors in human muscle fatigue: Evidence for suboptimal output from the motor cortex. *The Journal of Physiology, 490*(2), 529-536.

Gauthier, G. M., Martin, B. J., and Stark, L. W. (1986). Adapted head-and-eye-movement responses to added-head inertia. *Aviation, Space and Environmental Medicine, 57*(4), 336-342.

Giblin, S., Collins, D., and Button, C. (2014). Physical literacy: Importance, assessment and future directions. *Sports Medicine, 44*(9), 1177-1184. doi:10.1007/s40279-014-0205-7

Gibson, J. J. (1966). *The senses considered as perceptual systems.* Boston, MA: Houghton Mifflin.

Gibson, J. J. (1979). *The ecological approach to visual perception.* Boston, MA: Houghton Mifflin.

Gibson, E. J. (1988). Exploratory behavior in the development of perceiving, acting, and the acquiring of knowledge. *Annual Review of Psychology, 39*, 1-41.

Gibson, E. J. (1994). *An odyssey in learning and perception.* Cambridge, MA: MIT Press.

Glaveanu, V., Lubart, T., Bonnardel, N., Botella, M., de Biaisi, P. M., Desainte-Catherine, M., . . . Zenasni, F. (2013). Creativity as action: Findings from five creative domains. *Frontiers in Psychology, 4*, 176. doi:10.3389/fpsyg.2013.00176

Glazier, P. S., and Davids, K. (2009). Constraints on the complete optimization of human motion. *Sports Medicine, 39*(1), 15-28.

Gleick, J. (1987). *Chaos.* London: William Heinemann Ltd.

Gobet, F. (2015). *Understanding Expertise: A Multi-Disciplinary Approach.* London: Macmillan International Higher Education.

Gordon, D. M. (2007). Control without hierarchy. *Nature, 446,* 143. doi:10.1038/446143a

Greenwood, D., Davids, K., and Renshaw, I. (2012). How elite coaches' experiential knowledge might enhance empirical research on sport performance. *International Journal of Sports Science and Coaching, 7*(2), 411-422.

Greenwood, D., Davids, K., and Renshaw, I. (2016). The role of a vertical reference point in changing gait regulation in cricket run-ups. *European Journal of Sport Science, 16*(7), 794-800.

Guadagnoli, M., and Lee, T. D. (2004). Challenge point: A framework for conceptualizing the effects of various practice conditions in motor learning. *Journal of Motor Behavior, 36*, 212-224.

Guerin, S., and Kunkle, D. (2004). Emergence of constraint in self-organized systems. *Nonlinear Dynamics, Psychology and Life Sciences., 8*, 131-146.

Guignard, B., Button, C. Davids, K. and Seifert, L. (in press). Education of foundational movement patterns to enhance self-regulation in aquatic environments: An ecological dynamics approach. *European Journal of Physical Education.*

Guignard, B., Rouard, A., Chollet, D., Hart, J., Davids, K., and Seifert, L. (2017). Individual-environment interactions in swimming: The smallest unit for analysing the emergence of coordination dynamics in performance? *Sports Medicine, 47*(8), 1543-1554. doi:10.1007/s40279-017-0684-4

Güllich, A. (2018). Sport-specific and non-specific practice of strong and weak responders in junior and senior elite athletics–A matched-pairs analysis. *Journal of Sports Sciences, 36*(19), 2256-2264.

Güllich, A., Kovar, P., Zart, S., and Reimann, A. (2016). Sport activities differentiating match-play improvement in elite youth footballers–a 2-year longitudinal study. *Journal of Sports Sciences, 13*(3), 207-215. http://dx.doi.org/10.1080/02640414.2016.1161206.

Hadlow, S. M., Panchuk, D., Mann, D. L., Portus, M. R., and Abernethy, B. (2018). Modified perceptual training in sport: A new classification framework. *Journal of Science and Medicine in Sport, 21*(9), 950-958. doi:https://doi.org/10.1016/j.jsams.2018.01.011

Haken, H. (1996). *Principles of brain functioning*. Berlin: Springer.

Haken, H., Kelso, J. A. S., and Bunz, H. (1985). A theoretical model of phase transitions in human hand movements. *Biological Cybernetics, 51*, 347-356.

Harris, L. R., and Jenkin, M. (1998). *Vision and action*. Cambridge, UK: Cambridge University Press.

Harrison, H. S., Turvey, M. T., and Frank, T. D. (2016). Affordance-based perception-action dynamics: A model of visually guided braking. *Psychological Review, 123*(3), 305-323. doi:10.1037/rev0000029

Hasan, H., Davids, K., Chow, J. Y., and Kerr, G. (2017). Changes in organisation of instep kicking as a function of wearing compression and textured materials. *European Journal of Sport Science, 17*(3), 294-302.

Hasan, Z., and Thomas, J. S. (1999). Kinematic redundancy. In M. D. Binder (Ed.), *Progress in brain research* (Vol. 123). Amsterdam: Elsevier.

Haugeland, J. (1991). Representational Genera. In W.Ramsay, S.P.Stich, D.E.Rumelhart (Eds.) *Philosophy and Connectionist Theory. (pp.61-90)*. Hillsdale, New Jersey: Lawrence Erlbaum Associates Inc.

Haywood, K. M., and Getchell, N. (2005). *Life span motor development*. Champaign, IL: Human Kinetics.

Headrick, J., Renshaw, I., Davids, K., Pinder, R. A., and Araújo, D. (2015). The dynamics of expertise acquisition in sport: The role of affective learning design. *Psychology of Sport and Exercise, 16*, 83-90.

Heft, H. (2013). Foundations of an ecological approach to psychology. In S. D. Clayton (Ed.), *The Oxford handbook of environmental and conservation psychology* (pp. 11-40). Oxford, UK: Oxford University Press.

Hodges, N. J., and Franks, I. M. (2001). Learning a coordination skill: Interactive effects of instruction and feedback. *Research Quarterly for Exercise and Sport, 72*(2), 132-142.

Hodges, N. J., and Franks, I. M. (2002). Modelling coaching practice: The role of instruction and demonstration. *Journal of Sports Sciences, 20*, 793-811.

Hofer, S. B., Mrsic-Flogel, T. D., Bonhoeffer, T., and Hübener, M. (2006). Prior experience enhances plasticity in adult visual cortex. *Nature Neuroscience, 9*(1), 127.

Horn, R., Williams, A. M., and Scott, M. A. (2002). Visual search strategy, movement kinematics and observational learning. *Journal of Sports Sciences, 20*, 253-269.

Hristovski, R., Davids, K., Araújo, D., and Button, C. (2006). How boxers decide to punch a target: Emergent behaviour in nonlinear dynamical movement systems. *Journal of Science and Medicine in Sport, 5*(CSSI), 60-73.

Hristovski, R., Davids, K., Araújo, D., and Passos, P. (2011). Constraints-induced emergence of functional novelty in complex neurobiological systems: A basis for creativity in sport. *Nonlinear Dynamics, Psychology, and Life Sciences, 15*(2), 175-206.

Hulteen, R. M., Morgan, P. J., Barnett, L. M., Stodden, D. F., and Lubans, D. R. (2018). Development of foundational movement skills: A conceptual model for physical activity across the lifespan. *Sports Medicine, 48*(7), 1533-1540. doi:10.1007/s40279-018-0892-6

Ibáñez-Gijón, J., and Jacobs, D. M. (2012). Decision, sensation, and habituation: A multi-layer dynamic field model for inhibition of return. *PloS one, 7*(3), e33169.

Issurin, V. B. (2013). Training transfer: Scientific background and insights for practical application. *Sports Medicine, 43*(8), 675-694.

Jacobs, D. M., and Michaels, C. F. (2007). Direct learning. *Ecological Psychology, 19*(4), 321-349.

Janelle, C. M., Barba, D. A., Frehlich, S. G., Tennant, L. K., and Cauraugh, J. H. (1997). Maximizing feedback effectiveness through videotape replay and a self-controlled learning environment. *Research Quarterly for Exercise and Sport, 68*, 269-279.

Jeannerod, M. (1981). Intersegmental co-ordination during reaching at natural visual objects. In J. Long and A. Baddeley (Eds.), *Attention and Performance,* Vol. IX (pp. 153-172). Hillsdale, NJ: Lawrence Erlbaum Associates.

Jedlickova, K., Stockton, D. W., Chen, H., Stray-Gundersen, J., Witkowski, S., Ri-Li, G., ... and Prchal, J. T. (2003). Search for genetic determinants of individual variability of the erythropoietin response to high altitude. *Blood Cells, Molecules, and Diseases, 31*(2), 175-182.

Jeon, H., and Lee, S.-H. (2018). From neurons to social beings: Short review of the mirror neuron system research and its socio-psychological and psychiatric implications. *Clinical Psychopharmacology and Neuroscience, 16*(1), 18.

Jess, M., Atencio, M., and Thorburn, M. (2011). Complexity theory: Supporting curriculum and pedagogy developments in Scottish physical education. *Sport, Education and Society, 16*(2), 179-199.

Johansson, G. (1973). Visual perception of biological motion and a model for its analysis. *Perception and Psychophysics, 14*, 201-211.

Johnston, K., Wattie, N., Schorer, J., and Baker, J. (2018). Talent identification in sport: A systematic review. *Sports Medicine, 48*(1), 97-109.

Johnston, T. D., and Edwards, L. (2002). Genes, interactions and the development of behaviour. *Psychological Review, 109*, 26-34.

Kaplan, D., and Glass, L. (1995). *Understanding Nonlinear Dynamics.* New York: Springer Verlag.

Kauffman, S. A. (1993). *The origins of order: Self-organization and selection in evolution.* New York: Oxford University Press.

Kauffman, S. A. (1995). *At home in the universe: The search for laws of complexity.* London: Viking.

Keele, S. W., and Summers, J. J. (1976). The structure of motor programs. In G. E. Stelmach (Ed.), *Motor control: Issues and trends* (pp. 109-142). New York, NY: Grune and Stratton.

Kello, C. T., Anderson, G. G., Holden, J. G., and Van Orden, G. C. (2008). The pervasiveness of 1/f scaling in speech reflects the metastable basis of cognition. *Cognitive Science, 32*(7), 1217-1231. doi:10.1080/03640210801944898

Kello, C. T., Beltz, B. C., Holden, J. G., and Van Orden, G. C. (2007). The emergent coordination of cognitive function. *Journal of Experimental Psychology: General, 136*(4), 551-568. http://dx.doi.org/10.1037/0096-3445.136.4.551

Kelso, J. A. S. (1981a). Contrasting perspectives on order and regulation in movement. In J. Long and A. Baddeley (Eds.), *Attention and Performance IX* (pp. 437-458). Hillsdale, NJ.: LEA.

Kelso, J. A. S. (1981b). On the oscillatory basis of movement. *Bulletin of the Psychonomic Society, 18*, 63.

Kelso, J. A. S. (1984). Phase transitions and critical behavior in human bimanual coordination. *American Journal of Physiology: Regulatory, Intergrative and Comparative Physiology, 15*, R1000-R1004.

Kelso, J. A. S. (1992). Theoretical concepts and strategies for understanding perceptual-motor skill: From informational capacity in closed systems to self-organization in open, nonequilibrium systems. *Journal of Experimental Psychology: General, 121*, 260-261.

Kelso, J. A. S. (1995). *Dynamic patterns: The self-organisation of brain and behaviour.* Cambridge, MA: MIT Press.

Kelso, J. A. S. (2008). An essay on understanding the mind. *Ecological Psychology, 20*(2), 180-208. doi:10.1080/10407410801949297

Kelso, J. A. S. (2012). Multistability and metastability: Understanding dynamic coordination in the brain. *Philosophical Transactions of the Royal Society B: Biological Sciences, 367*(1591), 906-918. doi:10.1098/rstb.2011.0351

Kelso, J. A. S., and Engström, D. A. (2006). *The complementary nature.* Cambridge, MA: Bradford Books, MIT Press.

Kelso, J. A., and Zanone, P. G. (2002). Coordination dynamics of learning and transfer across different effector systems. *The* Journal *of Experimental* Psychology: *Human Perception and Performance, 28*(4), 776-797.

Kim, W., Veloso, A., Araújo, D., Machado, M., Vleck, V., Aguiar, L., . . . Vieira, F. (2013). Haptic perception-action coupling manifold of effective golf swing. *International Journal of Golf Science, 2*, 10-32.

Kiverstein, J., and Rietveld, E. (2015). The primacy of skilled intentionality: On Hutto and Satne's the Natural Origins of Content. *Philosophia, 43*(3), 701-721. doi:10.1007/s11406-015-9645-z

Komar, J., Chow, J. Y., Chollet, D., and Seifert, L. (2015). Neurobiological degeneracy: supporting stability, flexibility and pluripotentiality in complex motor skill. *Acta Psychologica, 154*, 26-35.

Körner, S., and Staller, MS (2018). From system to pedagogy: towards a nonlinear pedagogy of self-defense training in the police and the civilian domain. *Security Journal, 31*(2), 645-659.

Kostrubiec, V., Fuchs, A., and Kelso, J. A. S. (2012). Beyond the blank slate: Routes to learning new coordination patterns depend on the intrinsic dynamics of the learner—experimental evidence and theoretical model. *Frontiers in Human Neuroscience, 6*, 222.

Krebs, R. J. (2009). Bronfenbrenner's bioecological theory of human development and the process of development of sports talent. *International Journal of Sport Psychology, 40*(1), 108-135.

Kugler, P. N., Shaw, R. E., Vincente, K. J., and Kinsella-Shaw, J. (1990). Inquiry into intentional systems: I. Issues in ecological physics. *Psychological Research, 52*(2-3), 98-121.

Kugler, P. N., and Turvey, M. T. (1987). *Information, natural law, and the self-assembly of rhythmic movement*. Hillsdale, NJ: Lawrence Erlbaum Associates.

LaBar, K. S., and Cabeza, R. (2006). Cognitive neuroscience of emotional memory. *Nature Reviews Neuroscience, 7*(1), 54.

Latash, M. L. (2000). There is no motor redundancy in human movements. There is motor abundance. *Motor Control, 4*, 259-261.

Lee, D. N. (1976). A theory of visual control of braking based on information about time-to-collision. *Perception, 5*, 437-459.

Lee, D. N., and Lishman, R. (1975). Visual proprioceptive control of stance. *Journal of Human Movement Studies, 1*, 87-95.

Lee, M. C. Y., Chow, J. Y., Komar, J., Tan, C. W. K., and Button, C. (2014). Nonlinear pedagogy: An effective approach to cater for individual differences in learning a sports skill. PloS One, 9(8), e104744. doi:10.1371/journal.pone.0104744

Lewis, S. T., and Van Puymbroeck, M. (2008). Obesity-stigma as a multifaceted constraint to leisure. *Journal of Leisure Research, 40*(4), 574-588. doi:10.1080/00222216.2008.11950153

Liu, Y.-T., Mayer-Kress, G., and Newell, K. M. (2006). Qualitative and quantitative change in the dynamics of motor learning. *Journal of Experimental Psychology: Human Perception and Performance, 32*(2), 380-393.

Liu, Y.-T., and Newell, K. M. (2015). S-shaped motor learning and nonequilibrium phase transitions. *Journal of Experimental Psychology: Human Perception and Performance, 41*(2), 403-414. doi:10.1037/a0038812

Mace, W. M. (1986). J. J. Gibson's ecological theory of information pickup: Cognition from the ground up. In T.J.Knapp and L.C.Robertson (Eds.), *Approaches to cognition: Contrasts and controversies* (pp. 137-157).London, Routledge.

Magill, R. A. (1994). The influence of augmented feedback on skill learning depends on characteristics of the skill and the learner. *Quest, 46*(3), 314-327. doi:10.1080/00336297.1994.10484129

Magill, R. A. (2006). *Motor learning and control: Concepts and applications* (8th ed.). New York, NY: McGraw-Hill.

Martensen, R. L. (2004). *The brain takes shape: An early history*. New York, NY: Oxford University Press.

Mason, P. H. (2010). Degeneracy at multiple levels of complexity. *Biological Theory, 5*(3), 277-288. doi:10.1162/BIOT_a_00041

Mazzeo, R. S. (2008). Physiological responses to exercise at altitude. *Sports Medicine, 38*(1), 1-8.

McCosker, C., Renshaw, I., Greenwood, D., Davids, K., and Gosden, E. (2019). How performance analysis of elite long jumping can inform representative training design through identification of key constraints on competitive behaviours. *European Journal of Sport Science*, 1-9.

McCullagh, P., and Weiss, M. R. (2001). Modeling: Considerations for motor skill performance and psychological responses. In R. N. Singer, H. A. Hasenblas, and C. M. Janelle (Eds.), *Handbook of sport psychology* (2nd ed.) (pp. 205-238). New York: Wiley.

Merriam Webster. (n.d.) Merriam-Webster Dictionary. Retrieved from www.merriam-webster.com

Michaels, C. F. (1998). The ecological/dynamical approach, manifest destiny and a single movement science. In A. A. Post, J. R. Pijpers, P. Bosch, and M. S. J. Boschker (Eds.), *Models in human movement sciences* (pp. 65-68). Amsterdam: Institute for Fundamental and Clinical Human Movement Sciences.

Michaels, C. F., and Beek, P. (1995). The state of ecological psychology. *Ecological Psychology, 7,* 259-278.

Michaels, C. F., and Zaal, F. T. (2002). Catching fly balls. In S. Bennett, K. Davids, G. J. P. Savelsbergh, and J. van der Kamp (Eds.), *Interceptive actions in sport: Information and movement* (pp. 172–183). London: Routledge.

Mitra, S., Amazeen, P. G., and Turvey, M. T. (1998). Intermediate motor learning as decreasing active (dynamical) degrees of freedom. *Human Movement Science, 17*(1), 17-65.

Moen, P. E., Elder Jr, G. H., and Lüscher, K. E. (1995). *Examining lives in context: Perspectives on the ecology of human development*. Washington, DC: American Psychological Association.

Moreau, D., Macnamara, B. N., and Hambrick, D. Z. (2019). Overstating the role of environmental factors in success: A cautionary note. *Current Directions in Psychological Science, 28*(1), 28-33.

Moy, B., Renshaw, I., and Davids, K. (2016). The impact of nonlinear pedagogy on physical education teacher education students' intrinsic motivation. *Physical Education and Sport Pedagogy, 21*(5), 517-538. doi:10.1080/17408989.2015.1072506

Moy, B., Renshaw, I., Davids, K., and Brymer, E. (2015). Overcoming acculturation: Physical education recruits' experiences of an alternative pedagogical approach to games teaching. *Physical Education and Sport Pedagogy, 21*(4), 386-406.

Mullineaux, D. R., Bartlett, R. M., and Bennett, S. (2001). Research design and statistics in biomechanics and motor control. *Journal of Sports Sciences, 19,* 739-760.

Newell, K. M. (1985). Coordination, control and skill. In D. Goodman, R. B. Wilberg, and I. M. Franks (Eds.), *Differing perspectives in motor learning, memory, and control* (pp. 295-317). Amsterdam, North Holland: Elsevier Science Publishing Company.

Newell, K. M. (1986). Constraints on the development of coordination. In M. G. Wade and H. T. A. Whiting (Eds.), *Motor development in children: Aspects of coordination and control* (pp. 341-360). Dordrecht, Netherlands: Martinus Nijhoff.

Newell, K. M. (1996). Change in movement and skill: Learning, retention and transfer. In M. L. Latash and M. T. Turvey (Eds.), *Dexterity and its development* (pp. 393-430). Mahwah, NJ: Erlbaum.

Newell, K. M., and James, E. G. (2008). The amount and structure of human movement variability. In Y.Hong and R. Bartlett (Eds.). *Routledge Handbook of Biomechanics and Human Movement Science* (pp. 105-116). London, Routledge.

Newell, K. M., Broderick, M. P., Deutsch, K. M., and Slifkin, A. B. (2003). Task goals and change in dynamical degrees of freedom with motor learning. *Journal of Experimental Psychology: Human Perception and Performance, 29*(2), 379-387.

Newell, K. M., Deutsch, K. M., Sosnoff, J. J., and Mayer-Kress, G. (2006). Variability in motor output as noise: A default and errorneous proposition. In K. Davids, S. Bennett, and K. M. Newell (Eds.), *Movement system variablity* (pp. 3-24). Champaign, IL: Human Kinetics.

Newell, K. M., Kugler, P. N., Van Emmerik, R. E. A., and McDonald, P. V. (1989). Search strategies and the acquisition of coordination. In S. A. Wallace (Ed.), *Perspectives on the coordination of movement* (pp. 85-122). Amsterdam: Elsevier Science.

Newell, K. M., and Liu, Y. T. (2012). Functions of learning and the acquisition of motor skills (with reference to sport). *The Open Sports Sciences Journal, 5,* 17-25.

Newell, K. M., Liu, Y.-T., and Mayer-Kress, G. (2001). Time scales in motor learning and development. *Psychological Review, 108*(1), 57-82.

Newell, K. M., Liu, Y. T., and Mayer-Kress, G. (2005). Learning in the brain-computer interface: Insights about degrees of freedom and degeneracy from a landscape model of motor learning. *Cognitive Processing, 6*, 37-47.

Newell, K. M., Mayer-Kress, G., Hong, S. L., and Liu, Y.-T. (2009). Adaptation and learning: Characteristic time scales of performance dynamics. *Human Movement Science, 28*(6), 655-687.

Newell, K. M., and McDonald, P. V. (1992). Searching for solutions to the coordination function: Learning as exploration behavior. In G. E. Stelmach and J. Requin (Eds.), *Tutorials in Motor Behavior II* (pp. 517-531). Amsterdam, North Holland: Elsevier.

Newell, K. M., and Ranganathan, R. (2010). Instructions as constraints in motor skill acquisition. In I. Renshaw, K. Davids, G. J. P. Savelsbergh (Eds.), *Motor Learning in Practice* (pp. 37-52). New York, NY: Routledge.

Newell, K. M., and Vaillancourt, D. (2001). Dimensional change in motor learning. *Human Movement Science, 20*, 695-715.

Ng, J. L. and Button, C. (2018). Reconsidering the fundamental movement skills construct: Implications for assessment. *Movement and Sport Sciences/Science and Motricité*. https://doi.org/10.1051/sm/2018025.

Noppeney, U., Friston, K. J., and Price, C. J. (2004). Degenerate neuronal systems sustaining cognitive functions. *Journal of Anatomy, 205*, 433-442.

Nourrit, D., Delignières, D., Caillou, N., Deschamps, T., and Lauriot, B. (2003). On discontinuities in motor learning: A longitudinal study of complex skill acquisition on a ski-simulator. *Journal of Motor Behavior, 35*(2), 151-170.

Oppici, L., Panchuk, D., Serpiello, F. R., and Farrow, D. (2017). Long-term practice with domain-specific task constraints influences perceptual skills. *Frontiers in Psychology, 8*, 1387.

Orth, D., Davids, K., Chow, J.-Y., Brymer, E., and Seifert, L. (2018). Behavioral repertoire influences the rate and nature of learning in climbing: Implications for individualized learning design in preparation for extreme sports participation. *Frontiers in Psychology, 9*(949). doi:10.3389/fpsyg.2018.00949

Orth, D., van der Kamp, J., and Button, C. (2018). Learning to be adaptive as a distributed process across the coach–athlete system: Situating the coach in the constraints-led approach. *Physical Education and Sport Pedagogy, 24*(2). 1-16. doi:10.1080/17408989.2018.1557132

Orth, D., van der Kamp, J., Memmert, D., and Savelsbergh, G. J. P. (2017). Creative motor actions as emerging from movement variability. *Frontiers in Psychology, 8*(1903). doi:10.3389/fpsyg.2017.01903

Ovens, A., Hopper, T., and Butler, J. (2013). *Complexity thinking in physical education: Reframing curriculum, pedagogy, and research*. London: Routledge.

Pacheco, M. M., and Newell, K. M. (2015). Transfer as a function of exploration and stabilization in original practice. *Human Movement Science, 44*, 258-269.

Pacheco, M. M., Hsieh, T.-Y., and Newell, K. M. (2017). Search strategies in practice: Movement variability affords perception of task dynamics. *Ecological Psychology, 29*(4), 243-258. doi:10.1080/10407413.2017.1368354

Panchuk, D., Davids, K., Sakadjian, A., MacMahon, C., and Parrington, L. (2013). Did you see that? Dissociating advanced visual information and ball flight constrains perception and action processes during one-handed catching. *Acta Psychologica, 142*(3), 394-401.

Passos, P., Araújo, D., and Davids, K. (2013). Self-organization processes in field-invasion team sports. *Sports Medicine, 43*(1), 1-7.

Passos, P., Araújo, D., and Davids, K. (2016). Competitiveness and the process of co-adaptation in team sport performance. *Frontiers in Psychology, 7*, 1562. doi:10.3389/fpsyg.2016.01562

Passos, P., Araujo, D., Davids, K., Gouveia, L., Milho, J., and Serpa, S. (2008). Information-governing dynamics of attacker-defender interactions in youth rugby union. *Journal of Sports Sciences, 26*(13), 1421-1429. doi:10.1080/02640410802208986

Passos, P., Araujo, D., Davids, K., Gouveia, L., Serpa, S., Milho, J., and Fonseca, S. (2009). Interpersonal pattern dynamics and adaptive behavior in multiagent neurobiological systems: Conceptual model and data. *Journal of Motor Behavior, 41*(5).

Passos, P., Davids, K., Araújo, D., Paz, N., Minguéns, J., and Mendes, J. (2011). Networks as a novel tool for studying team ball sports as complex social systems. *Journal of Science and Medicine in Sport, 14*(2), 170-176.

Passos, P., Milho, J., and Button, C. (2018). Quantifying synergies in two-versus-one situations in team sports: An example from Rugby Union. *Behavior Research Methods, 50*(2), 620-629.

Paulo, A., Davids, K., and Araújo, D. (2018). Co-adaptation of ball reception to the serve constrains outcomes in elite competitive volleyball. *International Journal of Sports Science and Coaching, 13*(2), 253-261.

Paulo, A., Zaal, F. T., Seifert, L., Fonseca, S., and Araújo, D. (2018). Predicting volleyball serve-reception at group level. *Journal of Sports Sciences, 36*(22), 2621-2630.

Peh, Y. C. S. (2018). *The effect of attentional focus instructions on skill acquisition of an interceptive task from a nonlinear pedagogical perspective.* Unpublished doctoral dissertation. Nanyang Technological University: Singapore.

Peh, S. Y. C., Chow, J. Y., and Davids, K. (2011). Focus of attention and its impact on movement behaviour. *Journal of Science and Medicine in Sport, 14*(1), 70-78.

Peper, C. E., Bootsma, R. J., Mestre, D. R., and Bakker, F. C. (1994). Catching balls: How to get the hand to the right place at the right time. *Journal of Experimental Psychology: Human Perception and Performance, 20*(3), 591-612.

Pessoa, L., and Adolphs, R. (2011). Emotion and the brain: Multiple roads are better than one. *Nature Reviews Neuroscience, 12*(7), 425-425. Retrieved from http://dx.doi.org/10.1038/nrn2920-c2

Phillips, E., Davids, K., Renshaw, I., and Portus, M. (2010). Expert performance in sport and the dynamics of talent development. *Sports Medicine, 40*(4), 271-283.

Pinder, R. A., Davids, K., and Renshaw, I. (2012). Metastability and emergent performance of dynamic interceptive actions. *Journal of Science and Medicine in Sport, 15*(5), 437-443.

Pinder, R. A., Davids, K. W., Renshaw, I., and Araújo, D. (2011). Representative learning design and functionality of research and practice in sport. *Journal of Sport and Exercise Psychology, 33*(1), 146-155.

Pinder, R. A., and Renshaw, I. (2019). What can coaches and physical education teachers learn from a constraints-led approach in para-sport? *Physical Education and Sport Pedagogy, 24*(2), 190-205.

Pinder, R. A., Renshaw, I., Davids, K., and Kerhervé, H. (2011). Principles for the use of ball projection machines in elite and developmental sport programmes. *Sports Medicine, 41*(10), 793-800.

Polskaia, N., Richer, N., Dionne, E., and Lajoie, Y. (2015). Continuous cognitive task promotes greater postural stability than an internal or external focus of attention. *Gait and Posture, 41*(2), 454-458.

Poolton, J. M., Masters, R. S. W., and Maxwell, J. P. (2005). The relationship between initial errorless learning conditions and subsequent performance. *Human Movement Science, 24*(3), 362-378. doi:10.1016/j.humov.2005.06.006

Port, R. F., and van Gelder, T. (Eds.). (1995). *Mind as motion: Explorations in the dynamics of cognition.* Cambridge, MA: Bradford Books, MIT Press.

Post, A. A., Pijpers, J. R., Bosch, P., and Boschker, M. S. J. (1998). *Models in human movement sciences: Proceedings of the second international symposium of the institute for fundamental and clinical human movement science.* Enschede: PrintPartners Ipskamp.

Potdevin, F., Vors, O., Huchez, A., Lamour, M., Davids, K., and Schnitzler, C. (2018). How can video feedback be used in physical education to support novice learning in gymnastics? Effects on motor learning, self-assessment and motivation. *Physical Education and Sport Pedagogy, 23*(6), 559-574.

Price, C. J., and Friston, K. J. (2002). Degeneracy and cognitive anatomy. *Trends in Cognitive Science, 6*(10), 416-421.

Prigogine, I., and Stengers, I. (1984). *Order out of chaos.* New York: Bantam Books.

Profeta, V. L. S., and Turvey, M. T. (2018). Bernstein's levels of movement construction: A contemporary perspective. *Human Movement Science, 57*, 111-133. doi:10.1016/j.humov.2017.11.013

Proffitt, D. R., Stefanucci, J., Banton, T., and Epstein, W. (2003). The role of effort in perceiving distance. *Psychological Science, 14*(2), 106-112.

Rea, T., and Lavallee, D. (2017). The Structured RePsychLing of Talent: Talent transfer. In: J. Baker, S. Cobley, J. Schorer, and N. Wattie (Eds.). *Routledge Handbook of Talent Identification and Development in Sport* (pp. 443-454). Routledge, Abingdon.

Reed, E. S. (1982). An outline of a theory of action systems. *Journal of Motor Behavior, 14*(2), 98-134. doi:10.1080/00222895.1982.10735267

Reed, E. S. (1996). *Encountering the world: Toward an ecological psychology.* New York, NY: Oxford University Press.

Reed, S. K. (1993). A schema-based theory of transfer. In D. K. Detterman and R. J. Sternberg (Eds.), *Transfer on trial: Intelligence, cognition, and instruction* (pp. 39-67). New Jersey: Alex Publishing Corporation.

Rees, T., Hardy, L., Güllich, A., Abernethy, B., Côté, J., Woodman, T., . . . Warr, C. (2016). The great British medalists project: A review of current knowledge on the development of the world's best sporting talent. *Sports Medicine, 46*(8), 1041-1058. doi:10.1007/s40279-016-0476-2

Reid, M., Crespo, M., Lay, B., and Berry, J. (2007). Skill acquisition in tennis: research and current practice. *Journal of Science and Medicine in Sport, 10*(1), 1-10.

Rein, R., Button, C., Davids, K., and Summers, J. (2010). Investigating coordination in discrete multi-articular movements using cluster analysis. *Motor Control, 14*(2), 211-239.

Rein, R., Davids, K., and Button, C. (2010). Adaptive and phase transition behavior in performance of discrete multi-articular actions by degenerate neurobiological systems. *Experimental Brain Research, 201*(2), 307-322. doi:10.1007/s00221-009-2040-x

Reis, H. J., Guatimosim, C., Paquet, M., Santos, M., Ribeiro, F. M., Kummer, A., ... and Palotas, A. (2009). Neuro-transmitters in the central nervous system and their implication in learning and memory processes. *Current Medicinal Chemistry, 16*(7), 796-840.

Renshaw, I., Davids, K., Newcombe, D., and Roberts, W. (2019). *The Constraints-Led Approach: Principles for Sports Coaching and Practice Design.* London, Routledge.

Renshaw, I., Araújo, D., Button, C., Chow, J. Y., Davids, K., and Moy, B. (2015). Why the constraints-led approach is not teaching games for understanding: A clarification. *Physical Education and Sport Pedagogy, 21*(5), 459-480.

Renshaw, I., Chappell, G., Fitzgerald, D., Davison, J., and McFadyen, B. (2010). *The battle zone: Constraint-led coaching in action.* Paper presented at Conference of Science, Medicine and Coaching in Cricket 2010.

Renshaw, I., Chow, J. Y., Davids, K., and Hammond, J. (2010). A constraints-led perspective to understanding skill acquisition and game play: A basis for integration of motor learning theory and physical education praxis? *Physical Education and Sport Pedagogy, 15*(2), 117-137.

Renshaw, I., Davids, K. W., Shuttleworth, R., and Chow, J. Y. (2009). Insights from ecological psychology and dynamical systems theory can underpin a philosophy of coaching. *International Journal of Sport Psychology, 40*(4), 540-602.

Renshaw, I., Oldham, A. R., and Bawden, M. (2012). Nonlinear pedagogy underpins intrinsic motivation in sports coaching. *The Open Sports Sciences Journal, 5*, 88-99.

Ribeiro, J., Silva, P., Duarte, R., Davids, K., and Garganta, J. (2017). Team sports performance analysed through the lens of social network theory: implications for research and practice. *Sports Medicine, 47*(9), 1689-1696.

Richardson, M. J., Shockley, K., Fajen, B. R., Riley, M. A., and Turvey, M. T. (2008). Ecological psychology: Six principles for an embodied–embedded approach to behavior. In P. Calvo, and T. Gomila (Eds.) *Handbook of cognitive science* (pp. 159-187). Elsevier: Oxford, UK.

Ridley, M. (2004). *Nature via nurture: genes, experience and what makes us human.* New York, New York: Harper Collins.

Rietveld, E., and Kiverstein, J. (2014). A Rich Landscape of Affordances. *Ecological Psychology, 26*(4), 325-352. doi:10.1080/10407413.2014.958035

Riley, M., Richardson, M., Shockley, K., and Ramenzoni, V. (2011). Interpersonal Synergies. *Frontiers in Psychology, 2*(38). doi:10.3389/fpsyg.2011.00038

Riley, M. A., Shockley, K., and Van Orden, G. (2012). Learning from the body about the mind. *Topics in Cognitive Science, 4*(1), 21-34.

Riley, M. A., Shaw, T. H., and Pagano, C. C. (2005). Role of the inertial eigenvectors in proprioception near the limits of arm adduction range of motion. *Human Movement Science, 24*(2), 171-183.

Roberts, W. M., Newcombe, D. J., and Davids, K. (2019). Application of a constraints-led approach to pedagogy in schools: embarking on a journey to nurture physical literacy in primary physical education. *Physical Education and Sport Pedagogy, 24*(2), 162-175.

Roohi, N., Sarihi, A., Shahidi, S., Zarei, M., and Haghparast, A. (2014). Microinjection of the mGluR5 antagonist MTEP into the nucleus accumbens attenuates the acquisition but not expression of morphine-induced conditioned place preference in rats. *Pharmacology Biochemistry and Behavior, 126*, 109-115.

Rosalie, S. M., and Müller, S. (2012). A model for the transfer of perceptual-motor skill learning in human behaviors. *Research Quarterly for Exercise and Sport, 83*(3), 413-421.

Rosenblum, L. D., Carello, C., and Pastore, R. E. (1987). Relative effectiveness of three stimulus variables for locating a moving sound source. *Perception, 16*, 175-186.

Rothwell, M., Davids, K., and Stone, J. (2018). Harnessing socio-cultural constraints on athlete development to create a form of life. *Journal of Expertise 1*(1), 94-102.

Rothwell, M., Stone, J. A., Davids, K., and Wright, C. (2017). Development of expertise in elite and sub-elite British rugby league players: A comparison of practice experiences. *European Journal of Sport Science, 17*(10), 1252-1260. doi:10.1080/17461391.2017.1380708

Runeson, S. (1977). On the possibility of "smart" perceptual mechanisms. *Scandinavian Journal of Psychology, 18*, 172-179.

Sartori, L., Straulino, E., and Castiello, U. (2011). How objects are grasped: The interplay between affordances and end-goals. *PLoS One, 6*(9), e25203. doi:10.1371/journal.pone.0025203

Savelsbergh, G. J. P., and van der Kamp, J. G. (2000). Information in learning to co-ordinate and control movements: Is there a need for specificity of practice? *International Journal of Sport Psychology, 31*, 467-484.

Savelsbergh, G. J. P., van der Kamp, J., Oudejans, R. R. D., and Scott, M. A. (2004). Perceptual learning is mastering perceptual degrees of freedom. In A. M. Williams and N. J. Hodges (Eds.), *Skill acquisition in sport: Research, theory and practice* (pp. 374-389). London: Routledge, Taylor and Francis.

Savelsbergh, G. J. P., Whiting, H. T. A., and Bootsma, R. J. (1991). Grasping tau. *Journal of Experimental Psychology: Human Perception and Performance, 17*, 315-322.

Schiff, W., and Oldak, R. (1990). Accuracy of judging time to arrival: Effects of modality, trajectory, and gender. *Journal of Experimental Psychology: Human Perception and Performance, 16*, 303-316.

Schmidt, R. A. (1975). A schema theory of discrete motor skill learning. *Psychological Review, 82*, 225-260.

Schmidt, R. A., and Lee, T. (2005). *Motor Control and Learning: A Behavioral Emphasis* (4th ed.). Champaign, IL: Human Kinetics.

Schmidt, R. A., Lee, T. D., Winstein, C., Wulf, G., and Zelaznik, H. N. (2018). *Motor Control and Learning: A Behavioral Emphasis (6th Edition)*. Champaign, Illinois: Human Kinetics.

Schmidt, R. C., and Fitzpatrick, P. (1996). Dynamical perspectives on motor learning. In H. N. Zelaznik (Ed.), *Advances in motor learning and control*. Champaign, IL: Human Kinetics.

Schnitzler, C., Brazier, T., Button, C., Seifert, L., and Chollet, D. (2011). Effect of velocity and added resistance on selected coordination and force parameters in front crawl. *Journal of Strength and Conditioning Research, 25*(10), 2681-2690. doi:10.1519/JSC.0b013e318207ef5e

Schnitzler, C., Seifert, L., and Chollet, D. (2011). Arm coordination and performance level in the 400-m front crawl. *Research Quarterly for Exercise and Sport, 82*(1), 1-8.

Schöllhorn, W. I., Mayer-Kress, G., Newell, K. M., and Michelbrink, M. (2009). Time scales of adaptive behavior and motor learning in the presence of stochastic perturbations. *Human Movement Science, 28*, 319-333.

Scholz, J. P., and Kelso, J. A. S. (1989). A quantitative approach to understanding the formation and change of coordinated movement patterns. *Journal of Motor Behavior, 21*, 122-144.

Scholz, J. P., Schöner, G., and Latash, M. L. (2000). Identifying the control structures of multijoint coordination during pistol shooting. *Experimental Brain Research, 135*, 382-404.

Schöner, G., Haken, H., and Kelso, J. A. (1987). A stochastic theory of phase transitions in human hand movement. *Biological Cybernetics, 53*(4), 247-257.

Schücker, L., Anheier, W., Hagemann, N., Strauss, B., and Völker, K. (2013). On the optimal focus of attention for efficient running at high intensity. *Sport, Exercise, and Performance Psychology, 2*(3), 207.

Scully, D. M. (1986). Visual perception of technical execution and aesthetic quality in biological motion. *Human Movement Science, 5*, 185-206.

Scully, D. M., and Newell, K. M. (1985). Observational learning and the acquisition of motor skills: Towards a visual perception perspective. *Journal of Human Movement Studies, 11*, 169-186.

Seifert, L., Boulanger, J., Orth, D., and Davids, K. (2015). Environmental design shapes perceptual-motor exploration, learning, and transfer in climbing. *Frontiers in Psychology, 6*, 1819. doi:10.3389/fpsyg.2015.01819

Seifert, L., Button, C., and Davids, K. (2013). Key properties of expert movement systems in sport an ecological dynamics perspective. *Sports Medicine, 43*(3), 167-178. doi:10.1007/s40279-012-0011-z

Seifert, L., Komar, J., Araújo, D., and Davids, K. (2016). Neurobiological degeneracy: A key property for functional adaptations of perception and action to constraints. *Neuroscience and Biobehavioral Reviews, 69*, 159-165. doi:10.1016/j.neubiorev.2016.08.006

Seifert, L., Komar, J., Crettenand, F., Dadashi, F., Aminian, K., and Millet, G. P. (2014). Inter-limb coordination and energy cost in swimming. *Journal of Science and Medicine in Sport, 17*(4), 439-444. doi:10.1016/j.jsams.2013.07.003

Seifert, L., Leblanc, H., Herault, R., Komar, J., Button, C., and Chollet, D. (2011). Inter-individual variability in the upper-lower limb breaststroke coordination. *Human Movement Science, 30*(3), 550-565. doi:10.1016/j.humov.2010.12.003

Seifert, L., Orth, D., Boulanger, J., Dovgalecs, V., Hérault, R., and Davids, K. (2014). Climbing skill and complexity of climbing wall design: Assessment of jerk as a novel indicator of performance fluency. *Journal of Applied Biomechanics, 30*(5), 619-625.

Seifert, L., Wattebled, L., L'Hermette, M., Bideault, G., Herault, R., and Davids, K. (2013). Skill transfer, affordances and dexterity in different climbing environments. *Human Movement Science, 32*(6), 1339-1352. doi:10.1016/j.humov.2013.06.006

Seifert, L., Wattebled, L., Herault, R., Poizat, G., Adé, D., Gal-Petitfaux, N., and Davids, K. (2014). Neurobiological degeneracy and affordance perception support functional intra-individual variability of inter-limb coordination during ice climbing. *PloS One, 9*(2), e89865.

Seifert, L., Wattebled, L., Orth, D., L'Hermette, M., Boulanger, J., and Davids, K. (2016). Skill transfer specificity shapes perception and action under varying environmental constraints. *Human Movement Science, 48*, 132-141.

Shafizadeh, M., Davids, K., Correia, V., Wheat, J., and Hizan, H. (2016). Informational constraints on interceptive actions of elite football goalkeepers in 1v1 dyads during competitive performance. *Journal of Sports Sciences, 34*(17), 1596-1601.

Shaw, B. K., McGowan, R. S., and Turvey, M. T. (1991). An acoustic variable specifying time-to-contact. *Ecological Psychology, 3,* 253-261.

Shaw, R., and Kinsella-Shaw, J. (2007a). Could optical 'pushes' be inertial forces? A geometro-dynamical hypothesis. *Ecological Psychology, 19*(3), 305-320. doi:10.1080/10407410701432352

Shaw, R., and Kinsella-Shaw, J. (2007b). The survival value of informed awareness. *Journal of Consciousness Studies, 14*(1-2), 137-154.

Shockley, K., Grocki, M., Carello, C., and Turvey, M. T. (2001). Somatosensory attunement to the rigid body laws. *Experimental Brain Research, 136*(1), 133-137.

Silva, P., Garganta, J., Araújo, D., Davids, K., and Aguiar, P. (2013). Shared knowledge or shared affordances? Insights from an ecological dynamics approach to team coordination in sports. *Sports Medicine, 43*(9), 765-772.

Silva, P., Chung, D., Carvalho, T., Cardoso, T., Davids, K., Araújo, D., and Garganta, J. (2016). Practice effects on intra-team synergies in football teams. *Human Movement Science, 46,* 39-51.

Silva, P., Esteves, P., Correia, V., Davids, K., Araújo, D., and Garganta, J. (2015). Effects of manipulations of player numbers vs. field dimensions on inter-individual coordination during small-sided games in youth football. *International Journal of Performance Analysis in Sport, 15*(2), 641-659.

Smeeton, N. J., Varga, M., Causer, J., and Williams, A. M. (2018). Disguise and deception of action outcomes through sports garment design impair anticipation judgments. *Journal of Sport and Exercise Psychology, 40*(2), 73-81.

Solomon, H. Y., and Turvey, M. T. (1988). Haptically perceiving the distances reachable with hand-held objects. *Journal of Experimental Psychology: Human Perception and Performance, 14,* 404-427.

Sparrow, W. A. (2000). *Energetics of human activity.* Champaign, IL: Human Kinetics.

Sparrow, W. A., and Newell, K. M. (1998). Metabolic energy expenditure and the regulation of movement economy. *Psychonomic Bulletin and Review, 5*(2), 173-196.

Stallman, R. K., Junge, M., and Blixt, T. (2008). The teaching of swimming based on a model derived from the causes of drowning. *International Journal of Aquatic Research and Education, 2*(4), 11.

Stattin, H., and Magnusson, D. (1990). *Paths through life* (Vol. 2). Hillsdale, NJ: Lawrence Erlbaum Associates, Inc.

Steinberg, L., Darling, N. E., Fletcher, A. C., Brown, B. B., and Dornbusch, S. M. (1995). Authoritative parenting and adolescent adjustment: An ecological journey. In P. Moen, G. H. Elder Jr., and K Luscher (Eds.), *Examining lives in context: Perspectives on the ecology of human development* (pp.423-466). Washington DC, American Psychological Association.

Stepp, N., Chemero, A., and Turvey, M. T. (2011). Philosophy for the rest of cognitive science. *Topics in Cognitive Science, 3*(2), 425-437. doi:10.1111/j.1756-8765.2011.01143.x

Stöckl, M., Lamb, P. F., and Lames, M. (2011). The ISOPAR method: A new approach to performance analysis in golf. *Journal of Quantitative Analysis in Sports, 7*(1), 10.

Stone, J., Strafford, B.W., North, J.S., Toner, C. and Davids, K. (2019). Effectiveness and efficiency of Virtual Reality designs to enhance athlete development: An ecological dynamics perspective. *Movement and Sport Science/Science et Motricité.* https://doi.org/10.1051/sm/2018031

Stone, J. A., Maynard, I. W., North, J. S., Panchuk, D., and Davids, K. (2015). (De)synchronization of advanced visual information and ball flight characteristics constrains emergent information–movement couplings during one-handed catching. *Experimental Brain Research, 233*(2), 449-458.

Strafford, B. W., Van Der Steen, P., Davids, K., and Stone, J. A. (2018). Parkour as a donor sport for athletic development in youth team sports: insights through an ecological dynamics lens. *Sports Medicine-Open, 4*(1), 21.

Swami, V. (2015). Cultural influences on body size ideals: Unpacking the impact of Westernization and modernization. *European Psychologist, 20*(1), 44-51. doi:10.1027/1016-9040/a000150

Swinnen, S. P. (2002). Intermanual coordination: From behavioural principles to neural-network inter-actions. *Nature Reviews Neuroscience, 3*(5), 348-359. Retrieved from http://dx.doi.org/10.1038/nrn807

Tallet, J., Kostrubiec, V., and Zanone, P.-G. (2008). The role of stability in the dynamics of learning, memorizing, and forgetting new coordination patterns. *Journal of Motor Behavior, 40*(2), 103-116.

Tan, C. W. K., Chow, J. Y., and Davids, K. (2012). 'How does TGfU work?': examining the relation-ship between learning design in TGfU and a nonlinear pedagogy. *Physical Education and Sport Pedagogy, 17*(4), 331-348.

Taylor, J. B., Wright, A. A., Dischiavi, S. L., Townsend, M. A., and Marmon, A. R. (2017). Activity demands during multi-directional team sports: a systematic review. *Sports Medicine, 47*(12), 2533-2551.

Temprado, J. J., Della-Grasta, M., Farrell, M., and Laurent, M. (1997). A novice-expert comparison of (intra-limb) co-ordination sub-serving the volleyball serve. *Human Movement Science, 16*, 653-676.

Tenenbaum, G., and Land, W. M. (2009). Mental representations as an underlying mechanism for human performance. *Progress in Brain Research, 174*, 251-266. doi:10.1016/S0079-6123(09)01320-X

Teques, P., Araújo, D., Seifert, L., Del Campo, V. L., and Davids, K. (2017). The resonant system: Linking brain-body-environment in sport performance. In M. R. Wilson, V. Waslh, and B. Parkin (Eds.), *Progress in Brain Research,* Vol. 234, (pp. 33-52): Amsterdam, North Holland: Elsevier.

Teulier, C., and Delignières, D. (2007). The nature of the transition between novice and skilled coordination during learning to swing. *Human Movement Science, 26*(3), 376-392.

Thelen, E., and Smith, L. B. (1994). *A dynamic systems approach to the development of cognition and action.* Cambridge, MA: MIT Press.

Todorov, E., and Jordan, M. I. (2002). Optimal feedback control as a theory of motor coordination. *Nature Neuroscience, 5*(11), 1226-1235.

Travassos, B., Araújo, D., Davids, K., Vilar, L., Esteves, P., and Vanda, C. (2012). Informational con-straints shape emergent functional behaviours during performance of interceptive actions in team sports. *Psychology of Sport and Exercise, 13*(2), 216-223. doi:10.1016/j.psychsport.2011.11.009

Travassos, B., Araújo, D., Duarte, R., and McGarry, T. (2012). Spatiotemporal coordination behav-iors in futsal (indoor football) are guided by informational game constraints. *Human Movement Science, 31*(4), 932-945.

Travassos, B., Duarte, R., Vilar, L., Davids, K., and Araújo, D. (2012). Practice task design in team sports: Representativeness enhanced by increasing opportunities for action. *Journal of Sports Sciences, 30*(13), 1447-1454.

Travassos, B., Araújo, D., and Davids, K. (2018). Is futsal a donor sport for football? Exploiting complementarity for early diversification in talent development. *Science and Medicine in Foot-ball, 2*(1), 66-70.

Tresilian, J. R. (1995). Perceptual and cognitive processes in time-to-contact estimation: Analysis of prediction-motion and relative judgement tasks. *Perception and Psychophysics, 57*(2), 231-245.

Turvey, M. T. (1990). Coordination. *American Psychologist, 45*, 938-953.

Turvey, M. T. (1996). Dynamic touch. *American Psychologist, 51*, 1134-1152.

Turvey, M. T. (2007). Action and perception at the level of synergies. *Human Movement Science, 26*, 657-697.

Turvey, M. T., Burton, G., Amazeen, E. L., Butwill, M., and Carello, C. (1998). Perceiving the width and height of a hand-held object by dynamic touch. *Journal of Experimental Psychology: Human Perception and Performance, 24*, 35-48.

Turvey, M. T., and Carello, C. (2012). On intelligence from first principles: Guidelines for inquiry into the hypothesis of physical intelligence (PI). *Ecological Psychology, 24*(1), 3-32. doi:10.108 0/10407413.2012.645757

Uehara, L., Button, C., Falcous, M., and Davids, K. (2014). Contextualised skill acquisition research: A new framework to study the development of sport expertise. *Physical Education and Sport Pedagogy, (21)*2, 1-16. doi:10.1080/17408989.2014.924495

Uehara, L., Button, C., Falcous, M., and Davids, K. (2018). Sociocultural constraints influencing the development of Brazilian footballers. *Physical Education and Sport Pedagogy, 1*(3), 162-180. and

van der Kamp, J., and Renshaw, I. (2015). Information-movement coupling as a hallmark of sport expertise. In *Routledge handbook of sport expertise* (pp. 50-63). New York, NY: Routledge/Taylor and Francis Group.

Van Gelder, T., and Port, R. F. (1995). It's about time: An overview of the dynamical approach to cognition. In R. F. Port and T. v. Gelder (Eds.), *Mind as motion: Explorations in the dynamics of cognition* (pp. 1-43). Cambridge, MA: MIT Press.

van Maarseveen, M. J. J., Savelsbergh, G. J. P., and Oudejans, R. R. D. (2018). In situ examination of decision-making skills and gaze behaviour of basketball players. *Human Movement Science, 57*, 205-216.

Vaz, D. V., Silva, P. L., Mancini, M. C., Carello, C., and Kinsella-Shaw, J. (2017). Towards an ecologically grounded functional practice in rehabilitation. *Human Movement Science, 52*, 117-132.

Vereijken, B., Van Emmerik, R. E. A., Whiting, H. T. A., and Newell, K. M. (1992). Free(z)ing degrees of freedom in skill acquisition. *Journal of Motor Behavior, 24*, 133-142.

Vilar, L., Araújo, D., Davids, K., Travassos, B., Duarte, R., and Parreira, J. (2014). Interpersonal coordination tendencies supporting the creation/prevention of goal scoring opportunities in futsal. *European Journal of Sport Science, 14*(1), 28-35.

Vilar, L., Araújo, D., Davids, K., and Bar-Yam, Y. (2013). Science of winning soccer: Emergent pattern-forming dynamics in association football. *Journal of Systems Science and Complexity, 26*(1), 73-84. doi:10.1007/s11424-013-2286-z

Vilar, L., Araújo, D., Davids, K., Correia, V., and Esteves, P. T. (2013). Spatial-temporal constraints on decision-making during shooting performance in the team sport of futsal. *Journal of Sports Sciences, 31*(8), 840-846.

Wagman, J. B., and Carello, C. (2001). Affordances and inertial constraints on tool use. *Ecological Psychology, 13*(3), 173-195.

Wagman, J. B., and Van Norman, E. R. (2011). Transfer of calibration in dynamic touch: What do perceivers learn when they learn about length of a wielded object? *The Quarterly Journal of Experimental Psychology, 64*(5), 889-901.

Waldvogel, D., van Gelderen, P., Muellbacher, W., Ziemann, U., Immisch, I., and Hallett, M. (2000). The relative metabolic demand of inhibition and excitation. *Nature, 406*(6799), 995.

Walker, M. P., Brakefield, T., Morgan, A., Hobson, J. A., and Stickgold, R. (2002). Practice with sleep makes perfect: Sleep-dependent motor skill learning. *Neuron, 35*(1), 205-211.

Ward, P., Williams, A. M., and Bennett, S. (2002). Visual search and biological motion perception in tennis. *Research Quarterly for Exercise and Sport, 73*(1), 107-112.

Warren, W. H. (1990). The perception-action coupling. In H. Bloch and B. I. Berenthal (Eds.), *Sensory-motor organizations and development in infancy and early childhood* (pp. 23-37). Dordrecht, Netherlands: Kluwer Academic Publishers.

Warren, W. H. (2006). The dynamics of perception and action. *Psychological Review, 113*(2), 358-389.

Warren, W. H., Kim, E. E., and Husney, R. (1987). The way the ball bounces: Visual and auditory perception of elasticity and control of the bounce pass. *Perception and Psychophysics, 16*, 309-336.

Weinberg, R. S., and Hunt, V. (1976). The interrelationships between anxiety, motor performance, and electromyography. *Journal of Motor Behavior, 8*, 219-224.

Wenderoth, N., and Bock, O. (2001). Learning of a new bimanual coordination pattern is governed by three distinct processes. *Motor Control, 1*, 23-35.

Whitacre, J. M. (2011). Genetic and environment-induced pathways to innovation: on the possibility of a universal relationship between robustness and adaptation in complex biological systems. *Evolutionary Ecology, 25*(5), 965-975.

Whitehead, M. (Ed.). (2010). *Physical Literacy: Throughout the Lifecourse.* Routledge, London.

Wilkerson, G. B., Nabhan, D. C., Prusmack, C. J., and Moreau, W. J. (2018). Detection of Persisting Concussion Effects on Neuromechanical Responsiveness. *Medicine and Science in Sports and Exercise, 50*(9), 1750-1756.

Williams, A. M., Davids, K., and Williams, J. G. (1999). *Visual perception and action in sport.* London: E. and F. N. Spon.

Williams, A. M., and Hodges, N. J. (2005). Practice, instruction and skill acquisition in soccer: Challenging tradition. *Journal of Sports Sciences, 23*(6), 637-650.

Wilson, P. H., Ruddock, S., Smits-Engelsman, B., Polatajko, H., and Blank, R. (2013). Understanding performance deficits in developmental coordination disorder: A meta-analysis of recent research. *Developmental Medicine and Child Neurology, 55*(3), 217-228.

Withagen, R., Araújo, D., and de Poel, H. J. (2017). Inviting affordances and agency. *New Ideas in Psychology, 45*, 11-18. doi:10.1016/j.newideapsych.2016.12.002

Withagen, R., and Chemero, A. (2009). Naturalizing perception: Developing the Gibsonian approach to perception along evolutionary lines. *Theory and Psychology, 19*(3), 363-389.

Withagen, R., de Poel, H. J., Araújo, D., and Pepping, G.-J. (2012). Affordances can invite behavior: Reconsidering the relationship between affordances and agency. *New Ideas in Psychology, 30*(2), 250-258. doi:10.1016/j.newideapsych.2011.12.003

Withagen, R., and Michaels, C. F. (2002). The calibration of walking transfers to crawling: Are action systems calibrated? *Ecological Psychology, 14*(4), 223-234.

Withagen, R., and van der Kamp, J. (2018). An ecological approach to creativity in making. *New Ideas in Psychology, 49*, 1-6. doi:10.1016/j.newideapsych.2017.11.002

Withagen, R., and van Mermeskerken, M. (2009). Individual differences in learning to perceive length by dynamic touch: Evidence for variation in perceptual learning capacities. *Attention, Perception and Psychophysics, 71*(1), 64-75.

Wood, J. M., Lacherez, P., and Tyrrell, R. A. (2014). Seeing pedestrians at night: Effect of driver age and visual abilities. *Ophthalmic and Physiological Optics, 34*(4), 452-458.

Woodworth, R. S., and Thorndike, E. (1901). The influence of improvement in one mental function upon the efficiency of other functions. (I). *Psychological Review, 8*(3), 247.

Wormhoudt, R., Savelsbergh, G. J. P., Teunissen, J. W., and Davids, K. (2018). *Athletics skills model for optimizing talent development through movement education: No specialists, but athletes with a specialization: A new avenue to think about movement.* London: Routledge.

Wulf, G. (2007). *Attention and motor skill learning.* Champaign, IL: Human Kinetics.

Wulf, G. (2013). Attentional focus and motor learning: A review of 15 years. *International Review of Sport and Exercise Psychology, 6*(1), 77-104.

Wulf, G., Chiviacowsky, S., Schiller, E., and Ávila, L. T. G. (2010). Frequent external focus feedback enhances motor learning. *Frontiers in Psychology, 1*, 190.

Wulf, G., Hoess, M., and Prinz, W. (1998). Instructions for motor learning: Differential effects of internal versus external focus of attention. *Journal of Motor Behavior, 30*, 169-179.

Wulf, G., Lauterbach, B., and Toole, T. (1999). The learning advantages of an external focus of attention in golf. *Research Quarterly for Exercise and Sport, 70*(2), 120-126.

Wulf, G., and Lewthwaite, R. (2016). Optimizing performance through intrinsic motivation and attention for learning: The OPTIMAL theory of motor learning. *Psychonomic Bulletin and Review, 23*(5), 1382-1414.

Yarrow, K., Brown, P., and Krakauer, J. W. (2009). Inside the brain of an elite athlete: The neural processes that support high achievements in sports. *Nature Reviews Neuroscience, 10*, 585-596.

Zajac, F. E. (1989). Muscle and tendon: properties, models, scaling, and application to biomechanics and motor control. *Critical Reviews in Biomedical Engineering, 17*(4), 359-411.

Zanone, P. G., and Kelso, J. A. S. (1992). Evolution of behavioral attractors with learning: Non-equilibrium phase transitions. *Journal of Experimental Psychology: Human Perception and Performance, 18*(2), 403-421.

Zanone, P. G., and Kelso, J. A. S. (1997). Coordination dynamics of learning and transfer: Collective and component levels. *Journal of Experimental Psychology: Human Perception and Performance, 23*(5), 1454-1480.

Zelaznik, H. N. (2014). The past and future of motor learning and control: What is the proper level of description and analysis? *Kinesiology Review, 3*(1), 38-43.

INDEX

Note: The italicized *f* and *t* following page numbers refer to figures and tables, respectively.

ABOUT THE AUTHORS

© Chris Button

Chris Button, PhD, is a professor and the dean of the School of Physical Education, Sport, and Exercise Sciences at the University of Otago in Dunedin, New Zealand. He received his PhD in sport and exercise science in 2000 from Manchester Metropolitan University in the United Kingdom. His doctoral research focused on coordination and interception skills and applying ecological concepts to the study of interceptive actions.

Button is accredited as a biomechanist through Sport and Exercise Science New Zealand. He is also an executive committee member of the Australasian Skill Acquisition Network. Button regularly works with the coaches and athletes of High Performance New Zealand and has provided sport science support in netball, football (soccer), swimming, and motor sports.

Button publishes his research in a variety of books and journals on sport science, pedagogy, and movement science. Such topics have attracted interest within both scientific and political circles, as evidenced by recent invitations to provide expertise for the New Zealand Ministry of Health, Water Safety New Zealand, High Performance Sport New Zealand, and others. He is also a soccer coach for junior and adult learners.

Ludovic Seifert, PhD, is a professor at the University of Rouen Normandy. He is the vice dean of the Centre d'Etudes des Transformations des Activités Physiques et Sportives (CETAPS) lab and the head of the master's program in sport performance analysis. He obtained a certificate in physical education in 1998 and a PhD in sport science from the University of Rouen Normandy in 2003.

© Ludovic Seifert

Seifert's field of research relates to motor control and learning and expertise and talent development following an ecological dynamics approach. His emphasis focuses on movement coordination and visual-motor skills, with a particular interest in swimming and climbing. Such topics have led him to work closely with several French sport federations (such as swimming, climbing and mountaineering, and ice hockey) and professional clubs. His research has been published and cited extensively in peer-reviewed journals.

Seifert is the university's representative for Ecological Dynamics & Sport Performance, an e-lab of UNESCO's UniTwin Complex Systems Digital Campus program. He is also certified as a mountain guide by the International Federation of Mountain Guides Association (IFMGA).

© Jia Yi Chow

Jia Yi Chow, PhD, is an associate professor in the physical education and sport science department in the National Institute of Education at Nanyang Technological University. He is also an associate dean in the Office of Teacher Education at the same institute.

A physical educator by training, Chow's area of specialization is in motor control and learning. His key research work includes nonlinear pedagogy, investigation of multiarticular coordination changes, analysis of team dynamics from an ecological psychology perspective, and examining visual-perceptual skills in sports expertise. He works closely with colleagues and practitioners in the Singapore Ministry of Education, local sport institutes, and international collaborators to enhance the work on nonlinear pedagogy.

Duarte Araújo, PhD, is an associate professor and director of the department of sport and health and faculty of human kinetics at the University of Lisbon in Portugal. He leads both the research center of this school, CIPER, as well as the Laboratory of Expertise in Sport. He is an associate editor of the journal *Psychology of Sport and Exercise* as well as the *Journal of Expertise.*

Araújo's research on sport expertise and decision making, performance analysis, and affordances for physical activity has been funded by the Fundação para a Ciência

© Duarte Araújo

e a Tecnologia. He has published more than 130 papers in scientific journals (with over 4,500 citations in the Web of Science) and more than 15 books about expertise, team performance, variability, cognition, and decision making in sport. He also supervises several doctoral students from Portugal, Italy, and Australia.

© Keith Davids

Keith Davids, PhD, is a professor of motor learning at the Sport and Human Performance Research Group at Sheffield Hallam University. He graduated from the University of London and obtained a PhD in psychology and physical education at the University of Leeds. He has previously held professorial positions in the United Kingdom (Manchester Metropolitan University), New Zealand (University of Otago), Australia (Queensland University of Technology), and Finland (Finnish Distinguished Professor in the faculty of sport and health sciences at the University of Jyväskylä).

Davids' research program investigates sport performance, skill acquisition, and expertise enhancement in sport and how to design learning, training, and practice environments to successfully achieve these outcomes. He collaborates on research in sport, physical activity, and exercise with colleagues at universities in Spain, Portugal, France, Netherlands, Iran, Macedonia, New Zealand, Australia, and Finland. A large proportion of his scientific and practical research has been undertaken in collaboration with the New Zealand South Island Sports Academy, the Queensland Academy of Sport, the Australian Institute of Sport, Diving Australia, Cricket Australia, GB Cycling, and the English Institute of Sport.